The American

From Poverty to Prosperity

The Story of the de Jong Family

Doug & Mariette
Hope you enjoy
Claudia

As told to Claudia Aragon

DEDICATION

    This book is dedicated to the de Jong family who has been so generous and candid while they shared the story of their lives with me. Their family's drive and desire to succeed was an instrumental factor in their family's decision to immigrate to America where they worked as one to make Hollandia Dairy a reality.

    The book is also dedicated to the memory of their loving parents Arie Sr. and Maartje de Jong and to the brothers who have passed on; Kees, Karel and Elso.

INTRODUCTION

Before there were cars, radios, TV, computers, video games and smart phones, people sat around campfires, dinner tables and living rooms, and talked. They shared experiences, exchanged stories about their daily events, and divulged the humble beginnings of how their families came to be. At times they may have even peeked behind the doors hiding family skeletons. Throughout time elders have passed a verbal form of family history down to each subsequent generation. They told stories regarding the immigration to new lands, the tragic effects of war, hopes, dreams, ambitions, failures and successes.

Now due to socio-economic dictates, families not only have varied work schedules and days off that keep them apart, but in many instances the family unit is scattered across multiple cities, states, our country and/or the world. The exchange of information within the family unit during sit down family dinners is slowly becoming a thing of the past. Arie de Jong and his family are a part of that generation who sat and talked during meal times or over coffee.

For more than thirty years Arie kept hearing the same statement, *"Someone should do a book about our family."* Yet, no one ever did. Not one step was taken forward to make a book

Arie in front of Milne Motors, Escondido, Ca 1949

about the de Jong family a reality until 2010. That was when Arie decided it was time to act before there was no one left to pass the stories on.

This book is Aries vision, based on a shared collaboration with his brothers and sisters, who generously told their stories. Arie's love for, his devotion to and faith in his family has never wavered.

ACKNOWLEDGEMENTS

Thank you to Marcel and Emily for your endless patience and understanding, during all those times when I sat at the computer typing for hours on end. Thanks also to Anneke de Jong for the coffee and lunches she made to help keep us going while we worked. And finally thank you to the numerous people who were instrumental in making this book a reality for Arie and the de Jong family by their invaluable contributions.

Front cover photos:
Top photo left to right:
Back row: Elso, Karel, Kees. Middle: Jet, Arie Sr, Marrie, Maartje. Front: Jan, Arie Jr, Ellie
Bottom photo left to right:
Back row: Arie Sr, Maartje. Front: Arie Jr, Tom, Pete, Karel, (cousin) Rudy de Jong

Cover page photos: see page 28 and 98

TABLE OF CONTENTS

TABLE OF CONTENTS (cont)

TABLE OF CONTENTS (cont)

Arie Sr-Growing Up on the Farm

This is the true story of a large farming family from Holland (the Netherlands), who immigrated to the United States shortly after the end of WWII. The Netherlands is a small country in Western Europe, bordered by Germany to the East, Belgium to the South/West and England across the ocean to the West and the North Sea to the North.

Our story begins in May of 1895, when the patriarch of the family, Teun de Jong, was scheduled to be married. All of the arrangements were made to take possession of the agreed upon dairy, once they had a completed marriage contract. Most marriages took place in May, when the feed inventory was low, the spring cleaning was done, and the animals were in the pasture. This ensured a much smoother and easier transition.

Family farm in Koudekerk a/d Ryn in the 1920's

Unfortunately, before his wedding could take place, Teun's fiancé' died. He told his *Vader* (father) Arie, although his fiancé had died, his *ome* (uncle) Boudewyn had a beautiful babysitter and he would like to marry her instead. The babysitter, Elsje Zandbergen, was the daughter of Karel Zandbergen, a very nice, religious man from Rijnsburg.

Teun's father, Arie, paid a visit to Mr. Zandbergen; and with the gift of a horse and buggy the deal was made. The wedding date itself did not change, just the bride. When Teun and Elsje got married, she was sixteen years old.

Once they were married they wanted to begin their family right away, but Elsje had difficulty with her first three pregnancies. She lost all three of the children within three months of becoming pregnant. When she became pregnant for the fourth time, her husband took her to see Dr. De Haas in Wassenaar.

Since she lost her first three children so soon in the pregnancy, Elsje was given a bag of herbs by Dr. De Haas. Whatever the herb mixture was, it worked. She carried her next pregnancy to full term.

The doctor told her, *"You are pregnant with twins and they shall not die. Here is a bag of herbs. You must make a tea of these and drink it every day. If you need more, come back. You must also butcher an old chicken or rooster every week and make soup. Drink the soup; eat both the chicken and the skin. If you do as I say, you and the children will be ok."*

On May 5, 1901, a six pound girl, Henrietta Gertruida and a three pound boy, Ary (later

Neighbors of the de Jongs in Alphen 1947

changed to Arie) were born in Koudekerk, a/d Rijn, Holland. Though she initially suffered three miscarriages, Elsje gave birth to a total of eighteen children. Eight of which died at a young age and ten grew to adulthood.

Arie only attended school through the 6th grade, but he could read, write, and do arithmetic. His parents felt that was all the education a person needed to survive and live a dairyman's life. They were not fans of their children continuing an education past this point, and when he had children of his own Arie held the same view toward their education.

As he grew up, Arie worked with a neighbor, Gerrit Van Veen in the fields. During their work breaks Gerrit smoked and over time he taught Arie to smoke as well. Gerrit and his wife had fourteen children. The Van Veens were a very nice family and Gerrit worked for Arie's *Vader*, Teun, for more than twenty-five years. The hours they worked were long and hard, over ninety hours a week, for a mere 7-1/2 guilders pay, approximately three U.S. dollars. There was a great class distinction between the laborers and employers during that time. The employees were not treated very well and a spirit of discontent began to brew.

Arie's family had been raised with a very strict, Calvinist background, and was hard-working and frugal. As the family hellion, Arie gave his father quite a bit of grief while growing up. Much to his dismay, he was also sympathetic to his father's hired help, who were very poor. This was a direct effect of living in a capitalistic society and a reflection of religious doctrine. All workers were expected to be pious, humble, and loyal to their boss.

The Calvinist religious doctrine stated God had blessed the rich, because they were wise and

Arie Sr. in the Dutch Army

made good decisions. The poor were poor, because that is what God determined was best for them. Basically, their plight in life was to be and remain poor and humble servants. Arie strongly disagreed with this way of thinking. He saw strong work ethics and character traits in all of the workers in his father's employment, and he also felt most of them were less selfish and more giving than his father.

Communism had begun in Russia and sprang up in several Christian nations, like France, Spain, Italy, and Germany. Arie was angry at the current system and put his allegiance with the workers. His father felt he was a rebel and called him a *socialist*.

Arie's, *Vader* (father), Teun was a good husband and father, and he was also a boss, who felt hard work was beneath him. Arie, however, always had lots of energy, and when he worked with the hired help, he worked just as hard, if not harder. He set the bar high and expected the workers to keep up and do the same. All of this desire for action caused him to stir up trouble. As the oldest son, he was instrumental in creating quite a bit of havoc within the family unit.

Arie's, *"I win. You lose,"* approach to life, created a lot of strife with his parents, and younger siblings. On more than one occasion, his father had to step in to restore harmony,

10

knowing very well Arie was responsible for starting it, because he was wild and not easy to manage.

When Arie was drafted for military service in 1921, at the age of twenty, he felt he was lucky on several levels. The service provided him with the opportunity for both escape and adventure away from home. He loved horses and was thrilled he'd been chosen for the cavalry, because they wore a more elegant looking uniform. He was extremely eager to have the opportunity to be working with horses.

However, because Arie was such a good worker, his father didn't want to be without him for too long a period. His father, Teun, had him changed to the infantry, so he could serve a shorter term of service. Arie was furious, but the deed was done, he had missed out on his chance to serve in the cavalry. Although he was sensible enough to understand the reasons behind his father's decision, this was one of the many things in his life, Arie never forgot.

The Courtship and Marriage of Arie and Maartje

Arie's friend, Willem Roeloffs, knew he was looking for a girlfriend, but had not been very successful. Willem knew of a girl in a nearby village. Once he arrived at the house, Arie was instructed to ask for the younger daughter, Maartje, because she would be more open to the idea of dating a dairyman.

When the time for romance came, Arie's father was happy to hear his son was going to court a girl from a small neighboring village. He felt it was well past the time for his son to become more serious about life and start a family of his own. Maartje, the girl in question, was from a well-respected family, and Willem told Arie she had never dated, so she was pure.

One afternoon, when the weather was fair and sunny, Arie rode his old, rusty bike along the road next to the River Rijn in order to visit Maartje. He had to ride a rather lengthy distance along another canal, so it was almost an hour before he arrived at her village.

Maartje's older sister, Margje, had quite a few suitors and was very protective of her younger sister, especially in regards to dating Arie de Jong, the son of a dairyman. Because he had not made his intentions known, Margje did not go for the idea of Arie courting her sister. However, her brothers, Kees, Jan, and Marius liked Arie, and believed he was open regarding his intent toward Maartje and felt he had plainly stated his purpose. Since her brothers spoke favorably regarding him, Maartje was willing to give it a try and agreed to court Arie. She had never had a date or been kissed before, so she was very insecure.

Arie was wild by nature and so the courtship was somewhat rocky. His father, Teun noticed the relationship was in turmoil and warned Arie he might not receive help obtaining a dairy of his own if he did not start to get serious.

He finally decided to take his father's advice. He and Maartje were married February 26, 1925, when he was twenty-four and she was twenty-one. This was the beginning of the de Jong family and their eventual immigration to America.

MAARTJE

After they were married, Arie and Maartje lived at Neptunus, the site of a windmill water plant located in Aarlanderveen. Years earlier after the windmill burned down, it was converted to a steam-driven watermill.

The windmill belonged to rich *ome* (uncle) Bastiaan Hus, the brother of Maartje's mother. He was the *polder meister* (district manager) of the Aarlanderveen Provincial Water District.

All the windmills in Holland were owned by the regional water district and helped to control the water level in the canals. Whoever lived on a property that housed windmills, or a watermill pump, became the *molenaar*, and would be in charge of running the windmill, or the watermill pump to keep the water at the optimum level. In California, a tax is paid to get water to the land, but in Holland a tax is paid to remove water from the land.

Shortly after their marriage, Arie went into business with his brother-in-law, Marius. Both men were fun loving, hard workers, and very thrifty. They got along famously and had a lot of fun working together. Both men worked the farm during the daytime and the watermill, which was now powered by a steam engine at night. This was a prosperous time for the young couple.

Maartje's father lived next door to the newlywed couple and he owned some cows and chickens. The neighbor who lived across the gravel road from him also had a flock of chickens, but instead of buying the grain to feed his chickens, the neighbor let his run free. The chickens kept going to Maartje's father's house and ate all his grain. When Arie's father-in-law told him about the matter, Arie was very upset, but listened quietly about the incident. However, without his father-in-law's knowledge, each week he began to take a few of the neighbors chickens at night while they roosted.

Arie took the butchered hens to his father-in-law and said, "Hey dad, I have some chickens. Would you like some?" Of course, he was always told yes, because chicken meat was a great treat. The young couple, Marius and his father-in-law had a lot of chicken dinners.

After he butchered the birds, Arie threw the guts and feathers into the canal. When the neighbor began to complain about his flock of chickens disappearing, Arie said he didn't know anything about it. He pointed to the feathers in the canal and suggested it was probably the *schippers,* the people who hauled the coal and supplies throughout the canals and lived on their boats. The neighbor never caught on.

Arie and Marius operated the steam powered pump used to move the waters from the surrounding pastures into the nearby canal. The water in the canal was approximately four feet higher than the hundreds and hundreds of pastures belonging to the area dairies and farms.

De stoomketel van gemaal Neptunus in de jaren twintig. In het midden de toenmalige machinist Pieter van Vliet.

Maartje's parents and grandparents had operated the original windmill, which burned down and was replaced by a coal fed steam engine, very much like the locomotives of the time.

Arie also worked the locks/gates used to assist boats in getting from one water level to another. They are very similar to the lock system in the Panama Canal. The Rhine River ran through the middle of Alphen and operated as the main transportation artery for the area. Practically everything at the time was transported by boat.

The family was very proud of their Dutch heritage and their work, even though they felt they were looked down upon by the locals, because they smelled like the dairy. Factory workers in the area only worked a forty-eight hour work week, while they worked ninety hours on the dairy farm. Some people treated them like they were less than human, but during the war those same people began to treat them with respect, because they were the ones with the food.

The newlyweds lived next to the watermill pump, in a small house located on the property, until October of 1927 when Marius and Marie Molenaar were married.

Arie sold his share of the watermill operation to Marius before he moved his family to Alphen a/d Rijn, a small village located on the Rhine River, between Arie's childhood home of Lagewaard 76, Koudekerk a/d Rijn and the farm he had owned with Marius at Aarlanderveen.

Teun and Piet are born

Teunis de Jong was born at 6am, on November 23, 1925, in the town of Aarlanderveen, Galgmachine, Holland. The word *Galgmachine*, translated, means gallows. It had been customary at the time to hang anyone guilty of a major crime in the town square of larger cities, but in small towns the gallows served to warn approaching travelers, to be on their best behavior. The practice of public hanging was abandoned in 1925.

Teun was born in a modest 25 x 25 foot home belonging to his maternal grandfather. The small home had been in the family for four generations. A converted closet doubled as the shared bedroom. Most of the houses in the area could not afford to be built with the addition of bedrooms, so the closets were used as sleeping quarters, with storage above and below the bed.

These small alcoves called *bedstede* had two doors which closed in the middle. The small houses had no air circulation and a large number of people from the surrounding communities suffered from severe outbreaks of tuberculosis. Many suffered the loss of half their family due to the prevalence of TB. One Large family in particular, the Heestermans, had thirteen children. Twelve of their children suffered early deaths, because they fell ill to tuberculosis. Their only surviving child, Gerhard, perished at the age of eighteen.

Teun was born three weeks earlier than expected, and the church elders questioned whether his parents had remained chaste during their courtship. Arie and his new bride Maartje had indeed remained pure before their wedding. Teun's premature birth had been accelerated due to a near fatal accident in the family buggy.

After a day of celebrating the 16th birthday of his twin sisters, Geert and Janna, Arie lost control of the buggy while driving back along the narrow road of the canal. The top of the two wheeled carriage became caught on the drawbridge chain and spooked the horse, which ran off the gravel road and came to a stop too close to the edge of the deep canal for comfort. The very steep and narrow road ran between two canals, and there wasn't a lot of room. A mistake on any level could have easily carried them into the deep, dark, cold water. Thankfully, even though he wasn't a careful driver, Arie was not prone to panic. The buggy had good springs and he regained control at the water's edge. He drove through a yard and into a hay stack before he came to a stop.

The Rhine River runs East to West from Germany to the Holland coastline. Arie was on the small narrow road which crossed the River Rhine from Rotterdam to Amsterdam, and was on top of the dike, driving between the two manmade canals. In Holland, the larger canals are on the left side of the dike and are ten feet deep and sixty feet wide. The smaller canals are on the right side and are only twelve feet wide and four feet deep, and they are six feet lower in the pasture areas.

During the frantic ride, Maartje was thrown from side to side within the buggy. Her fear mounted as she saw they were rapidly covering the distance to the deep, shiny waters of the canal. Unable to swim, she panicked at the thought of what would happen to the baby, if they did go into the water. Due to the accident and her heightened anxiety, Teun was born within the next twenty-four hours. Maartje quickly began to suffer the effects of post partum depression soon after the birth, and was institutionalized for several months. Arie's sisters Jet and Petronella took turns helping to care for baby Teun.

Maartje struggled with mental illness her entire life. The episodes seemed to be triggered by hormonal changes, especially close to her monthly cycle, more commonly known as PMS (pre-menstrual syndrome). Her family had her institutionalized once after her first menstrual cycle, and a second time just after the birth of Teunis.

No one understood about post partum depression in the twenties. They simply locked you away. It was something Maartje's parents kept silent about and hidden from her future husband, Arie, and his family. Her parents felt he would never have married her if he knew. This information was also kept from the American immigration department; out of fear the family would be denied entrance to the United States.

Teun has always been affectionately known to his family as, "*the talker*". He was pontificating from within the confines of his play pen before he could walk. As a baby he focused all his energy on talking and trying to learn about the world around him, giving everyone the illusion he hardly moved a muscle. He finally started to walk at eighteen months, and his legs never quite caught up with his desire to learn and talk about everything around him. Teun was an inquisitive child with an unquenchable thirst for knowledge. As he grew older, he became the "*go to*" person whenever someone in the family or neighborhood sought information, or answers regarding world religion, politics, health and history.

Teun grew up quickly, assuming the responsibility for his siblings at an early age. Feeling the full weight of that responsibility, he experienced separation anxiety when apart from his younger siblings. His earliest childhood memory revolves around his duties as the oldest son, when he went with his mother and father to visit his paternal grandparents, leaving behind Piet, who was just too young to go. Piet was born second and came into the world on February 20, 1927. Teun remembers driving away, waving to Piet and how awful it was to watch him looking sad.

For the most part, the de Jong family was very easy going. Maartje felt Arie who had a fun loving personality, was far too lenient with the children. She possessed a great love of adventure and Arie provided plenty of that throughout their marriage.

Elso I and Kees are Born

Elso I was born April 14, 1929, followed shortly by the birth of Kees, on November 28, 1930. Having previously been blessed with the birth of three sons, Maartje had hoped for a girl when

Kees was born. A daughter would not only have been a welcome addition, but would have

brought the added benefits of giving her future help in the house.

The neighborhood next to the farm was filled with row houses. This provided a wonderful playground for the de Jong children, with an abundance of playmates and lots of neighbors.

Teun remembers how his paternal *oma* (grandmother), Elsje de Jong, impressed upon him to be loving and caring towards his siblings and his mother. She told him to make sure he was always obedient and helpful to his mother, because his father was always busy and too easy going. He became fearful that something could happen to one of his siblings if he were not there to protect them. Sadly, this came to pass when Teun was only six years old.

Canals Prove Tragic

For the summer vacation of his first grade year, Teun was taken to his grandmother's home leaving behind Piet, Elso I and baby Kees. Piet, was only five years old at the time, and was not used to caring for anyone else and he was still too young to take care of himself. Caring for his brothers was a huge responsibility for someone so young, especially when he had never previously been given such a task, even for a moment.

On a warm, sunny day in August of 1932, during Teun's absence, while Elso I played alongside the canal, he must have either slipped, or fallen into the water. He was very young and lacked the ability to swim. His drowning caused the family great sorrow.

A multitude of friends, family and neighbors came to offer comfort. The remaining children were still too young to understand the implications of the tragic loss. That is, except for Teun, who felt guilty because he wasn't there to save Elso I.

The de Jong's dairy was comprised of almost seventy acres of land, with approximately four miles of ditches running through it. The Dutch farmers and dairymen dug the ditches to drain and carry water away from the farms. The ditches surrounded the farms like castle moats and ranged from twelve to fifteen feet wide, with depths of about five feet.

The de Jong farm house was built to allow access to the canal water from both inside and outside the house, enabling them to easily clean the milking and cheese utensils. They were also able to pump drinking water for the animals housed in the barn during the winter.

There were no childproof guards or fences to protect the children from falling into the multitude of water filled ditches. To warn her children to stay away from the edge of the water, Maartje used stories of the "*Bullebak*," a fierce water monster that would grab children close to the water's edge, pull them in and drown them.

Teun was fraught with anger, guilt and sadness, over not being there to protect his brother. He questioned over and over, why God hadn't protected Elso in his youthful innocence? Teun's religious views for the rest of his life would drastically be altered by this one event.

In school he learned such beautiful Bible stories and songs. One song in particular gave him comfort: *"Er gaat door alle landen een trouwe kindervriend. Geen oog kan hem aanschouwen."* Translated: "There goes through every country a faithful children's friend. No one can see him."

The song goes on to say that he sees every child and protects them. Teun began to wonder, why God would let something this sad and tragic happen, especially to someone as young and innocent as Elso I.

He recalls how the minister told his mother; God needed another angel in heaven, so Elso

 was in a better place. The minister went on, saying he hoped Maartje had the strength of Job, who had lost ten children to God, yet continued to praise the Lord. Teun remembers thinking the minister was not handling his mother's grief properly, and given the choice, at even such a young age, Elso I would have chosen to live. The Dutch-Reformed minister's statements and explanations concerning Elso's death, led Teun to rethink and later change his religious affiliation to Jehovah's Witness.

Drowning was a big problem in the area and quite a few local children were lost. Most of the homes were built near the water and the children weren't taught to swim. The de Jong's lost many childhood friends to drowning deaths. After losing Elso I to drowning, Arie Sr. took the children to swim in the Rhine River. The goal was for them to learn to swim distance and build endurance while their father swam next to them. He never wanted to lose another child. Elso II fell in the canal and almost drowned before his father had the opportunity to teach him how to swim.

Except for Jet and Mary, all the de Jong children learned to swim in the canals of Holland. Their father would take the children to where the water was only three feet deep in order to teach them how to swim.

In 1938, Arie I passed away from polio. Karel who was only four at the time, remembered Arie I being placed in a wooden box with a window in the lid, enabling the family to see him. The box was placed in the guest room for a few days and Maartje allowed the children to go into the room to see him a few times daily. A few of the children, like Karel, were too young to know what was happening, but older children, like Teun and Piet had experienced the death of Elso I and they helped to comfort and explain what was happening to the younger children.

Arie Sr. implemented a new family rule. The children were prevented from attending church, unless they were old enough to attend school. Karel desperately wanted to go to church, but his father felt since he was only five years old, Karel was far too young to attend. Karel remembered one occasion while the family was at church; he was playing next to the waters of the Rhine, and pushing at a piece of trash pretending it was a boat. The piece was pushed too far out and as Karel stretched to get it back, he fell into the water. Unable to swim he went under, but thankfully came back up.

Swimming in the canal at the farm in Alphen A/D Ryn

He remembered seeing a dog and grabbing a pole, holding on tightly as he was pulled back to the shore. Karel and the family do not recall who had the pole and helped to pull him back to shore, but he recalled there were other children playing there as well. It would be three more years before Karel finally learned to swim.

It was fairly common in Alphen for children to fall into the rivers or canals, and be pulled safely to shore. Children usually played in groups and were trained to act right away when someone fell in the water by screaming or running for help. This occurrence happened to almost all of the de Jong children at one time or another. Eventually, they all learned to swim. Of course tragedies occurred. Some local children fell into the waters unnoticed and were unable to be saved. Sadly they perished.

Many people living along the edge of the Rhine built outhouses above the water along the river banks. The waste would fall into the water. It was not uncommon for anyone swimming or diving in the river to come across a piece of floating waste, which they simply pushed aside.

Elso II, Karel, Jan and Arie I are born

Maartje was pregnant the year Elso died, and she gave birth on October 16, 1932 to another boy she named Elso. She truly believed God had given her another Elso to replace the first. Like his brothers, he was born at home in the guest room at Alphen a/d Ryn, which doubled as a birthing room. Since it was the middle of the depression, Arie Sr. and Maartje didn't want to have so many children, however, they were uneducated in how to prevent pregnancy.

Elso II was always very small and looked younger than he was. When he was three years old, they went with his *Tante* Mag to spend a day at the ocean. He remembered playing in the sand with all the other children. In order to make the trip, the family would get on a boat and travel the ten miles along the River Rhine to reach the ocean. Elso said it was his earliest and happiest memory, because it was the first time he had French toast.

The sixth child, Karel, was born two years later on January 30, 1934. He was an extremely mellow, easy going baby, not boisterous or prone to crying like his siblings were as babies. Maartje was used to the way the other children wailed when hungry and listened for Karel's crying to give her clues. Since she was busy working on all the chores around the house, Maartje relied on and waited for his cries to signal her in to the fact that he needed attention.

Pictured left to right: Maartje, Kees, Elso, Karel
Front row: Jan, Arie Jr. Ellie

Since Karel never cried he almost died from malnutrition when he was six months old.

Jan was born May 29, 1935, at the family home at Alphen a/d Rijn. The children were being born so close together, Maartje began to feel overwhelmed. Jan was the seventh child born in a ten year period. Caring for an infant on top of the other children was just too much for her to bear. It was decided, until Maartje was better able to care for him, Jan, who was only two or three at the time, would be taken to her sister Mag's home in Aarlanderveen to be cared for.

Fortunately, Mag only lived five miles away and the family could see Jan quite frequently. He stayed with his Tante Mag for a year until she married Arie Veninga, in 1937. Her stepson Otto also lived with them after the marriage. She became pregnant soon after the wedding. It was decided, that with the addition of a new baby and her stepson in her house, Jan would be returned to his parents' home.

Jan was a scrawny child, which he attributes to his mother underfeeding him when he was small. He felt he was average in his ability, plain looking and possessed no extraordinary skills to make him stand out from the crowd. He also held no desire to go to school.

Jan felt his mother always worked too hard. So much so, she was never able to fully embrace and enjoy the blessings of the family. That's where Teun stepped in. He was instrumental with both the raising of the children and running of the house. His mother had very little time to enjoy her life, and the birth of Arie I and Ellie came soon after.

Ellie, the First Girl, is Born

After giving birth to eight boys, two of which died, a girl was finally born into the family. Sara Elsje Frederica, affectionately known as Ellie, was born December 21, 1937. She was named after both her maternal and fraternal grandmothers. Ellie was a very strong and muscular baby with broad shoulders. When Doctor Pillon performed the delivery, he held her up, he said, "This baby should have been a boy." Not only was she a physically strong girl, she was just as strong willed. Having to contend with so many big brothers, Ellie grew up tough.

The house in Alphen had a separate birthing room, and the children stayed away from that room, because of the scary noises Maartje made when she gave birth. Everyone in the family was in the living room when Ellie was born. Doctor Pillon carried her in, lifted her by one leg, indicated her pubic area, and said, "Now do you see this? You have a girl."

Ellie began to walk at nine months, and with a typical child's curiosity her hands and eyes were everywhere. Teun had repeatedly warned his mother not to leave the tea kettle too close to the edge of the stove, but she was so busy with all the children and forgot. Sadly, Ellie pulled down the kettle of hot water and was scalded horribly. She was burned so severely, her skin came off when Maartje removed her sweater to see the extent of her injuries. Her foot and arm still bear the scars from that day.

Oma de Jong, her paternal grandmother, thought girls should be inside the house, and didn't like seeing them play outside after school. She remembers her *Oma* saying, "Good girls don't play on the street."

After that Ellie could no longer play outside with her brothers and friends, she had to go to her *Oma's* house and learn to knit instead.

Ellie was always a Tomboy and never wore a dress until the day they immigrated, when she was eleven. She was always bigger than Arie Jr. and Jan. Her brothers, and the other boys alike, treated her like one of them, which was fine with her because she wanted to be a boy. She hated housework and only wanted to work and play with her brothers.

Always a hard worker, Ellie peeled potatoes, milked the cows and helped Maartje with the housework from the time she was eight years old, until the family immigrated when she was eleven. She would do anything to get away from housework and loved going to the fields with her father and brothers to milk the cows.

Pictured left to right: Cousins Ellie and Rena and Ellie seated

Ellie was not only accident prone, but was everywhere she shouldn't be and she always got into trouble. Like the time when she was seven and her *Vader* Arie cut down a tree for firewood. Because she wasn't paying attention, everyone moved except Ellie. She was hit with the back of the axe cutting open her chin.

On another occasion when she was seven, Jan accidentally shot her. She and Arie Jr. had been eating berries. Piet had been with Jan and told him not to load the gun, but he did it anyway and forgot to put on the safety. While walking Jan tripped and the gun flew out of his hands. It discharged shooting Ellie behind the ear. There weren't any pain killers available and her pain was unbearable. Her four brothers had to physically hold her down while they took the bullet out.

Ellie was extremely close to her brothers, and began to hate being a girl. She cried when she got older and her mother said she couldn't sleep with them anymore.

Discipline and Religion

On Sunday afternoons Maartje took the children to the cow barn where they sat in the hay singing songs. She loved to sing both Dutch and Christian hymns. One song she loved to sing in particular was about brothers that had been lost, but would meet once again in heaven.

pictured left to right: Pete, Kees, Elso, and Teun
seated: Ellie, Arie Sr, Maartje, Karel
front: Arie Jr, Jan

She felt the song was far better at explaining death than she was. With so many children to care for, she just did not have the luxury of extra or free time. There were times the children said their mother was so busy she didn't even have the time to stop and feed them. That's when Teun stepped in as the caregiver to his siblings.

Maartje was the family disciplinarian. Although Karel was the quietest of all the children, he loved to pester and aggravate his younger brothers and sisters, so he received quite a few spankings from his mother. However, Arie Sr. used to spank the older children quite harshly, that is, until he overheard Teun and Piet talking one day. He had been out looking for them and found them sitting inside a wooden barrel used to make butter that had been laid on its side. As he walked up, he overheard Piet saying to Teun, "I wish *Vader* was dead.'

Arie Sr. had been estranged from his own father growing up and did not want history to repeat itself with him and his children. He decided then and there to change. Karel felt they could never have had a better dad. He remembered how his father cried, as he told stories of how he and his father never got along.

Education

Since Arie Sr. did not benefit from or have a formal education himself, he didn't believe or feel an education was necessary to succeed in life. He recalled how his father said, *"All you need to know is how to be a dairy man. For you will always be a dairy man."*

Elso de Jong

That was in 1932, and the belief at that time was you only had to work the land. Education was an unnecessary luxury the farmers and dairymen could just not afford. They felt it took their children away from the daily operations, where they were needed the most.

It was required by the Dutch government that all children had to attend school from the age of six to thirteen, so even though Arie Sr. disagreed, all the de Jong children attended school. Arie Sr. told Teun; even though he had to go to school he was not required to participate. His upbringing made Teun uninterested in the benefits of a formal education, which frustrated his teacher. The teacher actively sought the help of Arie Sr. to change his son's mind about school, which he eventually did. Teun was an excellent student, which was fueled by his unquenchable desire to seek knowledge from infancy.

In Holland, the de Jong children attended school six days a week, from 9am to 4pm, with a two hour break at noon. On Wednesdays and Saturdays they only attended school for three hours in the morning. When he was in the 1st grade, Arie Jr. always looked forward to Wednesdays, because after school he went to his *Oma* de Jong's house for lunch. She always prepared an extra special treat for him, brood *pap,* which is hot milk poured over stale bread. He remembers how he could hardly breathe on those visits when his *Tante* (aunt) Janna, a large and big busted woman greeted him with an enormous hug and pulled him into her chest. She always affectionately called him *"lekkere drol,"* which means little turd.

Sports and physical education were not part of the Holland school curriculum, but they did have art lessons for one hour each week. The school day started with prayer. They were then taught about church history and the Bible, followed by the country's history. On Mondays, the lessons consisted of learning/memorizing Psalms. Studies regarding Church doctrine or children's songs were taught on different days.

Teun (Tom) is quoted as saying: *"A 6th grade education in Holland was like completing high school in the states, because we went six days a week in Holland and had very little vacation time away from our studies. That's why we are all good readers and possess a decent knowledge regarding history, geography and are good in arithmetic."*

When Teun was in agriculture school he was taught organic farming. At Alphen a/d Rijn they had thirty-five milking cows and young stock, plus fifty pigs, thirty sheep and fifteen goats. There was never a shortage of natural fertilizer. The canals and ditches were abundant with grass and plants. Due to the high water content, the vegetation would be soft and was harvested to keep the canals clean. The muck from the decomposed grasses provided the dairy farm with an ample supply of natural compost.

Kees de Jong

Although harvesting the manure and the compost proved to be a large undertaking for the family, it kept the soil naturally rich and healthy in nutrients. Commercial fertilizers would never be able to enrich the soil with an abundance of natural benefits.

Teun was a very good and protective brother to all the de Jong children. Piet admired him and his natural caregiver ability. There were no child labor laws in Holland and it was very common for children to work before and after school. Teun and Piet formed a team. Teun was a natural leader and Piet knew how to follow. The early morning hours before school were tough. Piet would get out of bed early and stoke the furnace, so the family had hot water to start the cheese making process. Hot water was necessary in order to bring the milk up to the proper temperature to make cheese. After doing their morning chores, all the children old enough, left for school. Piet was playful and a dreamer by nature and did not like school. He felt the discipline at school was too severe.

Even though children in Holland usually only stayed in school until the age of thirteen, Arie Sr. made Teun quit when he was twelve, to learn more about farming. He attended agriculture school for the next four years until he was sixteen. In Ag school, he learned how to feed and care for animals, fertilize the land, and how to harvest the crops.

Jan and Karel were both very shy children and preferred to be in the company of the family. Jan remembers the tender, loving way Karel held his hand to encourage him, when he started kindergarten, which was about a half a mile from the farm.

Both boys preferred it when the German soldiers occupied the schools during the war, because they didn't have to attend. With the onset of war, the school system was at least six months behind in teaching. Despite Jan not liking school, he was at the top of his class. When they had cold weather storms, they had to skate over the ice covered streets to get to the school.

Karel did his studies and tried really hard to succeed, but came away feeling as though he was only a mediocre student. He found no help from his brothers regarding his studies, for they were all far too busy helping around the dairy. Karel was very quiet and reflective, quite unlike his brothers, especially Teun, who was very talkative and boisterous.

Karel attended the same school as his siblings, even though he didn't really like school. He recalled how he and Jan, a year and a half younger, tried to get into the kindergarten classroom, but couldn't open the door and they walked all the way back home. When Piet asked what happened, they said the school was locked. Piet was dutiful and strict when it came to following the rules and he walked them back to the school and opened the doors for them. However, everyone agrees that if the two boys had seen Teun first, he would have simply said, "Well, it's your day off, enjoy yourselves."

Left to right: Jan, Ellie, Karel (back) and Arie

Teun was very involved in his siblings schooling and was instrumental in insuring they completed their school work. Like his older brother, Jan only went to school as far as the 6th grade, and then he attended Ag school. It was decided Jan would take a year of Ag school, and would only attend classes two days a week. This ended when he was thirteen, a short time before his family immigrated.

All the teachers from 1st thru 3rd grade in Holland were women. On one occasion in the 1st grade, while the children went outside for a break, Karel had to stay inside for detention. When the teacher stepped out of the room for a moment, he became frightened, because he wasn't used to being alone and he ran for the door, putting his hands on the wall kicking at the baseboard. Once he opened the door, he ran all the way home. Karel felt his teacher was nice, because she never mentioned the incident and he never got into trouble.

Mr. Van Beieren, their fourth grade teacher, was pro-German in some of his philosophies and beliefs, but very nice. Academic years during the war were difficult. The Germans seized the schools in order to use them as barracks. Local farm sheds became the new classrooms. It was up to the neighboring farmers, painters, or carpenters to vacate one room on their property in order for classes to continue. The desks and other furniture were moved to the makeshift classrooms which were scattered about the area. The individual classes stayed together, but the schools were split out of necessity.

The school children would go home for a two hour break, in order to have their afternoon meal. There was a fifteen minute break reserved for play. The children would play in the loose hay, and Mr. Van Beieren would join them, laughing as he was overtaken by numerous children, and buried in the hay.

One war memory of Jan's, was of the Jewish families in their area being rounded up like cattle. He remembered how the Jews were docile while being taken to the train station in town, for relocation to work camps, concentration camps or worse. The citizens of Alphen were ignorant to the atrocities taking place in the camps. The family learned of the horrors later on, and remembers when they heard the term, *"death camp,"* for the first time.

There was a dark haired Jewish boy in Jan's class, by the name of Hans de Jong (no relation). After the war was over they never saw Hans again. He was gone, and so was his family. At the time Jan was unaware that Hans was Jewish, he just remembered Hans was the only kid in the school with black hair. Out of the ninety plus Jewish families taken away from Alphen, no one ever returned from the death camps.

In 2012, Kees Visschedijk, wrote a book about the Jews of Alphen a/d Rijn, titled, *"Waar ze ook heen gaan, ze hebben in elk geval mooi weer" Herinneringen aan de wegvoering van de Alphense Joden in 1942."* ("Wherever they are going, they will have nice weather" Memories of Jews being transported from Alphen a/d Rijn in 1942)

Arie Sr. was a big promoter of work, not school, saying education wasn't important. If he wanted or needed help in the fields, his children simply stayed home from school.

Mr. Verhey was the 5th grade teacher. While the boys read, the girls learned knitting. He never had them continue with the reading from where they left off. The class would reread the same material over and over again. He was a very sour man and not very friendly at all. He was considered a bit of a bad ass.

Karel was very impish and always finding new ways to cause trouble. On one occasion during recess while in the 5th grade, Jan Marbus, a boy in Arie Jr.'s class wanted to have a look into their classroom through the window and Karel obliged and hoisted him up so he could see.

Unfortunately, a little too much force was used and Jan's head went through the window. Of course, Karel was sent to the principal's office. This was during the war and because there was no glass to replace the broken window, Karel's mother, Maartje had to take the glass from a picture frame to make the repair. The incident made for exciting dinner conversation among the de Jong children.

While in the 7th grade, Karel attended school half of the week and farm school two days a week, under the guidance of Johan de Jong. The students were given an extreme amount of homework to do. Karel finished third out of the forty students in the class. Johan was Karel's favorite teacher. He studied under him for four years while in agricultural farm school.

Some teachers steal the hearts of their pupils, while others make them fall asleep. And then there are special teachers like Johan, who was not only able to capture and hold his students attention, but always looked for and found new ways to help them learn. He was an excellent and well rounded teacher.

After the family immigrated, Johan stayed in touch and came to visit them at the dairy in Escondido. Tom felt Johan took better care of his cattle than he took care of himself, because he was unwilling to give up smoking. Karel remembered how Johan sported a finger stained brown by years of smoking and exposure to nicotine. The smoking would eventually cause Johan's death in 1974, at the age of sixty-two. On one Escondido visit, while Johan was driving, he told Tom he felt like he was going to die. Six short years later he was gone.

The de Jong family has always had an open door policy, where friends and family can come and go as they please. Because there were no strict rules in place, some people may have viewed the home life as chaotic. The de Jong home was always the one neighboring children gravitated to.

Arie Jr. is Born

With the threat looming of another World War, Arie Jr. was born on January 24, 1939.

After his birth Arie Jr. had a rough start. He has suffered from respiratory problems his whole life, which began in the very cold winter of 1939, when he was only five days old. Undressed so his mother could change him, Maartje left the room forgetting all about him. When she eventually returned, he was blue and barely breathing. That was the beginning of his asthma and respiratory problems. Although, the asthma was not diagnosed until later in his life.

Left to right: Ellie, Moeder Maartje and Arie

Arie Jr. didn't like work and would rather be out playing with his friends. He, Jan and Ellie were always together.

There was a trash dump located behind their dairy in Holland and the children were always in the dump scrounging around for something to play with or eat. At times they would eat the leftover jam in a jar, or gather cigarette butts, so their father could roll his own cigarettes.

The de Jong children played at the dump so often, that when they were asked where they were born, they simply replied, "We were born on the dump."

Even as a very young child Arie Jr. was always extremely competitive. With six older brothers he had to be.

He was ten years old when the family came to California, and the only brother who grew up the American way. He has always been success oriented and never did or accepted half hearted work.

Daily Life and Struggles in Holland

Times were tough and Arie Sr. and Maartje took in many boarders that were usually between the ages 18 to 25. The boarders worked long hard hours for only one to two dollars a week and worked eighty to ninety hours a week in exchange for food and lodging. Maartje would also do their laundry and clothing repairs.

Holland was a rich country. There were many Colonies and not too many taxes to pay. The rich lived well and the poor suffered. Teun was angry at a capitalistic government he felt was neglecting the poor, creating an impoverished nation. His mother, Maartje, felt the government needed to raise both the unemployment wages and the minimum wage, to enable people to not only increase consumption of goods and also, by doing so, the economy would improve throughout the region.

pictured left to right: Elso, Kees, Teun, Cousin Rita, Arie Sr, Karel, and Ellie front: Jet and Jan

All the de Jong children grew up in a tight knit family under strong leadership, with a loving mother who was overwhelmed and too busy to look after the children. Maartje was in charge of making the family cheese and butter and she enlisted Teun's help at every opportunity. When Maartje couldn't stay ahead of everything, Arie Sr. promised to take over some of the work, like making the cheese. However, he was too carefree and did a lousy job. Teun said they needed to change things, because having his father make the cheese would drastically change their income. For the worse.

Karel was the first to take over as the cheese maker, but that didn't last long. The responsibility was eventually given to Jan, who was a much better and more diligent worker. He never took shortcuts and always produced quality cheese.

They would make cheese twice a day after the cows were milked. Jan didn't mind, because he didn't have to get up extremely early, or in the middle of the night to milk the cows. Teun took over making the butter.

Maartje was brought up in a family that consisted of bakers and was very finicky about the quality of her work. Her *Vader* (father), Piet Van Vliet, was both a farmer and a miller. Her *Opa* (grandfather) operated the windmill. He was a small farmer and very thrifty. Maartje's *moeder* (mother), Sarah Hus and her *Oma* (grandmother) were both refined, whereas, her father was a common man with a good heart.

Though Arie Sr. was no help in maintaining the cleanliness of the farm, he did however, look for help and hired farm hands and was instrumental to the farm in that way. The downside; he always looked for cheap labor, and his wife, Maartje wanted someone who could work independently, without her having to guide them every step of the way.

Piet stated his *Vader*, (father), Arie Sr. preferred to hire flunkies, because they were cheap which enabled him to have a lot of help on the farm for very little cash layout. Times were tough and farming did not pay, so often it was difficult to pay the rent. He knew by having fun with his laborers he could help them to perform better by using competition. He was a hard worker and knew his helpers did not want to fall behind, so they would try to keep up with him and work at his level.

By this point in their marriage, Arie, and Maartje, had five sons. Maartje had quite a workload facing her each day and she wished she had a daughter to help with all the work. Between herself, the children, Arie Sr., a farmhand and a maid, it was a household of nine. She worked just as hard as the men. She made the cheese and butter daily, but was not the best when it came to managing and directing the workers.

In January of 1934, shortly after Karel was born, Arie Sr. was sent to prison for a few months, after he had purchased some stolen tools from one of his workers. He went before the judge and was placed in jail due to his belligerent attitude. After he returned from prison he looked extremely pale and frail. Karel smiled as he recalled his father telling the story of how, during his jail time a small bird came to sing at the window of his cell every day.

The first thing Arie Sr. asked for when he returned home was for someone to fetch his black Van Nelle tobacco pouch, so he could make and smoke a cigarette. He told the family how lucky and grateful he was to come back home to his family alive and not in a cheap pine box.

Friends and neighbors began to worry about Maartje, because she never seemed to show any emotion. She felt Arie was her rock, even though he failed to show her the tenderness and warmth she desired and desperately needed. Arie Sr. also lacked the ability to show her his appreciation for all she did to run the house, the farm and the family. The de Jong family was still young and the children thought the behavior their father showed toward their mother was normal.

In 1933, seven years before the start of World War II, the depression had already begun and made a great impression on Teun, even though he was only eight years old at the time. The family was going bankrupt, and he could see the threat of failure all around him. The Dutch people could no longer afford to buy milk. During the depression, a quart of milk sold at the dairies for one American penny and for three U.S. cents at the market. The price of cheese was four cents a pound at the dairy and eight cents at the market. Unemployment was also at an all time high and many people found it very difficult to live a normal life. It was heartbreaking to bear witness as the Dutch government destroyed food surpluses that could have fed the poor and hungry. Even though he was a young child at the time, it made Teun extremely rebellious to witness such atrocities.

Due to the drastic economic effects of the depression, a change had taken place within the family and their lives. Because of their livestock and farming, the de Jongs were in a group of the fortunate and lucky few, who were able to take care of themselves. Due to the lack of jobs and no money, their friends and neighbors who weren't as lucky, began to feel the harsh reality of the food shortage.

In the years during the depression, Teun saw a great opportunity to make money. In 1935, when he was ten, he started to sell products from the farm to surrounding families. He sold eggs, rhubarb, lima beans, and other produce as well.

A real hot item was colostrum, the first milk of a fresh cow. The newborn calves need to ingest it in order to get their digestive systems started. Colostrum is more than twenty percent protein and contains anti-infectious properties. When heated, the colostrum thickens until it resembles the consistency of a pudding. Dutch people are crazy about it. Teun sold it for three American pennies a liter. The equivalent of ten cents in Dutch currency.

Whenever a calf on the farm died during birth, Arie Sr. would butcher the calf and run the meat through the grinder, producing about twenty-five pounds of hamburger meat. He sold the meat for twenty cents a pound, which totaled five guilders, approximately two dollars in American money. This was twice the amount a live calf was worth. It didn't matter how illegal this venture was, Arie Sr. felt it was a great return financially and the risks were worth it.

At the age of fourteen, Teun continued to feel angry at how the capitalistic government not only neglected the poor, but in reality created poverty. That anger fueled and motivated him. He was determined to get his family out of poverty and to never be poor again. He felt each person was a product of both their education and environment. His economic situation and environment made him feisty and tenacious. He never wanted to go broke and was willing to do anything to survive.

Arie Jr. never knew his *Opa*, (grandpa) de Jong in Holland, who passed away from a heart attack in 1931. He was only fifty-nine years old when he died. His *Vader*, Arie Sr.'s extended family; siblings, parents, etc lived on the same farm in Koudekerk a/d Rijn, (Lagewaard), Holland. Arie Sr. only left the family farm after he married Maartje, and moved to Aarlanderveen. They later moved to Alphen a/d Rhine, where they raised their family.

In 1933, National Socialism got the economy in Germany rolling again, and Holland benefited as well. The selling prices of some of their products doubled and some of the unemployed from Holland found work in Germany.

After losing her husband, Arie Sr.'s mother, and sister, Janna, moved the next street over from them in the town of Alphen. Two of his brothers, Karel, and Teun, took over the running of the family dairy in Koudekerk. His brother Bouw, ran a dairy store in Den Hague and his youngest brother Elso, was a butcher's apprentice.

Ellie loved her *Oma* living so close, but being such a Tomboy, she hated the knitting lessons. She wanted to run and be wild with her brothers, but her *Oma* felt she should act like more of a lady and stay indoors. When the family immigrated Ellie took a knitted bathing suit she'd made. She was mortified, the first time she got wet while wearing the suit, because the crotch hung down to her knees and the top sagged so badly, her breasts were exposed.

World War II

After World War II began, in order to allow other people besides his own family to have food, Arie Sr. began slaughtering pigs to sell on the Black Market. With his concerns for his growing family, he realized he needed to be considerably more cautious. Each time Arie Sr. was arrested, the family felt there was no shame, because he had been helping other families obtain food to eat. The children had a lot of admiration and respect for their father. In their eyes, he could do no wrong.

Arie Sr. had a hired hand who housed a ham radio in his home. Normally this would be of no consequence, except this particular radio sported an English radio channel. That fact in itself could have resulted in a death sentence. Arie Sr. and his hired hand were both found guilty of owning the radio and were imprisoned. The prison food was so scarce; some prisoners desperate for any morsel of food would keep and suck the bones of a salted herring from the previous evening's dinner. Fortunately, both men returned home safely.

During the early part of the 1940's, no one in Holland seemed overly concerned about Austria and the Sudetenland. Both countries had been annexed by Germany and the Saar area had already been returned to German control. Holland as a country was neutral and had a waterway of canals which could be used for defense. This proved useless. The Germans kept coming even though the canals of the waterways had been used to flood the farms of Eastern Holland. This caused the Dutch farmers from the eastern region of the Netherlands to move their cattle and families West to where the de Jongs lived. However, by the time those farmers made their move, the Germans were already occupying the western region as well.

The farmers from the East had to remain in the West until they could pump the flood waters away from their homes. Even after those farmers returned to their homes, it was a while before their animals could return.

The war had proven to be a very interesting time for the family. As they saw airplanes, bombings, dead cows and devastation all around, the children were more excited than scared. During the war, Teun learned to speak German by studying books written in the language and he practiced by speaking to the German soldiers. He mastered the language so well; he became the interpreter for his family, friends and neighbors, as well as the German soldiers.

During the four day war, large German Junkers were flying low overhead and the de Jongs were feeling bad, because the Dutch fighters were nowhere to be seen.

By the end of Teun's schooling at the age of sixteen, World War II had already been in progress for two years. The German occupation continued even though the invasion by the Germans ended about five days after they entered Holland, in May of 1940. Many dairymen from the east side of Holland traveled over sixty miles and brought their herds with them, because the canals surrounding their farms and dairies had been used to flood their land in order to try to stop the Germans. Of course this didn't work and the Germans continued to come.

While on a family excursion to the neighboring township of Koudekerk, where Arie Sr. was born, the de Jong children bore witness to the post bombing devastation. Piet became afraid when he witnessed the destruction, but Karel was absolutely fascinated by everything he saw, especially the planes. Though the de Jong family did not live in a war zone, they witnessed the variety of smoking and wounded planes and bombers that had been shot, and went down on farm pastures only a half mile from their home.

Many of the Dutch women became anxious and concerned, when the German army rounded up the young men and forced them to work in the German factories and farms. During the last two years of the war the German factories needed workers. The German soldiers went to specific cities on certain days and picked up every capable man or young boy they found walking around the big city railroad stations or traffic hubs and took them away to work in the factories.

Teun and all his brothers liked the German soldiers they spoke to, and thought they were interesting and exciting. When the Germans invaded Holland, they were very nice to the Dutch children. They talked of how they had been drafted and were comfortable with being soldiers, but were not happy being so far away from their families. Some were from the Ukraine and Hitler had promised to liberate their country. When the war came to Holland, it was over in the blink of an eye. It only lasted four days.

After the German troops invaded, Jan, who was five, quiet and smart, admired how his family welcomed other Dutch families into their home, allowing them to stay in the cow barn to escape the fighting and bombing. Many times the de Jongs stayed in the barn also, in case the Germans bombed the house.

All of the Dutch soldiers who had been placed in German prison camps had to sign a paper stating they would not be involved in any retaliatory or hostile activity against the Germans. Once they signed the agreement, they were released and sent home to be reunited with their families and have some semblance of a normal life.

When Arie Sr. was first exposed to the overall intrigue and pageantry of the war and soldiers, he was swept off his feet. After witnessing the brutality and devastation of the four day German invasion he cried telling his family, "I wish I could have been in the army. I would have given my life for our country."

Teun immediately replied, "Father, you don't realize what you're saying. Holland would have lost anyway. Nothing could have stopped the war, or the invasion of our country. You have seven children. In order to survive we need you to be with us and survive we will. We have been very poor in a rich land. Now I want to know how it feels to be rich in a poor land."

The de Jongs felt the German people were just like them, and learned in their schools and churches to fight for God and country, the same way the Dutch did. The Germans had the same Psalms, the same Heidelberg's catechism and were either Catholic, or Lutheran just like the Dutch.

When the de Jongs got to know the Germans soldiers as people, they liked them. Deciding not to get into politics, Teun felt if they treated the Germans as friends, the family could make a lot of money. At the age of fifteen, Teun told his father his idea for making the family money and they put his plan into action.

During the war Teun and Piet's friend, Kees Roos, seventeen, became pro-German in his beliefs and enlisted into the Dutch SS. After the war ended there were repercussions for anyone that joined and followed the Germans/Nazis. Kees was arrested and sent to prison. Later, he was transferred to work in the coal mines in Limburgh, a province in Southern Holland close to the German border, where he remained working until he died.

Teun was impressed with Hitler at the beginning of the war, because of his economic views, which helped to boost the German economy; improving all Europe's economic growth overall as well. He convinced the family, that when the war was over, if Germany won, they would immigrate to the Ukraine, in Russia. However, if Germany lost the war, they would go to California instead, which is where they wanted to immigrate to anyway, because they already had family there.

Early in the morning while returning from milking during the German occupation, the de Jongs could hear the German soldiers singing as they marched all over the countryside. For them it was the temporary thrill and experience of peace time, although they knew the soldiers were being drilled for their next campaign.

To the de Jong children, it was beautiful; to see and hear the goose stepping, highly disciplined German soldiers. It was easy for the children to be impressed. They had heard many stories of how the Germans were victorious everywhere they went. However, the goose stepping pageantry and singing was not inspiring to the more sensible, older generation. To them the marching song, *'Wir Ghen Fahren...Nach Engeland, '*(After England We Go) was threatening.

Karel was impressed by the synchronized marching, singing and discipline of the German soldiers and felt the German uniforms were impeccable. This was another of Karel's life experiences he said he wouldn't have missed for a million bucks. He felt living through the German occupation was a very educational experience.

Units of German soldiers used the local schools as temporary living quarters. The surrounding communities were forced to house makeshift schoolrooms in workshops, sheds, barns, or in the council rooms of the local schools and churches. It was potentially a wild time for the children. If no buildings could be found to be used for classrooms, there would be no school. The children would stay home to work or play instead.

From the winter of 1944, to spring of 1945, the children had no school, because the Germans were using the schools as barracks. The community lost many of their teachers, who were mainly men, who had been forced to go to Germany to work in labor camps. Common use products like paper were hard to find due to the ravages of war. The winter that year was extremely cold and severe.

There was no heat in the makeshift classrooms and no paper to write on. Everything was being used for the war effort. Ever resourceful, the de Jongs had kept the school papers of the older siblings, and the younger children used those same papers to do their lessons by writing between the lines. John remembers the school children in his class exercising every ten to thirty minutes in order to keep warm. His teacher favored jumping jacks and they kept their wooden shoes on in class, because it was far too cold to take them off.

The Germans dug trench shelters around the farm and deep indentations pressed into the ground wherever the horse drawn cannons were placed. Many neighbors were lost during the exchange of military artillery fire. Holland and the de Jongs witnessed the peaceful withdrawal of the German troops, due in part to the peace treaty signed after Adolf Hitler was pronounced dead.

Food in the area was very scarce and the effects of starvation began to rear its ugly head. The government leaders of Alphen organized a make-shift soup kitchen where the needy town citizens could fill a small pail with a watery soup made of cabbage leaves and tulip bulbs. Every day the de Jongs saw the ever-increasing parade of people heading back and forth to get something to feed their families.

Schoolmates of the de Jong children would approach them begging for a slice of bread, or any small morsel of food, in order to keep the pangs of hunger at bay. It was tragic to watch as they wasted away.

The town of Alphen had a community slaughterhouse where people would take their animals that were either lame, or injured, to be butchered. A health inspector was there to insure the meat was safe to eat. The cost to use the facility was a portion of the slaughtered animal. When there was meat to purchase, the town crier would ride his bike through the neighborhoods, banging on a brass cymbal and would announce the type of meat and the price per pound. Everyone who could afford it, rushed to buy whatever meat was available.

The neighborhood in Alphen wasn't the best area, and at times it was like living amongst a den of thieves. Teun Vis, one of the people living across the street from the de Jongs, had a neighbor lady by the name of Mrs. ter Louw, who owned a cat he referred to as a "pain in the ass."

It was in the wintertime when her cat went missing. Vis had captured the cat and butchered it. He went to Mrs. ter Louw's just before Christmas and he told her, "I caught and butchered a rabbit and wanted to give you half for your Christmas dinner."

She was so happy to have some meat to eat and grateful he was so thoughtful. The whole neighborhood knew what happened, but no one had the heart to tell her she had eaten her own cat.

Fuel to heat their homes was scarce for many citizens in the Nederlands during the war. Most of the de Jong's neighbors in Alphen had no oil, coal or wood to use for cooking and warmth. The local children searched the canals, the dumps and streets for anything that could be burned. Doors were taken from empty buildings to chop up for heat. It was illegal to cut down trees in Holland, but the people were so cold they cut them down anyway. By the end of the war there were hardly any trees left in Alphen.

To help heat their home the de Jongs would harvest and dry the decomposing grasses and roots from the drainage ditches close to the canals. They would cut them into turf bricks to use for cooking and to heat the water needed to make cheese. To keep the cooked food warm for her large family, Maartje would place the pots of hot food inside a large wooden box built by Reinus Fase. The box, a type of homemade incubator, had several compartments that were first lined with a layer of hay and then covered with thick velvet fabric from old drapes. This was very effective in keeping the food warm.

During the German occupation of Holland, the German soldiers were quartered in some of the local horse and cattle barns, including the de Jongs. Although they had a hard time understanding them, the de Jong children found many nice Germans who willingly shared their leftovers with them. Many times they ate with the enemy. Arie remembers licking the remains from the German soldier's pots of pudding.

The German soldiers stayed on the de Jong family farm as occupational forces, until Holland was liberated by the Canadian Allies, on May 5, 1945. The German soldiers had been nice enough to stay in the barn with their horses, and allowed the de Jong family to remain in their home, but shared the cook stove used to prepare the family meals.

The older boys remember watching as German soldiers went across the Rhine by boats, where there was quite a bit of partying with plenty of girls and lots of alcohol. Hoping for a better life or a way to escape, the girls freely entertained the soldiers, it didn't matter what country they came from.

There are many things in life that can't be controlled by war. A prime example of this is the human heart and physical attraction. The only women available to the German soldiers were the local Dutch girls.

The German soldiers dressed sharp, were well behaved and good looking. The young Dutch girls of course became interested. They were thinking with their hearts and hormones, not giving a second thought to religious or political viewpoints. They simply saw available men that were young and good looking.

During the five years of the German occupation a vast number of young girls gave in to temptation. They would travel across the Rhine to be with the young soldiers. Of course, there was plenty of drinking, dancing and physical comfort offered. The soldiers were hungry for love and companionship and they offered money and cigarettes in return.

Most of the Allied soldiers during the liberation were Canadian and their popularity had also grown with the Dutch girls. Liberation day was great, as the Canadian soldiers marched through Alphen a/d Rhine to Leiden, with lots of heavy machinery and tanks. The majority of the allied soldiers did not use the local township for their living quarters. This was very fortunate for the citizens of Alphen, who were finally able to have their homes back. The residents of Holland were very thankful for their country's freedom from the Germans and the immediate supply of food being dropped by the same planes that had once carried bombs.

The Dutch girls were grateful for the country's Liberation and the food supplies, yet some were met with hostility from local boys who were angered over the way the girls went with soldiers from other countries, including the German enemy. The men and boys felt the women and girls of Holland belonged to them.

Many of the girls were treated poorly. The girls who consorted with the German soldiers were treated exceptionally bad. They were shunned by the men and other women as though they suffered from a contagious disease; as if they were lower than the lowliest prostitute.

The girls were repeatedly warned by political and religious factions, not to get romantically involved with the Germans, because they were the enemy. Of course, some of the young Dutch girls did not heed the warning, and many married soldiers from other countries. On Arie Sr.'s birthday, May 5, 1945, (D day), those political and religious organizations rounded up as many girls as they could and cut off all their hair to shame and make examples of them. Of course, this happened wherever there was a war, or soldiers. The same held true when the Dutch soldiers went to Indonesia and other countries. In Germany, Tom met his first wife Karin, while he was serving in the American Army and they were married shortly after. His father, Arie Sr. was against him marrying a German girl.

In May of 1945, the Allied forces marched across the big rivers of Holland into the central area of the small country. It was a truly indescribable feeling of hope and joy when the Allied forces, which included the American soldiers, came to liberate the country. The de Jong family, who was used to seeing the sharp looking, no nonsense uniforms of the German army, felt the American uniforms fell short in comparison. Germany had signed an unconditional surrender and rumors were rampant regarding Hitler's suicide. Because of this, the local atmosphere was much more relaxed during this time.

The German troops being marched off as prisoners still looked impressive in their tightly synchronized marching formation and uniforms, however, their singing had stopped. A great portion of the German soldiers were lucky enough to be captured by the Allied forces. Those who were unfortunate enough to be captured by the Russian soldiers were not treated as well, because of the way the Germans had treated the Russians with excessive harshness and very little respect. A million and half German soldiers went into the Russian prisoner of war camps, but only a mere 8,000 survived.

The Dutch people feared the Communists more than the Nazis.

The Dutch people found it difficult not to be caught up in the joy of LIBERATION, including the de Jongs. Teun and Piet took all their brothers and Ellie to the celebration, paying three cents for each of them to be ferried across the Rhine. The festivities were held in a large field across from the City Hall, which also doubled as an ice skating park in the wintertime.

It was exciting for the kids, especially young Arie Jr. There were carnival games and rides, food, music and dancing. Everyone went a different direction depending on their interest, and to celebrate with neighbors and friends. Left to his own devices Arie Jr. spent most of his time hanging around the rides, even though he had no money. The happy party goers, drunk with joy and alcohol saw he wasn't able to ride and paid his way over and over again. Excited, Arie Jr. kept running from ride to ride, and was unaware his brothers and sister had gone home leaving him behind.

It wasn't until the crowd thinned out around one in the morning that his neighbor Wim Scherpenzeel and his group of friends, saw that Arie Jr., only six, at the time, was alone and took him home. Because their house was always unlocked, no one heard him when he returned and went to bed. The next day he relayed the story of his great adventure and everyone was impressed with how well he had done on his own.

The Liberation celebratory feasting lasted for several days.

By the end of the war the American airplanes were dropping crackers, chocolates and Lucky Strike cigarettes throughout Holland. Some people took advantage and sold the cigarettes on the black market for seven guilders each, the equivalent of an American dollar. Although Teun encouraged his brothers to sell the cigarettes, he warned them not to start smoking.

The allies dropped food from planes during the last month of the war, which was very helpful in the fight against hunger. Jan thought the dry crackers were delicious. Due to the lack of money most families could not afford to buy new clothes or the fabric to make them. The women were resourceful and would gather up the parachutes to make clothing for their children, including Arie Sr's mother, who made shirts and dresses for her grandchildren. The green material was thin and the shirts and dresses didn't last very long.

Arie Sr with his sister Janna and his mother

After the war there was also a great shortage of building supplies, which made the community reconstruction and rebuilding efforts a challenge. Without having the ability to rebuild, the country did not receive the jumpstart it needed for economic recovery.

There were many times during the war when the de Jongs would find flies in the milk, rats in the cheese and maggots in the cow troughs. Some cows suffered from hoof and mouth disease, while others contracted Tuberculosis. Occasionally they found rats in the bottom of the milk buckets they had placed in the canal to cool after milking. Despite these occurrences Teun says they were never ill and he can't remember anyone ever having the flu.

The children grew strong and healthy despite the impoverished conditions. They ate a lot of fruit from the local trees, ignoring the portion where the birds had already pecked out the sweet flesh. Without strong immune systems some of the family members probably would have died.

One of the de Jong children, Jan, came down with a very severe case of tuberculosis in 1945. The doctor said his lungs resembled a net from the effects of all the scarring. Many children in the war torn area had died from T.B. It's a miracle he somehow overcame the disease.

Piet de Jong regarding World War II: "We were very thankful for the armed might of America. It was astounding to us what they sacrificed to save Europe from Hitler's insanity. If only they had stopped the Russians too from flooding Eastern and Southern Europe with the Communist plague. This has been very sad for Poland, Hungary, Rumania, etc, who had seen or heard enough about war time death."

The de Jong boys had heard wondrous stories from their father concerning World War I and how Prime Minister Chamberlain of England had been a champion for peace, with the message *"Peace in our time"*.

Since the pageantry associated with the German soldiers during World War II was an exciting time for the boys, they found peace time somewhat disconcerting. They wanted to find out for themselves what it was all about, but now that the war was over, the emphasis shifted toward immigration to America to start a new life.

The Family Joins the Black Market

Maartje's uncle, Bastiaan Hus

In 1929, the first landlord of the family farm in Alphen was Maartje's, rich *ome (*uncle), Bastiaan Hus. Because he had no children of his own, he had deep concerns regarding the family. He remained the family landlord, until the depression hit in the 1930's and he was backed into a corner financially and forced to sell off some of his assets. Unfortunately, the farm and dairy where the family lived in Alphen were among the properties and assets sold.

The new landlord, Myn Heer Rippe, was a textile merchant, who had started his business carrying his pack of wares on his back, selling door to door to the local farmers and merchants throughout the countryside. Oma de Jong, Arie Sr.'s mother, had been one of his

- Huswinkel op de hoek van de Hoefkade en de Jacob Catsstraat in de jaren '50.-

best customers. He never forgot her loyalty and support when he became the owner of a successful clothing store in Leiden, the nearest city to the west of Alphen along the Rhine. He was a good man and landlord. Once again good fortune blessed the family.

In 1942, local residents were starting to feel the negative effects of the food shortage once more. The country's government had implemented ration cards for food, as well as everything else. The rations were meager at best. Just a few years earlier, Holland had been the land of plenty. Now the only thing in abundance was the massive amount of people suffering from the food

De HUS-winkel aan de Jan Luykenlaan in 1953. ARCHIEFFOTO

shortage. Arie Sr. saw this as an economic opportunity and joined the Black Market. The dwindling local food supplies were a direct result of farmers being put into a position where they had to feed their food supplies to the German army.

The Black Market was a way to finally make some money for his growing and struggling family. As good church members he and his family had always faithfully supported the country's political system and by doing so had almost gone broke, losing everything. It was only by the grace of God and the mercy of the landlord they were able to keep the farm.

Arie Sr. was an adventurer at heart and always ready to take a risk. He had gone to jail five times. Each time he somehow charmed the German officers and was subsequently released. He would tell his captors how he, his wife and seven children made cheese and butter for the German Army. Because he had such a large family to care for they must have repeatedly taken pity on him. He also confessed that he had only

- Een voor die tijd erg modern en blits bestelwagentje van Hus in 1960.-

butchered his own cattle, in order to feed his large family. If farmers were arrested, the Germans usually let them go.

War is a finely tuned machine that consumes and destroys anything and everything in its path. Forced into a corner with no other option, people were willing to pay a high premium to obtain anything to eat. The German army closely monitored and guarded everything the farms and dairies produced; hay, wood, coal, oil and gas were requisitioned. Because of the war and its aftermath the economic situation of the entire world was now in trouble.

Whenever the pigs got sick and died from hog cholera, Arie Sr. buried them. He would dig them back up the next day and in most cases the meat would be white and good again. To test his theory he would give some of the pig meat to the neighbors, Hein Groeneveld and his wife, to eat first, always encouraging them to eat the meat straight away. If the neighbor failed to either get sick or die, he would ask how the meat tasted. He knew he had options and he could either sell the meat, or the family could eat it themselves.

Of course, there was never any malicious intent on his part; the main reason driving his decision was to earn money for the family. It was mainly for health reasons this practice was prohibited by the government, who wanted any animal raised for consumption to be given inspections for disease.

Arie Sr. saw the Black Market as his chance to finally make money from farming. There was only one problem: The Germans monitored everything and made it dangerous to take food away from the system. Thinking about the future of his growing family, he threw caution to the wind and decided to utilize the Black Market to take care of his growing family's needs.

Arie Sr. was suspected of illegally making cheese to sell on the Black Market, and was friends with several people on many levels within the differing political parties. He was alerted by someone in the Gruen Polizi that his dairy was going to be searched. He informed his friend and barber, Jakobus (Kobus) Vierbergen, who his children affectionately referred to as *Ome* (uncle) of the situation.

Kobus agreed to hide the cheese in the basement of his barbershop/home. Using the cover of darkness, the de Jongs quickly and quietly shuttled the cheese they had stored in their basement, across the street in a wooden cart, to Kobus' home. The Germans ascended on the dairy in what they believed to be a surprise inspection, but they were the ones surprised, when they found nothing and left empty handed.

Kobus came back to Arie Sr. and told him they needed to move the cheese again and quickly. He was afraid he was under suspicion and would be searched, because his customers asked why his barbershop smelled like cheese.

The Germans that occupied the dairy in Alphen, never suspected small children regarding the smuggling of contraband items and food products. During the latter part of World War II, young Arie Jr. was a courier for his father's Black Market business.

Jan was also a courier for his father. On one occasion he was supposed to deliver the food to Mr. van Heiningen, who was the comptroller for an oil distributor friend of Arie Sr. However, Jan made the delivery to the man's neighbors in error, who were thrilled to receive such a generous and welcome package.

Koos Verhagen a neighbor in Alphen

During the war, the landlord, Myn Herr Rippe also ran out of food. Arie Sr. would have the children deliver Black Market food; eggs, milk and meat to pay the rent. The German soldiers monitored the roads, river and bridges in order to prevent Black Market activity. During that time there were no cars. No one could afford them. Everything was pretty much horse and wagon. The Germans even had large horse drawn artillery guns on the fields of the de Jong farm.

The Germans searched the adults, but never suspected the smaller children of smuggling. During the war Karel, Jan, Kees and Ellie walked fifteen kilometers one way in the snow, to the city of Leiden, pulling a three wheel cart with wooden wheels. Because of the snow, the children had nails on the bottom of their shoes to give them traction and to prevent them from slipping. To take food to the landlord, two of the children would pull the wagon with ropes, while one pedaled. The cart filled with meat and eggs, was topped with fire wood in order to disguise the food hidden below. The food was given to the landlord in lieu of rent for the family's dairy, until they could afford to pay rent again. The first real money the family made was during the war, because of the Black Market.

On the days the children made the deliveries to the landlord, they usually spent the night, because it was such a long distance back home. The guestroom beds were rarely used and the sheets would be freezing cold. Used to sleeping on flannel sheets, Karel remembers how the linen sheets were so cold it was like sleeping on ice. The three children would huddle together in order to try to stay warm.

However, it was always a treat for them the next morning, because Mrs. Rippe, the woman of the house, had her stepdaughter Agnes hard boil some eggs for their breakfast. Because eggs were worth so much money, the children were never given eggs to eat at home.

The children always had fun, even while working, so it wasn't a burden. When the children did have time off to play, they shot mud balls through hollow brass curtain rods, at the homes of people they didn't like. They also played marbles frequently, but couldn't afford to buy them.

One time Ellie stole a penny, and Arie Jr. said if he was going to steal any money, he was going to do it right. He took a quarter from the jar his mother put the money from the sale of milk. Maartje found out and Arie Jr. was spanked severely. Ellie cried. Although she had stolen also, he had gotten spanked and she didn't.

In 1944, Arie Sr. bought some sheep from a neighboring farmer about 4 kilometers away from the farm. Jan remembers going with his father to pick them up. They herded the sheep over the road next to the canal. The neighbors had a little boat used for hauling vegetables. U.S. Allied fighter planes flew over the boat and warned them to evacuate the boat

immediately, because they were going to shoot it full of holes.

Arie Sr., Jan and the sheep hid in the ditch opposite the canal. One neighbor didn't get off the boat in time and was shot in the shoulder, rendering his arm useless. While the de Jongs hid in the ditch, bullets continued to fly all around them. They could see the bullets dancing and splashing across the surface of the water. Fortunately, neither of them was hurt or hit by a stray bullet and no sheep were lost.

When it came to the art of smuggling, Teun was very useful to his father. Piet however, attempted to help butcher and stow away the meat from hogs, sheep and cows. Arie Sr. was very skilled at skinning and cutting the meat. He tried to teach the art of butchering to Piet, who was satisfied to just help his father and watch. Piet was able to sell the dried and stretched skins of moles for ten cents each. It was a bloody business, but he had learned a lot by watching his father and paying attention.

The whole family pitched in around the farm and the chores were shared to ensure everything was done daily. The three youngest children were in charge of peeling the potatoes every day. Teun would divide the amount of potatoes between them according to their age. Jan received the most, then Ellie. Arie Jr., the youngest and slowest, got the least, and because no one was allowed to help anyone else finish their chores, he was left in the milk *stahl* by himself to finish. Nothing was wasted. The potato peels would be fed to the cows and goats. Jan hated peeling potatoes and felt milking would be a much better job. Although, once he started getting up early in the morning to do the milking, peeling potatoes didn't seem so bad after all.

The milk *stahl* was actually a barn, which was attached to the house and kept the animals and farmers safe from the cold during the winter. Many families like the de Jongs used the loft above the milk *stahl* as sleeping quarters. Whoever was the last to get into bed at night was responsible for turning off the light. Arie Jr. hated being last because he had to walk to his bed in the dark. Karel, always the prankster, made sure Arie Jr. was always last and when he got halfway to the light, Karel would jump out of bed. Arie Jr., thinking Karel was now last would start running in an attempt to get into bed first, but he never made it. Karel beat him every time, causing Arie Jr. to walk back toward the light, only to have Karel repeat the prank over and over, while the other boys laughed.

When he was nine years old, Jan helped his father with the butchering of hogs, horses and cows. This practice wasn't allowed by the German soldiers, who confiscated food to send back to their families in Germany. Because of this, all of the butchering had to be done in secret, and then the meat was sold on the Black Market.

The Dutch gaming police had suspicions concerning Arie Sr. early on. He was known throughout the surrounding areas as an adventurer. After shadowing the family's movements they found meat at one of his customer's home. The gaming police took Teun back to the customer and confronted them; stating he had delivered the meat, which he of course denied, resulting in a negative outcome for the police.

The first people Arie Sr. had to deal with to protect his Black Market enterprise were the government agents. He was very personable and even made friends with some of the agents, which enabled him to know ahead of time when a surprise inspection of the farm was planned. It was the same with the Dutch Police. Unfortunately, there was also the *Grune Polizei* (Green Police), the Gestapo and even the Dutch SS. It was not an easy task for him to stay a step ahead of all of those agencies.

Arie Sr. had been picked up and imprisoned on several occasions, five of which were during the war. It was very hard for people to grasp and understand how and why the police never kept him in jail.

The country was divided by the pro-orange and the pro-German factions. To protect themselves and find favor with the Germans, the Dutch pro-Germans turned in their pro-orange neighbors. The Germans were vigilant and used any reason, or means necessary to arrest anyone they felt was anti-German.

Jan van der Broek, a neighbor, owned goats and would come to milk them at the corral next to the de Jongs. On one occasion in 1943, Arie Sr. sold Jan two pigs to butcher. Since Jan and his helper were riding bicycles, he had no way to get the pigs home alive, so Arie Sr. used his stun gun to kill the pigs. They hoisted the pigs into the bicycle baskets and the two men were on their way. A short while later, Jan and his helper were arrested by the *Grune Polizei,* the pro-German Dutch Police; after they were caught butchering the pigs in Jan's shed.

Van der Broek told the Germans about Arie Sr, and he was later arrested and taken in for questioning. When the Germans asked Arie Sr. what he got out of the deal, he said, "I only got a couple of shots of schnapps for killing the pigs. That's all."

The Germans confiscated his stun gun and let him go. However, Jan and his helper were pro-German in their political views, and he was always expressing his pro-German beliefs. The remarks Jan van der Broek made about the great power of the Germans did not sit well with the de Jongs, because his remarks came across as anti-Dutch.

Because he had illegally butchered the pigs, Van der Broek and his helper were taken to concentration/work camps by the Dutch CCD-Crisis Control Dienst and they never returned.

The depression had been extremely hard on the Nederlands, and when Hitler started to build his ever-increasing army, Germany's focus shifted from agriculture to building weapons of war. Their close neighbor, the Nederlands had an abundance of farms and dairies and Germany started purchasing produce, meats and dairy products, which helped to jumpstart the small country's economy again. Because of this, many Dutch citizens became pro-German, especially the farmers.

During the war, it was illegal to own a radio because of the English and Allied broadcasts into the Netherlands. Arie Sr. knew owning a radio was illegal, but owned one anyway. The de Jong family had acquaintances that were pro-orange or pro-German. Before the war, Arie Sr.'s friend, Willem van der Wel married a German girl named Paula. Of course, she was pro-German in her political beliefs and she knew about the radio.

Arie Sr. hid the radio beneath a floorboard in the hallway of his friend Jaap Metselaar's, parent's home. The Germans came for the radio and threatened Arie Sr. with death if he did not turn the radio over. He went to Jaap's home, retrieved the radio and turned it in. He and Jaap were both arrested and sent to prison. There was great speculation regarding whether or not it was Paula who alerted the Germans as to the location of the radio.

Farmers were considered a valuable commodity and highly regarded by the Germans, because they kept the Germans supplied with food. Since Arie Sr. was a dairyman/farmer and he had so many children he was released shortly after his arrest. Thankfully, Jaap was also released a few days later.

Post War Economics

The de Jongs already had family members living in America before the war who were doing very well. Teun was happy the war was finally over. Although he had once supported Hitler, he changed his mind when he realized the man had become a monster.

On the dairy in Alphen, 1946. Piet (left), Teun and Jopie Verhagen

In 1945, after the war, the new Dutch government changed both the value and look of the country's currency. Overnight, the de Jongs currency went from being worth $100,000 to $25. The value of the family's livestock inventory changed as well. They owned thirty-five cows, young calf stock, a hundred sheep, forty pigs, eighteen goats and lots of feed, etc. The mature cows were worth $100 and the twenty head of young stock was worth $60 each. The family also owned one hundred head of sheep, valued at $25 a head, forty pigs at $20 each and eighteen goats worth $20 a head. The sum total of all the livestock was $8,360. The previous worth of the same amount of livestock was five times as much. (Note: The figures have been converted into American dollars.)

When the Dutch government began printing new money, all of the country's existing currency was rendered worthless. The choice was simple; they could either pay it in taxes or destroy it all, because now it was of no value.

Though the family had lost the monetary value of their currency, they still had the value of the livestock and its offspring. The new government took several months to print the new currency. The de Jongs did not put any of their money into the bank, because most of the money they had was earned during the war, from the "Black Market." According to the new Dutch government laws, the family was required to sell all of their products in the post war distribution system, but of course, they did not. After running a profitable covert business for five years during the war, it was difficult to stop their Black Market activity.

When the war ended, every Dutch citizen received ten guilders, the equivalent of $2.50 per person and could buy twenty loaves of bread, or ten pounds of cheese. The ten member de Jong family pooled their money together, putting it into the family business.

They continued to make money using their "Black Market" system. Meat was in short supply throughout the country and still being rationed, so of course, the de Jongs slaughtered some of their sheep and pigs to sell, because butchered meat brought over three times the value of a live animal. The de Jongs felt they were simply doing themselves and the country a service by supplying the demand for fresh meat. Fresh milk, pigs, goats, chickens and eggs made up the inventory of goods for sale by the family's money making enterprise. It didn't take the family long to make new money. They multiplied and built on the one hundred guilders they started with.

The ocean off the coast of Holland was rich with an abundance of fish, and the Dutch fishermen in the industrial fleet used post-war fishing to their advantage. However, this was one enterprise the de Jongs did not participate in and none of them ventured close to the shores, because of the multitude of sea mines placed there during the war.

Under the new Dutch government, taxes were so incredibly high; they became the family's main expense. With the higher taxes and such a large family, the de Jongs barely had enough to survive, let alone save for the future, despite the family's "Black Market" success.

In order to get ahead and survive, they continued selling under the table to people individually. If anyone sold goods to government run outlets, they had to report the money they made. This added even more to the outrageous tax already imposed upon the citizens of Holland. The family kept their money hidden; desperately saving to prepare for leaner times. Hopefully they would emigrate and have a new start for the family in America.

Even though the family continued to run their covert enterprise after the war, the de Jongs persisted in being frugal. Food was rationed among all of the family members, especially special treats like pudding and candy. On Sundays, Maartje would make pudding that she separated into bowls and cups of various sizes and designs; most of them scavenged from the local dump. To make the distribution of the portions fair, each Sunday Teun selected a different child to decide which bowl's portion the other children would receive.

The child making the choices would face the corner, so they couldn't see the size of the bowls. Teun would point to a random bowl and say, "Who gets this one?" He normally pointed to the largest bowl first, and Kees knew this, so when it was his turn, he always chose the first portion for himself. Once Teun realized what Kees was doing, he started to mix up the order of the bowls and portions to make it more random.

Every week their mother, Maartje, also purchased a pound of caramels from the corner grocer and divided them equally among all the children. Tom, Piet and Karel would save their candies to eat over time, while the younger kids devoured theirs instantly and then envied the older boys, who always had candy, while they didn't. To make matters worse, the older boys would pour the candy out onto the table in front of the smaller kids and count them, while the little ones looked on with their mouths watering.

During the war, the neighbor across the road from the dairy in Alphen, Willem Vis, a cattle dealer, wanted to borrow some money from Arie Sr. He had no way to repay the loan and Teun cautioned his father not to give Willem the advance, because he was a bad risk and he'd never get his money back.

Arie Sr. stated he would loan him 300 guilders, if Willem used his Sunday suit as collateral and an agreement was made. Willem was prone to violence when he drank and it was well known he drank a lot. Time passed and he wanted his suit back, but still hadn't repaid a single guilder. One Sunday evening while Arie Sr. and Maartje were at church service, Willem went to the house and demanded the return of his suit.

Teun had been left in charge of the children and fortunately, the door was bolted, because Willem was drunk and tried to force his way in. Teun got a large butcher knife and swore if he broke in, he would stab the unruly neighbor in order to protect the family. In the meantime, Willem was outside yelling obscenities, calling Arie Sr., a "Son of a bitch" and a few other choice words. When he went to a window to break his way in, he noticed Kees standing there with a shotgun, and immediately went to try the backdoor instead.

He raised so much commotion the neighbors all came out of their homes. His wife and children were too embarrassed to come out and watched through the windows. Someone called the police. After officer van Straaten arrived on the scene, he attempted to calm Willem down and told him leave to the house. He refused and became even more violent and struck out at van Straaten, who knew Judo and flipped Vis head over heels in the front yard. Willem quickly went back home with his head hanging and his tail between his legs. Feeling sorry for him, Arie Sr. returned his suit a few weeks later. Willem's family immigrated to Canada after the war, in 1947

The new Dutch government's tax base and economic structure was in place. Teun knew he needed to learn to understand every aspect of the laws and policies, in order to keep up with the new system, just to keep one step ahead of the government. It was 1946, and he began going to night school to study economics, social security, and taxes. Most of his classmates were businessmen with high school diplomas seeking to start a business, not the son of dairyman like himself with a limited education.

It usually took the business men two years to complete the course work, yet it only took Teun one year. He crammed twenty hours of study into his already long and exhausting work week. He got up extra early each day in order to study from 3 am to 5 am, before starting his workday. Three nights a week he went from work, which ended at 7 pm, straight to his 7:30 pm class. His long day ended at 9:30pm. He felt a sense of urgency; because the family's economic future was at stake.

Teun never took credit for his schedule juggling and time management. He gives all the credit to his brothers, who covered him when he needed extra time to study during work hours. The family knew the importance of what Teun was trying to accomplish. It was for the benefit of them all. At the course completion, he graduated at the top of his class of three-hundred students, earning perfect ten scores in the three main areas of study: business administration, social security laws and bookkeeping.

He remembers how excited his professors were as they called him up to the front to congratulate him. Knowing Teun would never have settled for less, the family had come to expect this form of perfection from him, and weren't as excited as his professors by his accomplishment.

He remembers how they never even complimented him when he graduated. It was what the family expected. They didn't worry about getting or giving compliments. However, they did respect his accomplishments, because he did the bookkeeping and they knew how important that was.

The reason Teun felt he did so well on his tests, was because initially his brother Piet started the class with him, but was drafted into the Dutch army halfway through the course. When Piet came home on the weekends, Teun taught him everything he'd learned, which only helped to reinforce all his knowledge even more. Arie Sr. now possessed a first class labor force. His confidence in them and their abilities grew daily. The farm's workforce was comprised of his children; a team he could fully trust. He knew they would do a great job, because they all had the same common goal. The family needed Teun for management, because of his knowledge of bookkeeping and his mind for business practices. Piet had more ability regarding field work.

Teun, nineteen at the time, was solely responsible for taking care of details the others failed to do. Piet, eighteen, was competing to prove himself and tackled whatever farm work needed attention. Though the work was hard, the boys still managed to have fun. At the age of thirteen, Kees was a very hard worker, and he was constantly being egged on and teased by Teun and Pete. Elso though younger than Kees, was a very hard worker, but less aggressive. Teun was always a very capable performer in whatever he chose to pursue. Whenever he and Piet worked together they were like a finely tuned engine. Everything ran smoothly.

The weather was beautiful during the spring and summer, but the fall and winter months could be extremely tough.   Piet remembers how he and Teun had dreamed about the weather in the more tropical areas of the world. Places where it was so warm a person didn't have to suffer as the cold wind ripped and cut through everything it came in contact with. No more cold hands and near frost bitten feet. The tropics would be a blessed relief. Piet remembers a song called, 'Sunny Madeira'. The romantic melody still haunts him to this day. Of course California was also a big part of their dream.

Because Teun did the books, and the boys worked the farm, Arie Sr. was enjoying his practically carefree life. The government controls were still very stringent, because Holland was still struggling as a country to escape the effects of poverty created during the war. The family had made war profits through the Black Market and the government was looking for money to level the playing field, and wanted to equalize the war profiteers with the rest of the population who had suffered through years of starvation.

This was a process that Teun knew how to fight tooth and nail, because the effects of the government's restrictions would have left the family considerably poorer. The tax-collectors were not dummies and were in the mood to rake the family over the coals. However, they became increasingly frustrated, because Teun, a mere farm boy thwarted them at every move and opportunity.

Teun's education paid off; the family business quickly grew. The value of their thirty-five cows was $3,500 and they made $2,850 in the first year. He felt it was like buying a business and paying it off in three years, when the value of the stock inventory was factored in. He remained the family bookkeeper for two years, until he taught Elso to take over, which gave him the freedom to immigrate to America. Piet, who had been drafted into the Dutch Army, had gone to Indonesia. He had been next in line to take over as bookkeeper.

Arie Sr. had a habit of looking for ways to cut costs when it came to hiring farm labor. This brought many colorful characters and experiences to the de Jong farm. One particular occasion he hired a worker named Hugo from the rehab service center. Hugo wasn't exactly the sharpest crayon in the box, but he could have beaten everyone else at being the hardest worker if he had chosen to. He only truly excelled in milking, because it was a sit down job.

Hugo had been in jail several times, but the family didn't judge him. The only thing that mattered to them was that he continued to do his job and do it well. The children enjoyed the stories he told regarding his life experiences. One story he told was how he was down on his luck and had gone to his minister for help, and he was clothed and well fed. After duly thanking the minister, he happened to notice a rather nice looking bicycle parked in the vestibule. Hugo told the children how he began speaking to the bicycle, as though it was fully able to understand everything he said.

"Are you going to come with me or do I take you?" Since the bike failed to give a reply, Hugo simply took it and found himself back in jail.

In 1947, not long after the war, local people began to talk about taking vacations. During the war there was no such thing as vacations, because everything including the barns, sheds, farms, schools, etc, had been taken over by the Germans. Elso, Karel, Jan and a friend wanted to go on vacation and they received permission from Teun to go, stating he and Kees would stay behind and would take care of doing all the chores. Everyone had failed to consult their father in the matter to ask his permission.

When the boys said where they were going, "on vacation," he told them he'd never been on a vacation before, so the boys asked if he wanted to join them. Of course, he said, yes. He grabbed his jacket and told Maartje he was going on vacation with the boys. They had no tents, raingear or extra clothing and took very little food.

The vacationing group was allowed to sleep in the haylofts of several generous farmers during their trip. Unfortunately, the wind would whip through the gaps in the barn boards, forcing them to burrow deep down under the loose hay in order to stay warm. They rode their bicycles through the towns of Lisse and Haarlem, before heading north to the Afsluit Dyke, built in 1932. When they were 40km over the dyke, the wind came up hard and fast blowing so hard it was difficult to stand or walk, let alone ride their bicycles. The wind was behind them, which helped them to obtain incredible speeds, although with some difficulty.

When they arrived in Friesland, located in the northern part of Holland, (known as the Nederlands), a severe storm started to approach. Luckily, their father had brought a little money with him and they went into a small café, while there they drank hot chocolate and heard a radio forecast, announcing the storm would last the rest of the week. Arie Sr. said they were going to put their bicycles on the train and head back home. It was very fortunate he had decided to join the boys. The storm was long and lasted another week.

After the *liberation*, Arie Sr. had more time to relax. It had taken all his energy during the war to make a decent living, yet stay out of trouble. Peace time was met with the blessing of two more children, daughters Henrietta Gertruida Wilhelmina, March of 1947 and Margje, November of 1948.

Jet is Born

Henrietta Gertruda Wilhemena, affectionately known as Jet, was the second girl born, on March 16, 1947.

Jet only lived in Holland until the age of 2 ½, and then the family immigrated to Poway, in America. Her most vivid childhood memories are of the years spent at 17th Street in Escondido.

Jet at the de Jong home in Alphen

Ellie and Jet in Alphen

Karel's Goats

When Karel was around ten years old; he cared for the goats of a family friend, Teun Van Rijn during the winter. His brother Teun promised to give him a newborn goat of his own the following spring. His father saw Karel had a knack when it came to caring for goats and bought him three more. With four goats, he had breeding stock and before long the herd had grown to fifteen. The goats could supply a gallon of milk a day and ate less feed. When you compared the amount needed to feed them, the goats were a much better investment than cows.

Everyone was impressed by the way Karel took full responsibility for his small herd. This was just another example of how the members of de Jong family showed strength of conviction and a great deal of business savvy early on in life. Because goat's milk wasn't susceptible to TB, Karel sold the goat milk to his father to mix with the cow milk to make the cheese. The mixture of the two milks enhanced the flavor of the cheese to insure a richer and more flavorful outcome. Karel became known as, *the goat farmer* in Alphen and the neighboring areas. Goats don't consume great amounts of hay and Karel was very thrifty. He serviced a route to pick up all the potato peelings and kitchen waste from neighbors to feed his goats. Whenever he needed to purchase feed, Karel paid for it. He also harvested the cut and wasted hay from the side of the public roadways.

Karel and his goats at the farm in Alphen

In the family's home town of Alphen there was an organization for goat keepers, called "Christelyke Geiten Fok Vereeniging," (the Christian Goat Breeders Association). The organization owned two male/Billy goats used for breeding; one large and one small. They were the best quality for breeding and were placed at the de Jong dairy. Billy goats are quite a bit more pungent than dairy cows and other livestock, so many of the other members preferred not to house them at their farms and only took possession long enough to breed their females,

before taking them back to the de Jongs. The Association paid Karel to care for and feed the Billy goats.

Whenever their goats were in heat, many members brought the females to the de Jongs to have them bred by the Billy goats. Annie, the de Jong family's maid and her father owned a goat and was also a member of the Christian Goat Breeders Society. So when members came to have their goats bred, she felt obligated as a member to assist in the breeding process. Karel of course, stood off to the side hiding and laughing. To add further embarrassment to Annie, the whole experience would be rehashed during dinner conversation.

Karel hired several of his younger brother, Arie's friends and classmates as helpers, but some of their mothers wanted them to quit. After working in the small shed with the goats, the boys went home smelling of the strong stench of the Billy goat, which was pretty overwhelming to the senses.

The "Christelyke Geiten Fok Vereeniging" organization held a yearly celebration with coffee, sodas and hard liquor. Arie Sr. never attended any of the school, church or dairymen meetings. However, he never missed the goat keeper meetings and always attended with Karel and Arie Jr. They sat off to the side drinking soda pop, watching as the men drank hard liquor and smoked. The men smoked so much; the air turned blue and was so thick you could cut it with a knife. They always had a roaring good time.

A neighbor, Jan Angenent, had ten children and worked 80 hours a week. He was amazed that a school kid like Karel was making far more money than most of the men in the area.

Karel was a hard worker and protected the stock and profits anyway he saw fit. On one occasion Karel and his friends took a boat to a neighboring area to harvest some hay. They left immediately after school, even though the sky was threatening rain. When the hay was loaded onto the small boat, they took off for home. They were at the halfway point on the return trip, when it started to rain. They pushed the piles of hay tightly together and took off their clothes to protect the hay and keep it dry. A half an hour later, the five naked boys docked the boat loaded with the hay, which still ended up a little moist from the rainfall.

Karel was an excellent manager who knew how to inspire the helpers he never paid. He made everyone feel it was an honor to work with the goats. The male goats which belonged to the "Christelyke Geiten Fok Vereeniging" received special care. The boy who was the most devoted was given the title of, *"1st, He Goat Servant."* (He also had a 2nd and 3rd)

In the winter when it became very cold, Karel's helpers took off their coats to warm the "Billy" goats. There were times the goats pulled the coats off their backs, and urinated on them. The poor mothers tried desperately to wash the stench of the goats out of the clothing, but it was difficult to do.

Karel was never one for sports. At the age of twelve he tried his hand at fishing and after sitting stagnant for five to ten minutes, he became antsy deciding it really wasn't for him and went back to tend his goats. On another occasion he tried his hand at soccer. He felt running around chasing a ball in the sun all day was pointless and once again decided it wasn't for him and went back to tending his goats.

During the winter when the fields were frozen over, the family had a big manure pit they used. Boards were placed across the top of the pit wall to allow the wet manure to be dumped in from wheelbarrows.

On one particular occasion, Karel's *first goat helper*, Jelle Houweling, was on the boards in the center of the pit, attempting to dump his wheelbarrow full of manure. When he tried to shake the contents free, the momentum caused him to lose his balance. He and the wheelbarrow fell into the three and a half feet of manure in the pit.

Jelle was buried in the manure up to his head and shoulders. Since he was unable to get out of his predicament, he screamed for help. Although Karel saw his situation, rather than rescue Jelle, Karel started screaming until a crowd of other children and adults surrounded the pit.

Karel didn't want to miss the opportunity to have as many people as possible view his manure covered friend. He felt it was such a comical sight and he knew whoever saw it, would never forget it and would talk about the incident for years to come.

Cold, smelly and embarrassed, Jelle was pulled out, but only after Karel had his fun. Karel and the boys took him home in a wagon and delivered him to his mother and father, who took his manure covered body through their very upscale clothing store and house, to rinse him off in the freezing waters of the Rhine River.

Mrs. Houweling did just that, she 'howled.' After cleaning Jelle, she ran over to the de Jong family farm screaming at Arie Sr. stating how irresponsible he was for allowing the whole incident to happen in the first place. Karel and young Arie stayed out of sight laughing as their father was being scolded by this irrational woman.

On another occasion, one of Elso's classmates, Gerrit Voss had just gotten a job at "The Star Laundry." While heading out to do a delivery of clean, pressed and starched shirts, he decided to show off and brag about his new job, and he headed to the de Jong farm in the fully loaded, brand new wagon. Before he knew what was happening, the de Jong brothers had jumped on board to take a ride.

In order to turn around Gerrit had to make a turn a little too close to the manure pit and when he began to make his turn all the brothers jumped off, sending him, the wagon and the clean shirts into the pit full of manure. The boys laughed as they pulled him out of the pit and decided to help him clean up the wagon. They wheeled it over to the edge of the canal, and laid it on its side. Then the boys used twig brushes to clean the highly lacquered wagon, but in doing, so they severely scratched the surface.

After it was clean they righted the cart, reloaded the manure covered shirts and sent Gerrit on his way. They watched and snickered as he headed back to the laundry, his head held down in shame and embarrassment. The de Jong brothers don't remember if he lost his job or not because of the incident.

All of Karel's goat helpers were comprised of Arie Jr.'s classmates and were much younger than Karel. This made it much easier for him to manipulate them into doing his work for free. Arie Jr. was never given any compensation from Karel either, even though he enlisted his classmates for Karel to use. The whole family benefited from the money earned from the goats.

Although, Karel showed a lot of hard work and dedication to his goats, he failed to show the same amount of dedication to the family home and business. As his goat business increased, his brothers became more and more dissatisfied. It was a family decision that his younger brother Arie Jr. would be trained to take over the goat operation, to enable Karel to focus his energy on the family business. Even though Arie Jr. had started his training to take over responsibility of the herd from Karel, he was unable to assume the goat operation, because the family immigrated to the United States.

Different Religious Philosophies

Religion has not only played an important part in Teun's life, but also played an important role in the lives of all the de Jongs. It has been especially important to him, that people come to understand and respect his decision to become a Jehovah's Witness. Teun prefaces the story of his conversion with this statement regarding his family:

"We have a family that really gets along. We have the ability to disagree without being disagreeable. We love and respect each other and accept each other just the way we are."

Teun's Christian-reformed education was very thorough. Besides Christian school, Dutch children always attended Sunday school until the age of ten. Attending group meetings with other young people from the ages of twelve to sixteen years old, and then as young adults they would meet together in groups. All children went to catechism. Teun was still haunted into his early adulthood by the words of the Dutch-reformed minister when his brother Elso died so long ago. He continued to question how a loving God could let something so tragic happen to someone so young and innocent.

In 1944, Teun came across Rienus Fase, a man who worked in a furniture manufacturing business next to the family dairy. Even though he had known Rienus for several years, Teun had not seen him at the furniture shop for well over a year.

Rienus had recently returned from a German Concentration camp. Because they were Jehovah's Witnesses, he and his wife had been arrested and suffered at the hands of the Germans. He was a good man, very nice and impressive with his philosophy, which was part of his faith. One might call him a true martyr. The one thing that resonated with all of the de Jongs, especially Teun, was the religion's idea of no war. After experiencing and seeing the aftermath and the effects of war, it was a beautiful thought and philosophy.

The Jehovah's Witnesses have only one allegiance and that is to Jehovah and to spread his word. The nations of the world are forever in one conflict or another, but the Jehovah's Witnesses have no part of it. When Teun decided to become a *Witness*, a doctrinal conflict became part of the de Jong family's life. The result of which can be seen in the fact that because they were conscientious objectors, all of the de Jong boys served in the U.S. army as medics. Teun was old enough to be drafted into the Dutch Army, but filed for and was awarded a deferment, enabling him to get his visa and emigrate.

Teun was surprised to learn Rienus, his wife and ten others had been arrested and placed in concentration camps for being Christians. The German soldiers and the Dutch police had gone into their homes at two in the morning and arrested them. His wife was taken to the concentration camp in Ravensbruck, Poland, while the others were scattered about various other concentration camps.

Rienus was released to care for his two young daughters, who were four and six years old at the time, but only after he promised not to preach, hand out or speak about the publications of the "Watchtower Association." They gave him back his Bible and he was instructed to speak of those teachings only. He agreed and was set free to work and care for his children.

Teun found it difficult to understand how the political element would persecute and prosecute Christians. All churches support their governments on some level, and chaplains are found deep in the trenches, praying with the soldiers. We, as a people, are all part of the system on one level or another.

Rienus showed references from his Bible, of what it said in the book of Matthew: *"Look I am sending you forth as sheep amidst the wolves.....Be on your guard against the men, they will deliver you up to local courts and they will scourge you in their synagogues. And you will be objects of hatred by all people in account of my name."*

He also quoted from the book of John: *"If the world hates you, you know that it has hated me before it hated you. If you were part of the world, the world would be fond of what is its own. Now because you are no part of the world.....the world hates you. A slave is not greater than his master. If they have persecuted me, they will persecute you also."*

There were many similar scriptures Rienus showed Teun. The change was not easy. Due to the deep saturation of his faith his whole life, this was a difficult change to embrace, but one he felt he needed to make. There was a simple lesson he learned and held onto, which was what Jesus said.

"Love your enemies, bless those that curse you. Do well unto those that persecute you and pray for those that hate you."

Teun felt a person didn't need to study theology to understand a simple basic message like that. The local community had ten different Christian denominations and none of them taught or practiced this simple basic philosophy.

He also remembered Jesus saying, *"By their fruits you will know them. A good tree cannot bring forth bad fruit and a bad tree cannot bring forth good fruit. Yes, by their fruit you will really know them."*

From Reinus he learned more about the trinity, eternal punishment, what he felt would happen when we died, predestination and most of all, what God's kingdom is. Millions of people pray daily, "Your kingdom come," and he learned to join them. After the war in 1945, Teun was the only one in the de Jong family who joined the Jehovah's Witness religion.

Piet Goes To Indonesia

Piet was attracted to the soldier's life. He felt the religious fervor of his upbringing did not overcome his longing for adventure. As a boy he dreamed of joining the Dutch Naval Academy, but with the onset of war, it was impossible for him to achieve that dream. His father told all of the de Jong children study was not for them. He continually stressed how his family were farmers, and everyone had to help do the work in order to keep the farm and help the family.

Piet was drafted into the Dutch Army in 1947 and began experiencing a new and exciting world as a soldier. The experience of military life was such a drastic difference from his life on the family farm. The Indonesia conflict was in its infancy. In contrast, Teun, always the practical one, wanted no part of that conflict or anything remotely connected to it. With his smooth talking ability he was able to circumvent the Dutch drafting process.

Piet ever the obedient one, did not try to dodge the draft. After undergoing basic training and seven more months of intensive military training in preparation for his trip he boarded ship and headed for Indonesia.

Pictured from the left: Piet, Teun, Teun van Ryn and Karel

Although Teun was glad he dodged the draft, he was enthused about Piet's military life and training. He always admired the way Piet was successful and capable in whatever task he undertook. The two brothers became even closer during this time. Teun had plans to immigrate to America, but in the meantime he was proud to witness his brother's success and adventures as a soldier in training. When Piet returned home on furlough, he and Teun spent a great deal of time together, because of Piet's pending deployment to Indonesia and Teun's immigration to America.

Pictured left to right: Elso, Piet, Kees, Maartje, John, Arie Sr (rear), Teun and Karel

If his parents were worried, they never let on to any of their children, or to Piet. They only wanted him to know how much they loved him and how very proud they were. In October of 1947, he boarded, The Nieuw Holland, a troop transport with fifteen hundred other men. Being twenty at the time, Piet was filled with plenty of excitement. The idea of being killed or killing someone else was remote. He knew his military division was suitably armed and well trained. The enemy used guerilla fighting techniques and they had been trained to anticipate that type of evasive warfare.

As a soldier in the Dutch army Piet was stationed on the island of Java and was fighting in Indonesia, when the rest of his family immigrated to America. Indonesia was just one of the many colonies held by the Dutch government. Sukarno-was Indonesian and he had regained control at the end of WWII. It was imperative for the Dutch government to regain and maintain power once again and abolish Sukarno's control over the Indonesian people.

During WWII, Japan invaded Indonesia to gain the natural resources, like rubber, oil and various other necessary supplies they needed for the war effort. The Japanese took control away from the Dutch government and the Dutch residents, men, women, and children were gathered up and taken to remote Japanese concentration camps where they were treated harshly. In 1947, after the end of the war, the Dutch government sent soldiers to Indonesia to take political control back from Sukarno. While Piet was stationed in Indonesia between 1948 and 1949, his company of soldiers, were instrumental in the capture of Sukarno's mother and sister.

Shortly after this incident and before they re-obtained their colonies, the Dutch government was ordered by the American allies to relinquish their Indonesian colonies and told to leave the country. Piet stated, "Although the soldiers were well armed and well trained, we ultimately lost the war to politics."

The Dutch soldiers were under strict orders to never go anywhere without their sidearm. After Piet initially went to Indonesia, Teun sent him a German revolver he had purchased from a Dutch SS Trooper. He felt it would be easier for Piet to carry the pistol for protection when he wasn't on maneuvers. Before leaving Indonesia, Piet sold his sidearm to an enemy soldier for ten times the value.

Piet was very good with languages and was frequently used as an interpreter. During his tour of duty in Indonesia he did quite a bit of traveling throughout the country and did extensive photography.

Marrie is Born

Born Margje de Jong, on November 18, 1948, Marrie was last in the long line of de Jong children. Weighing in at a whopping ten pounds, she was the largest baby Maartje had ever delivered. Like her brothers and sisters before her, she was born in the birthing room in the house at Alphen a/d Rhine. Her father was forty-seven and her mother was forty-five when she was born.

Mary and Moeder Maartje in Holland

Because they were so close in age, their mother, Maartje always dressed the youngest girls alike, even down to their blond braids. Her father said Mary was the quietest of all the children.

A New Country, a New Beginning for Teun

Teun still wanted to go to the United States and pursue the family's dream and purpose, so in the spring of 1948, he went to the consulate. He was told it would take two years to get his papers in order to immigrate to the states. He obtained the name of the man at the immigration office, and looked him up in the phone book. He kept calling all the names listed in the phone book, until he finally found the right man. After finding the right person, Teun then went to the man's home and told him stories of the war, and the tough life his family had endured. He was finally able to talk the man into giving him a letter of permission to allow his immigration to the states. He basically bribed the man to obtain his visa. When all was said and done, he received his papers in six months, instead of two years.

Arie Sr.'s, twin sister, Henrietta, Jet, for short, had immigrated to the United States in the 1920's. She had married a man by the name of Sam Bruinsma. They decided to sponsor Teun, with a job and a place to live.

In the fall of 1948, Teun received an early birthday gift, he received his visa. He left by boat in November. While in the middle of the Atlantic, he received a telegram, informing him his sister, Marrie was born four days before his twenty-third birthday. He was very happy regarding the news that he now had three sisters. With the birth of Marrie and his departure for America, the family began a new chapter in their lives. Now Arie Sr.'s first born son would be the first in his immediate family to venture to the United States. Teun made the trek across the Atlantic Ocean alone, with a mere twenty dollars in his pocket.

Arie Sr.'s youngest brother, Elso was single. Although crippled at birth, he was considered the wild man of the family. He loved driving his Norton motorcycle. The bike was very loud because he had removed the baffle from the exhaust pipe. In 1947, Elso was involved in the Holland Black Market and he was hiding out for illegal butchering and there was a warrant out for his arrest. At that time, all the food in the country was still being rationed.

Realizing he would need to flee the country, Elso had submitted his paperwork to emigrate and had received his passport and visa. He purchased his plane ticket to the U.S. and had barely boarded the plane when the police, who were too late, came to arrest him at the airport. The plane had already taken off and was in mid-air.

After he arrived in America, Elso wrote a letter to the police. Basically the letter said, "You just missed me—I slipped through your dirty, greasy fingers you etc, etc, etc."

Shortly after his arrival Elso relocated to Artesia and became a milker.

Their *Tante* (aunt) Jet had been married previously to a man by the name of Henk Stam. He was a very good looking son of a Dutch dairyman. Against her father's wishes they got married in 1926, after her brother Arie Sr. married Maartje. She and Henk started a dairy products store in Rotterdam, but it didn't do very well and they eventually went broke. With what little money they had, and their marriage already on the rocks, they immigrated to California in 1930. She and Henk had two

Sam Bruinsma at his Artesia Dairy

daughters, Gertie and Alice. While Henk worked milking cows, Jet took in boarders to earn extra money. One of those boarders was a young man by the name of Sam Bruinsma, he was from Friesland in Northern Holland, and he also worked as a milker.

Henk was lazy and Jet found herself not only cooking and cleaning for the boarders, but doing the milking for Henk. She became more and more tired and frustrated from doing all the work, while he just sat around doing nothing. She divorced him, and kept her children. She and Sam were later married.

In 1939, just before the war started, Jet and Sam drove from Los Angeles to New York. From there they boarded a ship bound for Holland. She and her husband brought with them a brand new, yellow Dodge car that had a radio in the dashboard. Their car was taken onboard to use during their vacation. After they arrived in Rotterdam, they drove to her mother's home in Alphen. Her brother, Arie Sr. was visiting with his family as well, and his son Karel, who was five years old at the time, remembers strange noises coming from inside the empty car while he played outside. Frightened, he ran into the house, and told everyone the car was talking. It was the first time he had heard a car radio.

While there she told everyone stories of how wonderful it was to live in America, especially California. Arie Sr.'s family was unaware at the time that eleven years later, they too would be living in California.

Their *Tante* (aunt) Jet took them on a day's vacation to the local lake. She rented a boat and they went swimming. That little mini vacation made the children feel as though they were in another world, experiencing another life.

Jets husband Sam Bruinsma, who was very aggressive and a good dairyman, invited the de Jong family to come to California. If the children hadn't been so young, and the war hadn't broken out, the family probably would have immigrated right then and there, instead of after the war.

Reflecting back, there was so much to do and learn. The whole family agrees that none of them would have wanted to miss their experiences during World War II.

Karel is quoted as saying: *"I wouldn't have missed the experience of the war for a million dollars!"*

Sam had dreams of being a rancher. He made good money during the war and in 1946, he bought the 800 acre, *'Bar C Bar Ranch'*, in Poway, California for $60,000. The purchase included the Wyoming Picnic Grove and three small rock houses. The actual location of the ranch was in Poway where Metate Lane is today.

Ernie, a cowboy from Wyoming worked for Sam. He was a slight man, old, and worn out with a crippled arm. Ernie's job was to ride his horse around the ranch every day to check on the beef cattle and make sure they had plenty of water. He was far from spry and just getting into the saddle physically challenged him. After work he'd meet friends at Robertson's Cafe, or go drinking, and dancing at the Big Stone Lodge, in Poway. Years later, after his trailer caught fire and burned to the ground, the small, close-knit Poway community rallied together and raised enough money to purchase him another small trailer next to Robertson's Cafe where he lived until he died.

Sam only wanted to be a rancher, but after Teun immigrated, he convinced his Uncle to build a dairy on the ranch as well. Teun was sent to Los Angeles by Sam to learn how to machine milk, something they didn't have in Holland at the time. Teun felt very fortunate and blessed to be given that opportunity. Most Dutch immigrants who settled in the Eastern U.S. and Canada made only $85 a month working on farms or dairies, and needed approximately $60 a month for their room and board and other living expenses.

Teun, now going by his American name of "Tom", made $15 a day and worked a full thirty days a month as a relief milker in Heinz/Paramount and Bellflower, located in the Los Angeles suburbs. The milking sheds in the Los Angeles area were all union, so the wages were much higher. He made $450 a month and, because he stayed rent free in his Uncle Hill Goedhart's bunk house he had next to no living expenses. He worked hard and had no extra time to pursue a social life. Because he worked so many hours and had no social activities, he was able to save over $400 a month, which was a substantial amount of money at that time.

Tom only worked as a relief milker for a couple of months in the Los Angeles area before he was hired by the Bouma Dairy. He continued to work there for three months, until Sam started his dairy in the spring of 1949.

Sam and Tom traveled to Utah, where Sam purchased two hundred head of cattle. He loved working for his uncle and didn't mind putting in ten hour days, seven days a week. This was a great improvement over the ninety-five hour work week he had in Holland.

Once his Uncle Sam began his dairy operation he was in a position to sponsor the remaining ten de Jong family members.

After Tom's immigration to America, he was never disappointed, because he truly believed it was the land of opportunity. The family's training and experience during the struggles of the depression and the war had enabled and strengthened him. He was now equipped to make full use of all his knowledge to become successful. The letters he wrote home told of all the opportunities for making money and being successful in American business. The family was very excited and dying to experience the same opportunity he had.

His father Arie Sr., was still clinging desperately to the life he knew and found it hard to believe the tall tales Teun was telling and he wondered: 'Could America really be that good?'

Arie Sr. knew in his heart just how tough it could be for the family to start all over in a new country and he was unsure if he and Maartje should take on that struggle with ten children. He had plenty of free labor on the family farm because of his large family. Kees, as well as the rest of his children were hard workers. With his family's strong work ethic and desire to succeed, Arie Sr. had no doubt they would achieve their dream if they went to America.

Tom had always been a good letter writer and a master story teller. The more information the family received from his letters regarding how good things were in Poway, the more convinced they were it was better to immigrate to California, than to stay in Holland with all the financial strife.

Tom recalls writing the family letters explaining and comparing how many hours he had to work to pay for certain things, like sugar, flour, coffee, oranges, shoes, etc. He told the family in his letters how he would be able to save more in a year by himself, than they would earn as a family unit in Holland. He spoke in his letters about the weather, the hills, trees, ocean and the desert. The town of Alphen had 12,000 people and Poway had less than a thousand residents.

Life was good and food was cheap. The family felt Tom had moved to paradise, and in a way he had.

The more letters Tom wrote about the beauty and the vast opportunities in America the more restless the de Jong children became. They longed for a better life in the states and were anxious to immigrate as well. Maartje was worried the family would soon be torn apart by the large void of the Atlantic Ocean and said the whole family should go. However, Arie Sr. was hesitant about making such a huge and drastic move with such a large family.

When Arie Sr. saw the spirit of hope in his children's eyes, he did not want his family split between two continents, with an ocean between them. He and Maartje had long discussions about the benefits and possible problems with regards to relocating such a large family to a new country. The decision was made to move forward to give the family the chance to live their dream and no one would be left behind. Before final plans were made, he had to see if Teun's stories had validity. He booked a flight from Amsterdam to Los Angeles.

It was understood by the family that he would be away for at least six weeks, in order to have an accurate and thorough understanding of life in America. He and the family would face many obstacles regarding culture and language. These were important factors to consider, in order to bring his family to the states for a new beginning.

When Arie Sr. arrived in Poway, February of 1949, Tom and Sam had already returned from Utah with two hundred head of dairy cattle. Loads of lumber were being delivered and bulldozers were leveling the land to build the new dairy. The family, who expected their father to be gone for over a month, was surprised at his swift return. He had no more arrived in America, before he turned around and headed back to Holland. He was supposed to be gone for six weeks but had returned in two.

The family was alarmed at his swift homecoming and wanted to know what had gone wrong. He simply stated, *"I didn't know there was still a heaven on earth!"* Because he was an ever practical man and a dairyman, his reference was not regarding spiritual treasures. He had seen how simple, humble people, not any smarter than his family had made their fortunes.

Karel recalled how his father's voice cracked with emotion as he told them about the dairy operation and the states. Everything Tom had said was true and it was decided, the whole family would immigrate to the United States, and live in Poway.

Then and there he came to the conclusion his family could make it in America and would be successful. Even though Tom was in California and Pete in Indonesia, the number of family members had not decreased.

The de Jong Family Immigrates to America

It was far easier to leave their home in Holland than one might think. The family didn't own the property they lived on and only owned thirty-five cows. The sale of the cows still needed to be completed before they could leave. Maartje with the help of the children carefully packed their possessions for the trip. Any items to large to take were left in the care of trusted friends, or family.

Pictured left to right: Ellie, Moeder Maartje, Jet (front) and Marrie (in the basket)

When the family left Holland, the Dutch government had set in place firm restrictions on how much money they could bring and even on how many pairs of shoes a person could own.

Each family member was only allowed to take one new pair of shoes and one used pair. That's how strict the laws were in Holland. Karel was determined to take both his new pairs of shoes. He took one pair of his new leather shoes and scuffed them on the flooring in the barn to make them look old.

The family had to be immunized for small pox before they could leave Holland. At that time vaccines were given in the left arm, just below the shoulder. The shot didn't affect anyone, with the exception of itching at the point of entry. Kees was prone to going around shirtless, even when he milked and he began to scratch the site of his vaccination while milking the cows, unaware he was breaking the skin and spreading smallpox to the cows. Slowly a few of the cows began to get sore teats.

Arie Sr. did not have a buyer for the cows while the family was still in Holland. The actual sale took place a few days after their departure to America. He left the details of the sale to his brother Teun and his trusted friend, Jake Biemond. By this time most of the cows experienced pain while being milked, because the udders had developed sores. No one seemed to really take notice, or pay attention to this.

After the cows were auctioned off and sold, they were moved to over twenty different locations in about ten days, and then a milker at one of the farms became very ill. Soon several milkers at different locations had gotten sick as well. The laboratories at the three main hospitals took blood samples from the sick men and the results revealed....small pox.

A few of the milkers nearly died from the disease and many of the herds were infected. The milkers were unable to milk the cows without wearing thin examination gloves, for fear of getting sick and spreading the disease. It was a terrible tragedy and cost the dairy industry thousands of dollars. By this time the family had settled into their new life in California and was unaware of the disaster. It was weeks later before they heard the news. This prompted the family to stay away from Holland for several years after the tragedy.

In May of 1949, with the exception of Piet and Teun, the whole family boarded the Holland/America line ship, the Veendam, bound for New York Harbor. The ten immigrating family members leaving aboard ship were Arie Sr., Maartje, Kees, Elso II, Karel, Jan, Ellie, Arie Jr, Jet and Marrie.

Holland/America line ship, the Veendam

The trip to America lasted two weeks by ship. They recall that when the family was boarding the ship, they were all so excited by this new opportunity and adventure; they left baby Marrie sitting on the dock in her crib basket. As they waved good-bye, their *Ome* (uncle) Willem Roeloffs shouted from the dock, "You've left the baby!"

The whole family was very enthused and excited; for it was rumored America was the land of milk and honey, a source of great opportunity. They knew this had to be true, because Teun constantly wrote letters to tell the family of his great fortune after his arrival in America.

Karel, fifteen, was seasick the whole boat trip across the Atlantic. He felt as though being seasick totally stripped away and knocked a large hole in his enthusiasm. Karel was resigned to spending twelve out of the thirteen day boat trip in bed. He was so ill, his mother grew concerned. The voyage was so rough, that after the first day at sea most of the plates on the dining room tables had fallen off and broken.

Thirteen days aboard ship was a long time and the children immediately set out looking for adventure, but only created mischief. Jan and Arie Jr. passed the time playing tag by running from one side of the deck to the other. The ship pitched violently from side to side and while running across the deck a huge wave headed for the ship. Jan was faster and made it to safety inside the huge metal doorway. Arie Jr. was not so lucky and he slid across the deck when the wave hit, smashing him into the guardrail. Fortunately, he wasn't washed overboard.

The food was abundant and unbelievably delicious. The children consumed so much food; they were full as ticks ready to pop. None of the de Jong children had ever seen a black person before. Arie Jr. remembers being startled when he walked into the dining room and saw a black waiter in a white uniform. He was so intrigued he ran to get Ellie and Jan, so they could see him too.

After the ship docked, the family was taken around New York City by Arie Sr.'s cousin, Bouw Philippo, who was a tulip broker there. Elso remembered the massive size of the Statue of Liberty and the Empire State Building, and how they were so much larger than anything he'd ever seen in Holland.

Within a few hours after their arrival to Ellis Island, in New York, the family had an eleven hour plane trip to Los Angeles. Everyone was still recovering from being seasick, when they boarded the plane to California. Karel swore he would never travel by boat or ship ever again. Little did Karel know or realize that he would indeed be subjected to seasickness once again after his enlistment in the military. He was aboard ship once again when he traveled to Europe and back while in the Army. Elso, like Karel, was also seasick on the boat trip when the family immigrated to the United States.

The family's departure from New York City, to Los Angeles made the newspapers. Before their departure, photos were taken of the whole family on the steps of the plane.

The family wanted to stay in New York to see the sights, but they were quickly running out of money. Using almost all the money they had, it cost $12,000 for the family of ten to sail aboard ship and then fly to California from New York. By any standards it was considered a small fortune at the time. By the time the family arrived in Poway, the only money Arie Sr. had left was $32. Although excited; the family viewed the immigration to America as a form of death and loss, as they left behind friends and family they might never see again.

The family wanted to be dairy farmers in America, because if there was ever a war, they could continue to have food, just like in Holland. Piet arrived soon after and had never seen a country as large as America. Comparatively, Holland was just a bit larger than San Diego County.

Being in an airplane and flying was an exciting experience for the whole family. Only Arie Sr. had flown previously. In New York City a family member, Bouw Philippo, spoke English and helped the family get through the harbor, as well as, the immigration process dealing with all the paperwork, and got the family to the airport on time for the flight to Los Angeles. During a short layover in Chicago, the de Jong children noticed a candy vending machine. They had never seen a vending machine before and a stranger noticed their fascination and bought a Hershey chocolate bar for the kids to share.

While they waited for their ride at the Los Angeles Airport, the kids noticed some dry grass and wondered if it would burn. Someone found matches and they built a fire in the field, which immediately started to burn out of control. In an effort to put out the fire, the boys began peeing on it, which of course had negative results. They resorted to taking off coats and various articles of clothing to successfully beat the flames out. Shortly after putting out the fire, they were greeted by Arie Sr.'s twin sister, Henrietta, Jet, for short, and her daughter Alice, who would drive them to Poway. Because the family was so large, they brought two vehicles. Jet drove a new 1949 Buick four-door sedan and Alice drove their new 1949 GMC pickup truck.

Most of the family had only been in a car once or twice before. The large group and their luggage crowded into the two vehicles. The boys rode in the back of the pick-up and were packed like sardines. To make matters even worse, the ride was bumpy and windy. Everyone was very tired, and the cramped driving conditions proved to be very taxing. Poway was not very impressive. Everything that should have been green and lush was dead, dry and hot. The family was used to the cool rich canals and pastures of Holland. The dry, arid conditions instantly made everyone homesick.

After the long ride from Los Angeles they arrived at Uncle Sam's; Bar-C-Bar Ranch in Poway, and Tom met them with a case of oranges for everyone to eat and enjoy. The children were thrilled with the juicy, fresh treat. Fresh picked oranges had not been available or imported to Holland because of the war. It was hard for the children to realize they could simply go outside and pick the delectable fruit from a tree. Everyone was used to the plush green, flat lands of Holland and had never seen a hill before. The truck had barely stopped before Arie Jr. jumped out and ran up the hill, where he could look over the whole valley.

In May of 1949, when the family immigrated, they already had jobs working on Sam's dairy.

Dairy Life in Poway

The de Jongs found the American people to be extremely hospitable and very nice. The Americans they met were happy for their quick success and not jealous of their progress.

In Holland the de Jongs worked twelve to fourteen hours a day, from 4am to 7pm, six days a week and only worked eight hours on Sundays. Working in the U.S. it was wonderful. They only worked ten hours a day, from 1am to 6am and then again from 1pm to 6pm.

Sam Bruinsma

Because Sam and Tom had brought back the heifers from Utah to stock the dairy there was more than enough work for the whole family.

Arie Sr. had plans for his family to work as a unit to achieve their dream of becoming successful dairy farmers. His dream was realistic and achievable. Tom possessed the same vision.

Kees was aware of the family goal and as long as there continued to be a progression forward, he was willing to work all the hard and long hours needed to obtain the family dream.

Arie Sr. and Tom felt since Arie Jr. and Ellie couldn't speak English, but were proficient in math, they should skip a grade in school. They were enrolled in the 6th and 7th grades. Arie Jr.'s 6th grade teacher was Mrs. Van Dam. Her husband was of Dutch origin, so she was well versed in the Dutch culture.

She was fond of Arie Jr. and helped him learn English. Many years later, Mrs. Van Dam lived in the Howell Heights Rest Home in Escondido. When she was ninety-nine, Arie Jr. organized a party for her and invited all her Poway students. They all pitched in and bought her a television set. The next day they held a reception and barbecue for her at the Big Stone Lodge in Poway.

She'd never been to the Big Stone Lodge before. When she was younger, it was a bar and it was considered inappropriate for a young girl to go there. It was mainly a military bar, so there was a lot of drinking, dancing and raising hell. It was understood only women of loose moral character went there.

Arie Jr. recalled how when he was a kid, he took soda pop bottles from the back of the Big Stone Lodge and then took them inside to get the cash deposit. He snatched the bottles again, but took them across the street to Koch's Bar and turned them in for cash.

As a smoker Arie Sr. didn't want to pay the high price for pre-rolled cigarettes. Instead, he rolled his own. While out collecting the soda bottles, Arie Jr.'s job was to harvest cigarette butts along the roadways and from the two neighborhood bars. In order to harvest the tobacco when he returned home, young Arie Jr. stripped off the papers, so his father could roll his cigarettes. The tobacco was a rich, smooth blend of Old Gold, Lucky Strikes, Chesterfields, Phillip Morris and Pall Malls. No two batches of tobacco ever tasted the same.

All Elso wanted was to fellowship and get a girlfriend, but like his brothers he went straight to work. They all worked very hard too, seven days a week. The neighbors felt Elso and his siblings should be in school, but Arie Sr. wasn't big on education and he put all of his children to work. Elso was a milker and hated working the split shift. The cows had to be milked twice a day, which meant he had to get up at one in the morning for the first milking and then he would re-milk them at one in the afternoon.

The difference between milking cows in the states versus Holland, was in America the cows were milked by machine and not by hand like in Holland, where they began milking at four in the morning. After the machine milking, the cows had to be stripped, which means to hand squeeze the last of the milk from the teats.

As a teenager, Elso wanted to stay up late. This played havoc in regards to him getting enough rest at night. He had a broken sleep pattern and never got more than six or seven hours sleep each night. He worked from 1-6am, had breakfast and then he laid down to rest for a bit. Someone usually had to shake him, to wake him up, so he could milk some more.

Before the family arrived, the 'Bar-C-Bar', was a ranch. When Sam agreed to build a dairy on his ranch in 1949, he had a partnership with the family in mind. To successfully run a dairy, a lot of water is required. However, there was a drought after the dairy was built, and Sam did not have a working well on the site of the actual dairy. He hired Joe Anderson's company, Anderson's Well Drilling, located in Lakeside, to drill the well and spent more than $30,000 trying to hit water. The water table beneath the dairy was dry, due to the lengthy drought.

The commute and the days were long and the work was hard. Joe was usually too tired to make the long drive Home and he decided to relocate to Poway while digging Sam's well and he rented a place behind the Big Stone Lodge, near Sam's ranch.

It was a slow and tedious, year long process to hand dig the four foot round well. The compressors supplied power to the jackhammers which ran all day, every day. Joe Anderson erected an 'A' frame over the opening and using a bucket hoisted his men down into the well to continue the digging process. The bucket was used to extract the continuous loads of earth from inside the well.

At one point the lack of water was so bad, the fire department brought water in pump trucks just so the cows had some to drink. It was during a drought year, and they dug almost a hundred feet before hitting water. Although the well was not dry when completed, it barely produced enough water to sustain the dairy and the cattle. The water retrieved from the well was pumped into a pressure tank to use in the dairy barn, to wash and clean the cows daily.

There were five de Jong brothers working for their Uncle Sam; Tom, Kees, Karel, Elso and John. The boy's boots leaked and their feet and socks got wet. They started using cotton milk strainer bags wrapped around their feet to keep them dry. Sam couldn't understand how they were using so many strainers and was unhappy when he found out they'd been wearing them on their feet and throwing them away.

Not wanting to go back to school, John, fourteen, went to work immediately, laying out the hay and catching the "hot" cows, (The cows in heat.). John was a hard worker and he did everything he could, from feeding the cows, washing the milk tanks and chopping weeds. He continued working for his Uncle Sam until he was fifteen.

The de Jong brothers earned $275 a month, but because John was the youngest, Sam only paid him $90 a month, or $3 a day. His wages paid the rent for the three little stone houses in Poway. John never received a paycheck, because it all went to pay the family rent.

Sam owned three of the six small rock cabins originally known as the Wyoming Picnic Grove. The de Jongs didn't understand why the people there were having picnics. In those days, it was common if you went to a picnic grove to pay an entrance, or use fee of twenty-five cents. The visitors to the picnic grove thought there was an entrance fee and paid it to the de Jong kids. They also gave them food to eat.

Young Arie thought, "America, what a great country. They feed you and then pay you."

The de Jong children didn't even know what a picnic grove was. In addition to the small rock houses there were picnic tables, bathrooms and stone fire pits located throughout the property their Uncle Sam now owned. Everyone, except for Pete, who was still in Indonesia, serving in the Dutch Army, was crowded into the three of the small stone cottages.

After their arrival to Poway, the family lived next door to a young married couple, Bob and Dolores Shidner. Bob was very friendly and walked the small distance to the de Jongs to introduce himself to the family. Arie Sr. invited him in, and Bob was touched and impressed by the way the family welcomed him in with their warm hospitality. It was an instant friendship. His wife Dolores, only seventeen or eighteen at the time, was young and beautiful. Elso admitted he had a crush on her. Bob and the de Jong family forged a strong friendship which has lasted the ravages of time.

Bob visited frequently and brought different foods for them to try, like watermelon. This became one of the long standing family favorites. Tom remembers how phenomenal the watermelon tasted.

In 1938, when Bob was a child, his family lived in Escondido's Felicita Park. His father was the park caretaker and they lived in the small caretaker's house next to the site of the current fire station. There was a gentleman who planted his watermelon fields close to the caretaker's house. Bob helped to harvest the melons which were taken to San Marcos and sold for three cents a pound.

In June of 1949, Bob and Dolores took John, Ellie and Arie Jr. to the Del Mar fair in Bob's 1936 two door Ford sedan. John was Bob's right hand man as translator, since he was the only

Cookie Gran

one of the three children that spoke some English. Bob bought the kids corn on the cob which they refused to eat. He felt he was giving the kids a special treat and the children wondered why he was giving them something for livestock to eat. In Holland corn was pig feed. They had a great time and tried different foods and rode the rides. This was the first of many cultural differences they encountered. Going to the fair was a big deal. Bob and Dolores also took the de Jong children on excursions to the beach.

Once while Arie Jr. was visiting Dolores' sister Gail, she tried to engage him in conversation, not realizing he didn't speak English yet. When she asked his name he just shrugged his shoulders. It wasn't until almost a year later, that Arie asked her what she had asked him. When she told him she was only asking his name, they both had a good laugh.

One of Arie Jr.'s school friends was Dolores' little brother, Tommy Gosnel. They attended the 6th grade together. His best friend was Gregory (Cookie) Gran, who lived next to the Big Stone Lodge. The two boys were inseparable throughout their school career. Cookie's family moved to Escondido not long after the de Jongs did, and his father owned and operated a radiator repair shop on Escondido Boulevard. Every day on his way home from school Arie Jr. would stop at the radiator shop to hang out with Cookie, who was always tinkering with one thing or another, along with his pet monkey Tonto, he bought from an old circus man.

At the time, the old 395 highway was the only road to San Diego, and ran close to the stone houses. Arie Jr. remembers lying in bed at night, hearing the big rigs as they shifted down, to climb the grade. Later, the 395 was expanded and relocated to where it is today. It was later renamed the Interstate 15 Freeway. The old road was turned into a dead end street.

In a form of dry land sledding, Arie Jr. and the other kids slid down the Oak tree covered hill behind Koch's bar in Poway, using pieces of cardboard or tin. It was there they first experienced migrant Mexicans walking through the hills looking for something to eat or drink. The de Jong children couldn't speak Spanish and the Mexicans couldn't speak Dutch. After giving the men help, they asked neighbors about these strange men and were told, "*Mexican wetbacks*." The de Jongs had no idea what that was. They only knew the men were poor and needed something to eat and drink.

Arie Jr. remembers there were gypsies in Poway, who lived in a travel trailer they pulled behind their pickup truck. They traveled to Sacramento to gather truckloads of willow twigs, and then returned to San Diego to make and sell the chairs and small tables crafted out of willow wood.

The de Jongs formed friendships with some of the gypsies, who invited them and Bob's family over for barbecues and to watch home movies. The de Jongs were fascinated, because they had never seen home movies before. The food was prepared and blessed, then slowly barbecued for several days before eating.

After they arrived in Poway, Ellie begged and begged her father for a horse and though he felt it wasn't a good investment, he got her a horse anyway when she was twelve. Ellie and her girlfriend, Gail Parrish rode the horse in the hills around Poway. Her daily work responsibilities were demanding and hard, and riding her horse was the only fun she had. One day when Ellie came home, the horse was gone.

Because the family needed meat to eat Arie Sr. had butchered it. Ellie was sad, but not mad about the situation. It was 1949, and although Ellie was upset, she understood the requirements of the family always came first and they needed to eat. Each day John, Ellie, Arie Jr. and their father would go into the hills to hunt rabbits, another source of food for the family.

When the family emigrated from Holland, certain foods were still being rationed or were in short supply. During World War II there wasn't any sugar available and the family found food in

America to be plentiful and cheap. Once the de Jong children started to experience Kool-aid and the sweetness of sugar, they couldn't get enough. Soon the family consumed twenty-five pounds of sugar a week.

They also consumed large quantities of white, Wonder Bread, donuts and cookies they bought from the Peter Wheat Bread delivery man. He always made sure the de Jongs were his last stop, because they emptied out his truck and bought all the day old bread items.

After Tom went to the dentist and found out several of his teeth were beginning to decay, he knew the family had to make a change in their eating habits. He felt the large amounts of sugar the family ingested were very unhealthy, so he began to monitor and ration the family's intake of sweets.

Attending church in Escondido in the early 1950's

He also contacted John Cnosseen, the sales rep from Coast Grain and had him add one hundred pounds of wheat to his Uncle Sam's grain shipment. The family ground the wheat to make their own bread.

Some of the family attended service at the Old Community Church, on the corner of Community and Hillery in Poway. They always wore their wooden shoes, which drew a lot of attention.

A Dutch church in San Diego heard about a large family in Poway that had recently arrived from Holland. The church elders wanted them to join their congregation and they sent a deacon to find them and visit the family. Soon after the visits began the family started to attend Sunday service, in San Diego. Arie didn't want to go to church anymore.

The de Jong family was so large the family was housed in three small rock cabins on the *Wyoming Picnic Grove*. It was rustic at best, but for Maartje it was a wonderful relief. It was nothing compared to the Dutch style of cleanliness, which was being extremely meticulous down to the tiniest detail. She found it less stressful and much less burdensome to do her cleaning in America.

When the family immigrated the original plan was for the family to take over ownership of Uncle Sam's dairy after working off their sponsorship. With this arrangement, Sam felt comfortable with the value he would receive in the transfer of ownership.

At the age of forty-eight, Arie Sr. was not entirely comfortable working as the subordinate of his younger brother-in-law. Even though he was a farmer in his own right, the work was physically taxing and was more than he wanted to tackle. Tom, the leader of the group was convinced they could earn the dairy farm after due effort.

To begin work each day, transportation to their Uncle Sam's dairy, consisted of Tom pedaling a bicycle, with Karel perched precariously upon the frame of the handle bars. One day while going down the hill on Pomerado Road, Karel's hat flew off his head. When he turned to see which direction the hat went, Tom lost control of the bike and they went flying into a ditch, and crashed into a barbed wire fence. Fortunately, neither boy was seriously hurt. In true de Jong style, they shook off the dirt and proceeded to the dairy to start the morning milking.

Because of his young age, Karel wasn't supposed to be milking at 1am. However, the day after the family's arrival, Tom had him working as a cow pusher and washer. Karel's pay consisted of $10.00 for a ten hour workday, the same wage the rest of the family earned. A pusher brings the cows from the corrals into the barn. The washer does precisely that, washes down the cows with a pressurized hose to wash and thoroughly clean the udders before they're milked, a very grueling and cold job, especially at night.

After a year of stripping and washing cows for his Uncle Sam, Karel went to work in the Artesia and Bellflower area, washing cows at one of the local dairies. A few months later, a family from Holland offered him a job as a milker and he accepted. This particular job gave Karel a vast amount of experience using a milking machine, which could milk one hundred cows during each shift.

The de Jong boys liked it when they went to work in the Artesia/Bellflower area to learn more about the trade, because it was a very large Dutch community. The boys were welcomed with open arms by the Dutch dairymen and instantly felt at ease.

Transportation needs were very different in Holland, where the family either walked or rode a bicycle everywhere. On some occasions they made good use of a horse and wagon or borrowed a three wheeled cart. Another common source of transportation was a small schouw, or flat bottom boat used to travel through the canal waterways. This allowed for the transporting of the milk cans to the fields where they milked the cows and to transport the manure or other commodities to other areas.

The boat was moved using a *"pol stok,"* a long pole that was wedged into the back of the boat, by someone walking on the bank of the canal to push and steer the boat.

When the de Jongs immigrated they bought two bicycles which the whole family shared, but they wanted to own an automobile. The Gossnell's grandpa, "Grandpa Soleigh", lived next to Robertson's café in one of the rock houses and he had an old 1928 Buick sitting out under his Oak tree that he was willing to sell. Bob and Dolores introduced her grandfather to the de Jong family and because of their help; the family was able to purchase the car for the lofty sum of fifty dollars. Later on, Bob taught everyone how to drive.

Pictured left to right: Ellie, Kees, Mary, Arie Jr, Jet and John

This investment served the family for many years. Elso and Karel both learned to drive at the same time. Eventually everyone learned how to drive that old 1928 Buick. It was a nice car and received a great deal of abuse from all the new and different drivers in the family.

No one in the family knew how to drive, so Bob and whoever else was available helped to teach them how to drive, including Arie Jr., who was only ten at the time. For the family driving the car was like going to Disneyland. Anyone who had a spare moment would take off in the car, but no one had a license.

Laughing, Arie Jr. said, "We looked like the Beverly Hillbillies."

The kids took possession of an old Buick, with wooden spoke wheels. During their time off they enjoyed piling into the car and going for rides around the countryside. The car was constantly being wrecked and repaired, because everyone in the family learned to drive it. Karel drove the car into a railroad tie that was used as a fence post at the entry of a chicken ranch. Another one of the boys hit an oak tree. The top was smashed beyond repair, and they cut it off to create a makeshift convertible. The car had a square shape and so it was real easy to cut the top off. The car was literally being held together with baling wire. Maartje never expressed the desire to learn to drive.

Arie Sr. was the last person who learned to drive the Buick and the car was wrecked again when he hit the "Bar-C-Bar" sign. By that time the clutch was pretty much shot as well. Kees and Arie Jr. were in charge of fixing the car, however, they didn't know what they were doing. They had never taken a car apart before. Bob Shidner suggested they travel to Cliff Ingraham's wrecking yard get repair parts.

Bob had gone to school with Cliff. The wrecking yard was on the corner of Ivy and Ohio in Escondido. The family decided someone needed to learn how to be a mechanic. Kees was tired of the same old routine of milking cows and was looking for more to do in his time off. It was a unanimous decision and he agreed to become the family mechanic. Kees went to work for Cliff between milking jobs. Arie Jr. swept and cleaned up the garage and worked for Cliff's mother mowing the lawn.

There were approximately eight hundred people living in Poway when the de Jongs immigrated. They were the only foreign family around and everyone knew who they were. They were viewed as a novelty by the community.   Everything was new to them and they enthusiastically explored the surrounding area. Bob Shidner remembered how the de Jongs sang Dutch folk songs as they drove to work in their 1928 Buick.

Poway was still very rural at the time, with an abundance of open country. One day while out exploring they happened upon a large ranch owned by Miss Florence Chambers, a wealthy single woman. When the children poured out of the car, she was very surprised, by their age and stature. Although they resembled a scroungy bunch of ragtag misfits, the boys were enthusiastic, muscular and quite intelligent. Although the boys spoke very little English they were extremely curious and eagerly investigated everything. Even with their limited English the children's visit with Miss Chambers was pleasant.

The upside was when Miss Chambers came to visit the de Jongs looking for a ranch manager. She wanted to know if anyone in their family could work for her. Arie Sr. recommended his younger brother Elso, who had immigrated to California a few years earlier. He was working in Artesia and was more than willing to relocate. When he took the position as the ranch manager he moved in with Arie Sr.'s family and lived in one of the small rock houses.

Elso liked how the relocation from Artesia would put him closer to his brother Arie Sr.'s family. In Holland, he had worked for his brother Arie Sr. and the children felt their uncle was fun to have around. The older boys in their Holland neighborhood loved to get together with him, because he always thought of some hare brained scheme causing a neighborhood commotion. He was Arie Sr.'s youngest brother and told great stories about the Wild West.

Miss Chambers' ranch was not a dairy so the nature of the work was much more relaxed. After a while, Arie Sr. decided it would be better if he worked there as well. However, he was far from impressed by his brother Elso's leadership skills, but was fine with fitting in wherever he was needed in order to get the job done. The result was a cut in his wages, which were already low.

Still in its infancy, there wasn't much to Poway besides the bars, a church, the egg and turkey ranches and a small post office. The family always attended church while living in Holland, but that wasn't the case when they first arrived in Poway, because Sam and Jet didn't go to church, the family didn't either. Instead of attending church, Arie Sr., his brother Elso and brother-in-law Sam went rabbit hunting and took John, Ellie and Arie along as spotters.

John and Kees with kids after hunting

While the kids rode in the back, the men piled into the cab of the truck, sitting on the .22 rifles. During one hunting excursion at Florence Chambers ranch, when the kids yelled "rabbits", Sam slammed on the brakes and everyone jumped out of the truck except for Arie Sr.'s brother Elso, who was sitting on the rifle in the middle. When Sam grabbed the rifle it went off accidentally and shot Elso in the ass.

Elso crawled out of the cab of the truck and collapsed on the ground. When Sam panicked thinking he had killed Elso, Arie Sr. thought Sam was suicidal and he told the kids to grab all the guns. When Elso came to they laid him on his stomach in the back of the truck and took him to a local nurse in Poway to be treated. Because the bullet had gone through both his butt cheeks there were four holes. The incident was rehashed as humorous dinner conversation for years.

Miss Chambers, was the only child of a wealthy banking family, had a financial adviser by the name of Mr. Van, and lived in her family home in Ocean Beach. She suffered from polio as a small child, so her father placed her in swimming therapy to strengthen her legs. She became such a good swimmer, and she began to win competitions. Florence earned a seat on the Olympic swimming team and competed at the 1924 Olympics in Paris, France.

On one occasion when Mr. Van needed to go to the house in Ocean Beach, he took along Arie Jr, who was amazed at the vast amount of trophies and medals Miss Chambers had on display throughout the house. In 1970, she was inducted into the Breitbard Hall of Fame by the San Diego Hall of Champions. There is a bronze plaque honoring her accomplishments at Belmont Park in Mission Bay, near the Plunge, an enclosed swimming pool, near the beach and her childhood home in San Diego.

Young Arie's father and his uncle Elso took him to Miss Chamber's ranch so he could help them with the chores. They'd start by milking the six cows, using a milking machine, which didn't take long. Manny the cook always asked them how many eggs each of them wanted to eat and Elso always said a dozen. The huge breakfast consisted of eggs, bacon, potatoes and toasted bread.

After breakfast, they cleaned the barn and churned the butter. Once while Arie Sr. carried a large chunk of freshly churned butter into the house, he dropped it on the ground. When he told Miss Chambers what happened, she told him it was ok and that he could take it home to his family. Even though Elso lived with Arie Sr's family, he was mad and accused his brother of dropping the butter on purpose. Which of course, he probably did.

Since his brother Elso and Florence Chambers were both unmarried, Arie Sr. tried to hook them up because she had a lot of money. However, her bookkeeper Ed lived at her ranch. They were usually gone most of the day checking on her other properties and business ventures. Arie Sr. and Elso were worried, because they thought Florence and Ed were involved intimately and devised what they felt was a foolproof plan to find out. In order to see if he was sleeping with her or not, they had young Arie Jr. place a piece of straw between her bed sheets. The next day they sent him back in again to see if the straw had been disturbed or not. They never did know for sure, but it made for good dinner conversation.

Since Florence and Ed were gone each day, Arie Sr. and Elso took a nap after they ate lunch, which left young Arie, who was only ten at the time, unsupervised. On one occasion, while his father and uncle were in the sleeping quarters above the garage taking a nap, Arie Jr. decided to teach himself to drive the tractor. He managed to back out of the garage without incident, or waking his father and uncle. He began driving in circles around the garage. The sound of the tractor passing underneath the window woke his napping relatives. They decided to teach him a lesson for being so fresh.

They filled a bucket with water, and the next time Arie Jr. drove under the window, they emptied the bucket on him. Startled, Arie Jr. lost control of the tractor and careened into the fence, taking out over one hundred feet of the barbed wire fencing. His father and uncle panicked. They knew they needed to have everything back to normal and the fence repaired before Miss Chambers returned.

Arie Sr. was the eldest of eighteen children. Only ten had lived and of those ten, his brother Elso was the youngest and even though he had a slightly misshapen body, he was sufficiently muscular. Elso was highly intelligent and given the opportunity he could have been a good lawyer. Now he was the manager of his former boss and older brother, who took it all in stride, because Arie Sr. thoroughly enjoyed the freedom that came with working at Miss Chambers' ranch.

Many humorous adventures occurred on the Chambers ranch. Like the time it was rumored the FBI was coming to arrest lovers Manny and Naomi who lived and worked on the ranch. Elso was infatuated with Florence and tried to impress by proving how brave and reliable he was. He told her not to worry, because he was in charge and it would be over his dead body before he let anything happen to the ranch or anyone working there.

Of course, everyone scattered like cockroaches. Florence and Ed left as usual. Manny and Naomi quickly left for an undisclosed destination, but returned the next day. Elso was supposed to be in charge, but quickly left to go on an errand and never came back that particular afternoon. The only ones left behind were young Arie Jr. and his father, who spoke very little English. The FBI never showed up, but once again it made for good conversation.

Once they learned how to drive, the de Jong kids explored the surrounding areas. On one excursion they came across a local slaughter house, specializing in horses. The family was used to eating horsemeat in Holland, so Tom made arrangements with the owner to purchase buckets of horse filets for around a nickel a pound. They made weekly trips to what the locals referred to as, *The Slaughterhouse,* to pick up their buckets of filets. The meat would be thinly sliced by Maartje and cooked for breakfast and sandwiches.

On another driving expedition, they came across the Scripps family, ranch, just off the old 395, where the town of Scripps Ranch is located today. The de Jong children were amazed and impressed at the scale of the massive, adobe hacienda style, ranch house and they were greeted by Mrs. Scripps who was very cordial. There was an old, Model "A" station wagon on the ranch they no longer used, and Mrs. Scripps sold it to the family for $15.

The Model 'A' wagon ran forever and ended up being one of the best cars the family ever owned. The de Jong brothers wanted a truck, so they took the station wagon over to Florence Chambers Ranch, where Karel cut the back off the car between milking shifts, to turn it into a pickup truck. Had the family realized how rare and valuable it was to own a Model "A" station wagon, they probably would never have cut up the car.

In 1950, while on another one of their driving adventures, the de Jong brothers stumbled upon the Cloverdale Dairy in San Pasqual. Zweitzer van der Meulen owned and operated the dairy and it happened to be for sale. The property was fully self-contained, with several working wells and 400 acres where they grew hay. The boys were excited and wanted to purchase the property. Unfortunately the family was unable make the purchase, but talked Miss Chambers into buying the property instead.

Arie Sr. told her his brother Teun in Holland would be willing to come and run the dairy for her, along with his brother Elso. She made the purchase and agreed to become the sponsor for Teun and his family. While waiting for them to arrive from Holland, Arie Jr. and his Uncle Elso moved into the large three story house to take care of the property.

There were several workers living on the Cloverdale Dairy ranch, including Zweitzer's cousin Dick van der Meulen. Zweitzer vacated the property as soon as the sale went through, but all of the workers stayed, including Zweizer's cousin, Dick, who was the maintenance mechanic. Arie Jr. only eleven years old at the time was excited, because Dick let him drive the company Jeep around the ranch.

Arie Jr. remembers how the large house was vacant, except for the bed they both shared. He was so scrawny and his uncle was so large, he slept under the covers in the huge void created by his uncle's massive frame. It was almost like sleeping under a tent.

The Cloverdale hay field irrigation was somewhat sub-standard, so Jesse a worker from Miss Chamber's Poway ranch, worked on the improvements. The dairy purchase occurred in the summer when it was time to harvest the hay, which was cut during the day to allow it to dry, before it was turned with a *swather* to create the wind rows. The baler would then be driven down the wind rows to create the bales of hay. Hay needs a certain amount of moisture during the baling process, so they did the baling at night. In those days the bales were tied by hand before being dropped off the back of the baler onto the field.

It was Arie Jr.'s job to tie the bales while his Uncle Elso drove the baler. The baling wire was in pre-cut strands with a loop at one end. Arie Jr. passed the wire under the bale and like threading a needle he ran the end of the wire through the loop before twisting it tight.

After their application to emigrate from Holland was approved, Arie Sr,'s brother Teun's family came to America and they moved into the three story house on the dairy in San Pasqual. Young Arie returned home and his Uncle Elso stayed to help with the dairy operation.

Over the years many Dutch visitors inquired how the de Jong's got their business enterprise started after they immigrated. They also wanted to see where the family lived initially, so Arie

Jr. took them to see the rock houses in Poway. The houses changed ownership over time and were eventually owned by Mr. and Mrs. Dahl.

Throughout the years, when Arie Jr. asked if he could show Dutch visitors the houses, Mr. Dahl, grumbled a little, but complied. Arie Jr. also told Mr. Dahl to let him know if he ever decided to sell the houses, because he was interested in buying them.

Mr. Dahl always emphatically stated, "No, I'm never going to sell them."

During one visit out of the blue, Mr. Dahl told Arie Jr. he might be interested in selling the houses, but never called back again to follow up. On another occasion when Arie Jr. took friends to see the houses, Mrs. Dahl told him that her husband had passed away. She had always been kept in the background and this was Arie Jr.'s first encounter with her. Her daughter lived in a travel trailer behind the houses. Arie Jr. said to call him if she ever decided to sell the houses.

Mrs. Dahl finally called Arie and asked if he was still interested in buying her rock houses. He said of course, but was curious why she changed her mind. She told him, her daughter was moving to Oregon, because her son-in-law had gotten a job there. Mrs. Dahl didn't want to stay alone in California, so she was going to Oregon as well. A meeting was arranged. She gave him a really good deal. He bought the three rock houses for $79,000, more than forty years after living there as a child.

Mrs. Dahl's neighbor, Dave Millard, had also wanted to purchase the property. When Arie Jr. asked her why she sold the houses to him instead of to her neighbor, she simply replied, "I wanted to sell it to the milkman."

Arie Jr. was the milkman.

Because Arie Jr. had bought the property, Dave Millard wasn't very fond of him. However, Arie Jr. had a bad property manager and after he fired her, he approached Dave and suggested he take the job. This insured he could pick out his own neighbors. He still manages the property and his wife does all the record keeping. Over the years Millard and Arie Jr. have become good friends.

The Birth of Hollandia Dairy

Sam felt he couldn't form a partnership with Arie Sr. until he had a proper working well. The wait was very long and Arie Sr. became impatient. Tom felt his father had a way of keeping the family together. Everyone worked as a team and pooled their money. After one year they had saved $7,000. Several things caused a shift in the family expectations.

The one and most significant event to help launch the de Jong family's path to success was the purchase of the small Escondido dairy. While Arie Sr. and Sam were on a trip hauling some butcher cows to the Talone Slaughterhouse in Escondido, they passed a small dairy with a *"for sale"* sign posted on the fence. Arie Sr. asked what it meant and Sam explained the owner wanted to sell the dairy.

Aerial view of the dairy on 17th Street in Escondido

After Arie Sr. learned the dairy was for sale, he talked to Tom about making it a reality for the family. Within a few days, Tom and his father returned to the small dairy in Escondido and the deal was immediately made to purchase the five acre Cash and Carry, from the Ratliefs in 1950. This was the location of the original Hollandia Dairy.

Although buying a dairy wasn't in the family plan, everyone considered the move a step in the right direction. The owner, Robert Ratlief, had been looking for a way to retire and get out of the business, so the family took over operation on May 1, 1950.

Money presented a problem, because the de Jongs only had $7,000. The fact they had saved that amount of money in such a short time, gave Mr. Ratlief confidence. His mortgage holder Mr. Wulff was willing to accept the transfer of ownership and Mr. Butler, a citrus grower from Escondido supplied them with a loan.

The total selling price was $35,000 for five acres, twenty-eight cows, and one bull and the processing equipment, including a fifty gallon vat pasteurizer, a fifty gallon per hour homogenizer, a two valve, and hand operated bottle filler and a milk route that included an old Chevy panel truck used for delivery and an existing customer base, bottles, caps, etc. The family was eager to learn the ropes and Tom did not lack confidence in the family's ability. The original dairy was a small cash and carry operation and the family felt it was a very good educational program for them all. The rest of the de Jong brothers left Sam's dairy in 1951, to work at various dairies in the Bellflower and Artesia area.

Running a dairy can be extremely grueling, requiring long hours, working seven days a week without being able to take time off. For the small dairy it was even more demanding, because there was a milk route attached, requiring deliveries seven days a week. Mr. Ratlief had not taken any time off for a long time. He felt he, and his family desperately needed a vacation, an opportunity to enjoy life. The timing couldn't be more perfect for everyone involved. The de Jong family was eager to take on the job of running the dairy, and the Ratliefs were eager to leave.

Standing in front of the milking barn at the Bar-C-Bar Ranch in Poway, 1949
(back row) Tom, Kees, Elso, Karel, John and Arie Jr.
(front row) Uncle Nick, Arie Sr, Uncle Sam, Cousin Ellie and Uncle Elso

After the family's arrival to Poway, John wanted to go to school, but his father said, "We didn't come to America to go to school. We came here to work and be successful."

After the family bought the 17th Street dairy, John was sent over to work and stay with the Ratlief's. John was nervous initially, because there was a lot to learn and it was a great responsibility to give someone so young. During the transition of ownership John shared a room with the Ratlief's son, Vernon, who was the same age as John. The first morning after he arrived, John thought he had overslept and ran to the barn to apologize to Mr. Ratlief.

Mr. Ratlief wasn't happy and said, "You didn't oversleep, boy. I sold the dairy to your father and older brother and they sent me a boy who should be in school."

Upset, John snuck away but watched to see how everything was done. He learned about the pasteurizer and homogenizer. He decided he was not going to have the same experience the next morning. There was no alarm clock and John got up before it was time and took the cows into the barn and washed them down. When Mr. Ratlief came into the barn he saw that the cows were cleaned and ready to be put onto the machine, he didn't say a word. He was very impressed by John's work ethic, considering his own son went to school, slept late and didn't do any work.

John was assigned to learn the processing. This was a strange turn of events for the Ratliefs, because here was a schoolboy, not quite sixteen, small in stature and who should be in High School that worked like a man. When the family bought the Ratlief's dairy in Escondido, Mrs. Ratlief felt sorry for John because he had to work and was not able to attend school. John was very serious, extremely eager and ready to learn the business.

The Ratlief's felt he should be allowed to develop normally and enjoy his youth. The de Jongs were not used to this kind of thinking and didn't notice any thoughts of disapproval.

Pictured left to right:
(back row) Elso, Maartje, Arie Sr., Ellie and Pete
(front row) Kees, Arie Jr., Mary, Jet, John and Karel

John learned very quickly. He became a part of their family and never had it so good. They spoiled him with ice cream and other goodies.

They milked the cows in Holland by hand, but here in America they milked by machine. During the transition the family would go to work at the dairy in Escondido and then drive back to Poway in the evening. John, however, continued to stay with the Ratliefs.

Once the deal was completed, Mr. Ratlief drove to Weseloh Chevrolet in Escondido, and purchased a new car and teardrop trailer. After the de Jongs initial training on the dairy's routes and general operation of the Cash and Carry store, the Ratlief's set off on their new adventure.

Tom liked it a lot when he took over the milk route. The work suited him. Kees was eager to get involved as well and wanted to start a milk route in Poway.

The house at the 17th Street dairy in Escondido had a garage that was converted to a bedroom where all seven boys slept. Because of the lack of insulation, the sweltering heat of the summer and the winter cold were unbearable, making it difficult to rest.

Arie Sr. had been worried originally about taking on such a large debt, but that changed when he noticed money was coming in. His new found independence was inspiring him. The family still worked for Sam, so there was money coming from outside the business as well.

His brother-in-law Sam was understandably upset when Arie Sr. bought the Escondido dairy. He felt he was being abandoned, when he thought they would form a partnership. When things finally began to turn around for Sam, he was resentful the de Jong boys whom he had fired had gone on to work in Artesia/Bellflower. Sam now saw that the family's heart was not set on building his business, but in building one of their own and he no longer expected Arie Sr. and the family to take over his dairy. By this time Tom and Kees, as well as the younger children, were already working in Escondido.

Not too long after the Ratliefs vacated the dairy and the de Jongs moved in, someone alerted the school district about John not attending school. When the truant officer came to the dairy on 17th Street to find him, John hid in the machine room between the wall of the cooler box and the wall of the building. When they were asked, Arie Jr. and Ellie pretended they didn't know where he was. The family believes the school district was alerted by Arie Sr.'s, sister Jet, because she felt the family deserted her husband Sam and she still harbored ill feelings.

It would take almost three years before Sam and Jet reconciled with the family. They traveled to the dairy in Escondido to attend Arie Sr.'s birthday celebration. Everyone was happy about the reconciliation.

Running the dairy in Escondido came naturally to Tom. He was taking on more and more responsibility and was very busy. Kees pursued making the dairy bigger and better, by adding new accounts. He was a natural born businessman and excelled at whatever he set his mind to.

John stated that when he was fifteen, he and Ellie fired their father, even though it was a difficult decision, because his work performance when stripping the cows didn't meet John's standards. Although their father was a great worker at two in the morning, and they were a great team and enjoyed his company; they felt there was no other option.

By this time the family had changed the name to, "Hollandia Dairy." While living in Holland, the family would place the full cans of milk produced by their cows next to the gate, where they were picked up daily and taken to the *Hollandia Creamery* to be processed.

When the time came to rename their dairy, Hollandia seemed the logical choice. It had always been a name they associated with quality. This was a matter of pride and a way to honor their family's Dutch heritage. The Escondido public also began to associate the Hollandia name with quality.

Piet Immigrates to America

In April of 1950, Piet returned to Holland from his tour of duty in Indonesia. He was sadly aware that all of the Dutch soldiers' war efforts in Indonesia, were not going to reward Holland with Colonial benefits. After World War II colonialism was abolished, directly due to the United States belief that all countries worldwide should have their independence. The family had immigrated to the United States a year earlier in May of 1949, and no longer resided in their longtime family residence in Holland.

Since his family home was occupied by another farming family, Piet stayed with his Uncle Sam's family in Wolsum, Friesland. He and his army friends still wore their uniforms. The local girls found the soldiers much more attractive and exciting than the local boys. Piet was the last de Jong family member to immigrate to America and he had no trouble achieving his visa.

After serving in Indonesia for over two years, Piet was more than ready to rejoin his family in America. Tom kept Piet informed by writing letters which created a picturesque and continuous daily journal while he resided in Holland, but once Tom and the family moved to America, there was no time for such in depth writing and detail.

The American Navy assisted in bringing the Dutch troops home. The troops boarded the *General Stuart Heintzelman*, a U.S. Navy troop-transport. Because he enjoyed doing the work, Piet volunteered for ships duty on the voyage home. He found the American crew very generous. During break-times they served large dishes of ice cream. Everything was better than what he was used to. The American sailors really enjoyed and liked the Dutch soldiers.

Coming home to Holland was a great experience for the Dutch soldiers, who were regarded as heroes and celebrated by their neighborhoods.   The soldiers were privy to free and unlimited train travel as well, which was used to real advantage.   By now Piet was staying with his *Oma* de Jong and *Tante* (aunt) Janna, not far from the farm where he grew up. It was close to summer and the weather was good for harvesting hay, so he volunteered to help at his Uncle Teun's farm.

While waiting for his emigration papers to be approved, Piet had lots of time to visit several buddies in the area. Their situations regarding settling back in and living a civilian life were somewhat different. For most of the soldiers it was easy to revert back to the old ways, but for some it was extremely difficult. Piet was in transition, getting ready to leave for America and so for him it was more like an extended vacation of sorts. Family members on both sides were extensive and Piet loved being able to visit all his aunts, uncles and cousins before setting sail for America. He continued traveling until August of 1950.

When his papers were ready he boarded the *Nieuw Amsterdam* for his trip to America. The consulate was very familiar with Piet, who had accompanied his Uncle Teun, when he was getting his papers to immigrate to California.

Piet became acquainted with the Van der Valks: Jo, Annie and their daughter Joey and traveled with them. Jo was a musician and was being sponsored by his uncle in the Los Angeles area. After they arrived in California, the friendship continued and their daughter, Joey spent time during the summer with the de Jongs.

During the war the *Nieuw Amsterdam* had been converted from a luxury passenger liner, to a troop ship for the Allies. It was the largest passenger ship belonging to the Holland-America Line at the time. Many of the passengers were immigrating to America and there was also a vast amount of tourists, mostly Americans, who were returning home. Piet was trying to learn American English, but he felt the language sounded very strange.

Piet noticed the Americans aboard ship were not very frugal. He watched as they made a hole in the skin of an orange, sucked out the juice and threw the rest away, instead of eating the meat of the orange, to take full benefit of the fruit. Being a victim of lean times during the war, he was not wasteful.

During his time aboard ship, Piet found himself annoyed with the fact the Dutch girls appeared to be more interested in the American military, than they were with him, or any of the other Dutch men on board. One girl in particular, a student, was constantly playing the piano; a skill Piet greatly admired and wished he could master. One melody in particular, *"Some Enchanted Evening,"* still haunts him, lingering in his memory to this day.

As an immigrant Pete was trying to fit into his new found position in life. This proved to be more of a challenge than he originally anticipated. After docking in New York, he boarded a Greyhound bus for the trip to Los Angeles. It was August, and the bus trip was suffocating because of the oppressive heat.

The bus ride from Los Angeles to San Diego was beautiful. The rich, blue ocean flanked one side of the highway and the scenery of homes and hills dotted the other. The drive from San Diego to Escondido was not quite as beautiful, or scenic. The land was brown, dry and hot, with too much desert and no visible water anywhere.

Pete felt it was good to finally see his family again. He was ready to dig in and help the family toward their common goal of owning and operating their own dairy. The first few days he was eased back into the hard knocks of civilian life. The family realized he was not used to the hard work and structure required for running a dairy. Pete ever resilient easily fell into the daily routine and quickly adapted to the chore of doing the job at hand.

His Uncle Elso took him to the stockyards in Los Angeles. It was a very interesting experience to a newcomer from Holland. It was a hot, dirty, messy mass of confusion. Pete thought his Uncle was impressive, because he already knew the ropes.

Pete with Mary and Jet with the 1953 Pontiac family car

A few days later, Pete was ready to pitch in and began working as a cow stripper. After the milking machine is taken off the cow, the stripper milks the last of the milk from the udder by hand. His brother Elso ran the milking machines and milked one hundred-eighty cows a day. The cows were milked twice a day, seven days a week, rain or shine, so Pete stripped one-hundred-eighty cows twice a day, every day. The milking would start in the middle of night when it was cold and then again in the heat of the day.

Although it was a simple job, it was very new to Pete. He had not milked for three years and his muscles had to get used to the milking motion and rhythm again. He was never prided himself on his milking ability. In Holland, he only milked and stripped six or seven cows a day. Coming off military duty he wasn't use to the stress dairy life had on his wrists. Stripping so many cows twice a day, made his wrists swell. He wrapped them in vinegar soaked cloths, because he was working so much. There were many nights Pete was unable to sleep, because of the pain. It took more than two weeks before he was finally used to the ebb and flow. Life of a dairy farmer was and is a hard life.

After the more leisurely life of a soldier, Pete found dairy life brutal. He was ready to give up and quit. However, his father Arie said to have patience and all hard work would eventually pay off. It helped for him to see and know that his brothers were working and suffering just as much as he was. Tom, the family cheerleader, always seemed to be full of enthusiasm. Pete's happy he listened to the council of his father and stayed in the family business.

Pete, Karel, Kees and Elso continued to work at their Uncle Sam's dairy to work off the sponsorship. Tom went to the new dairy in Escondido, to help his father milk the cows and run the business. It was May of 1950, when his parents purchased the site of the original Hollandia Dairy, on the north-west corner of 17th Street (now Felicita Avenue) and Centre City Parkway, in Escondido.

Pete and Elso were fortunate, because their Uncle Teun (Tom) had immigrated a few months after them, to become Miss Chambers' foreman. He hired them to work for him at the Cloverdale Dairy in San Pasqual. It was a big change from working on their Uncle Sam's dairy in Poway, and a great improvement.

Arie Sr and his brother Elso

Pete was close to his Uncle Teun and felt the pressure cooker atmosphere was a thing of the past. Not too long after they started work at the Cloverdale Dairy, the boys heard rumors that the milkers in Artesia earned wages considerably higher than the ones in San Diego. It was decided that Elso and Karel should find work there.

Los Angeles had an abundance of Dutch dairymen and cows. Because the boys were small in stature they looked more like schoolboys than dairymen and were met with some hesitation. The Dutch families not wanting to turn the boys away offered food and shelter in exchange for odd jobs. This helped them to get their foot in the door to become milkers.

There was a Christian Labor Association in Artesia. Mr. Sybesma, the Labor boss, helped the boys find employment. Elso went to work as a milker and Karel as a cow-washer. They were very pleased with the level of their wages while working in Paramount. They earned more than enough to supply room and board with the Feenstras, a nice Christian family from Friesland.

Elso's boss, Mr. Warrentjes, was impressed by Elso's work and when he lost one of his milkers; he asked if Elso had any brothers who could work for him. A call was made and Pete joined his brothers in Artesia. Once there, Pete, like Elso, was given sixty cows to milk. There were times Elso was given the cows experiencing udder problems. They required the more gentle touch of being milked by hand. There was a great deal of work available to the de Jong brothers once the dairy owners realized the full extent of their knowledge and abilities.

The boys were new to the country and had no time to develop a real social life. For them, there was only work and the family. Now that they worked in an area with a rich Dutch population and had more opportunity to meet young people; especially girls they could relate to. On Sundays, the boys attended church, but spent most of the time checking out the Dutch girls from the local families.

Although they were young, the de Jong brothers had become known as the best in time and performance. Elso and Pete grew close and during the time off between milking, he looked for a diversion. He always took Pete along to acquaint him with interesting people he spent hours talking to.

Pete and Elso worked together in the barn. It was nice for them both to be able to work alongside someone with the same work ethic. They discussed purchasing similar machinery to milk the cows in Escondido. They knew while they were away learning and earning money for the family, good things were beginning to happen on the dairy at home.

Karel was the cow-washer, a tough job to do, especially at night, because it was wet and cold. With whatever time he had left each night, Karel ran the milking machines with Pete and Elso. On more than one occasion Karel confided to Pete, how Tom's enthusiasm worked in reverse and failed to motivate him.

The Feenstras were concerned about the boys and how they were behaving with the young girls. For fun and relaxation the boys would often go ice-skating. This gave them a welcome break from the daily trek between the bed and barn and helped to stave off boredom.

Karel had a different set of problems. His boss liked old cows that gave a great deal of milk, but had low udders. This made Karel's job as pusher and washer even more tiring than usual. The more he slept; the more sleep he needed. He began to get bored and craved something that would challenge his creativity.

Milk sales at home were steadily increasing and Arie Sr. increased the number of cows from thirty-five to seventy in order to meet the increased demands. Tired of cow-washing, Karel wanted a milking job and he met an old dairyman by the name of Brandsma, who was willing to give him a chance to prove himself.

Because of Karel's keen eye for mechanics, he was the best thing that ever happened to Mr. Brandsma. After a short time, Karel noticed the vacuum on the milking machinery was insufficient and irregular, so the cows weren't being milked properly. He discussed this with

Mr. Brandsma who felt there wasn't a problem. Karel didn't give up. He went to his Uncle Hill Goedhart, to borrow a vacuum gauge/meter. Once Mr. Brandsma looked at the meter, the vacuum was fixed and his milk production increased thanks to Karel.

The boys arranged it with their bosses to finally take some time off to go home for a mini vacation. It was only for the week-end, but it was a well needed and well deserved rest for them all. Fortunately, Elso and Karel managed to get the same days off. The day was beautiful and sunny, and their excitement mounted in anticipation of being home with the family. The family car, a 1941 Chrysler, had been entrusted to the boys to use, due to the sheer logistics between Los Angeles and Escondido, to travel home for visits. The boys hopped into the old Chrysler and were on their way.

The journey home had barely begun when they became aware of a high pitched whistling. At first they ignored the sound, not realizing there was a mechanical problem that is until the car started to lose both speed and power. They pulled to the shoulder and just stared at each other in disbelief. With only a few days off, they wondered how they were going to get home and back to work.

Karel called his boss, Mr. Brandsma, to see if it was possible to borrow his old car for the weekend. Knowing how badly they missed their family, his boss decided to loan the boys his old Pontiac. The car was structurally sound, ran well and they were quickly on their way again. Later, Karel told his brothers, the gas station attendant had told him the Chrysler needed an oil change and a lube job, but he felt they were only after his money and turned down the offered service.

The Family Buys Wharton's Dairy

Grand opening at San Marcos Cash and Carry 1956

The Wharton's Dairy operation, on Grand and Ivy in Escondido was owned by Herb Lievers and he was in a state of declining health. His route drivers had complained to him on numerous occasions about a Dutchman named Tom, who had been systematically taking their customers away. Mr. Lievers was a wise businessman, and realized some of the route customers Tom had taken away, were really a pain in the neck to his overall operation, and he was better off without them.

Tom knew Lievers well, because there were certain products he stopped to purchase at Wharton's for his Escondido Dairy customers; like buttermilk, cream, half & half, butter and cottage cheese. He had met Tom previously and liked what he saw; an excellent salesman who had a good head for cultivating new business and expansion.

With the onset of his failing health, Mr. Lievers couldn't think of anyone who would be more suitable than

The grand opening of the San Marcos Cash and Carry 1956
Ellie (left) and Mary (right)

Tom and his large family to take over the growth and development of his operation. He made the tough decision to cash out and turned the reigns over to the de Jong family. It was an exciting time for the de Jongs, because Wharton's Dairy, Inc. had connections to Arden Farms.

The original dairy they purchased in Escondido on 17th Street just the year before, was only five acres, with twenty-eight cows being milked daily. Due to Tom's excellent sales ability the demand had grown to such great proportions, they began milking seventy cows a day on the

small dairy. Their business simply outgrew the Escondido location.

Approximately four months later, Karel returned from Artesia to work with the family at the San Marcos dairy. They bought Wharton's before anyone in the family went to work there. Before he sold the dairy, Lievers was being pushed to go union, but he refused to join. He loved Tom's enthusiasm and felt the de Jong family was large enough and strong enough to fight and beat the union. He talked to Tom about the family purchasing his dairy. Tom stressed the fact that the family had no money for such a grand endeavor.

Mr. Lievers continued with his proposal for the sale. He agreed to sell the family the seventeen acres of land, including a house, ninety-eight milking cows, four milk trucks, the

customer routes and the creamery and processing equipment for $100,000. The creamery building was rented in Escondido on Main Street, which is now the corner of Grand Avenue and Ivy. Mr. Lievers had faith that the family would make it and said they could pay him later. On October 1, 1951, the de Jongs officially became the owner/operators of the San Marcos dairy facility.

In September of 1951, while the boys still worked in the Los Angeles area, they received a call from Tom. "You boys need to come home right away, we bought Wharton's Dairies!"

This was the beginning of an exciting and unbelievable series of events. The dairy's creamery was in the middle of Escondido. The purchase came complete with retail routes throughout Escondido and Vista. The family literally bought "*THE*" local dairy and was finally on the way to financial and business success.

Karel and John machine milked the cows in San Marcos, while Arie Sr. took care of the milking in Escondido. Karel's engineering skills were by far his biggest contribution to the family's business. He was always finding new and creative ways to get the job done better, while increasing efficiency. He was so good at building and engineering dairy machinery, yet, he never had any formal engineering education. It just came to him naturally.

The family also made and bottled orangeade and fruit punch to sell on the milk routes and in both Cash and Carry stores. The well water at the San Marcos dairy was the best for this purpose. The water would be hauled in the ten gallon milk containers to the processing plant in Escondido to be mixed and bottled.

At the time, there were two health department inspectors in the county Bob Clayton and Mr. Stewart. They operated like good cop, bad cop. Where Mr. Clayton was nice, Mr. Stewart was the hardnosed code enforcer. Health code protocol was that all milk shipments being hauled to the processing plant not only had to have sealed lids, but also had to be covered by a tarp.

Koos Brouwer

On more than one occasion Arie Sr. had been warned to cover the shipment of milk cans before transporting them, or the milk would be dumped the next time he was in violation. He knew the inspector was out to get him, and felt he was being followed, so Arie Sr. was being cautious. Stewart staked out the dairy and waited, certain he would catch him red handed. He saw the truck leave the San Marcos location with a load of uncovered milk cans, and he followed the truck to the Escondido processing plant and quickly pulled in behind it.

He became excited, since he thought he nailed Arie Sr. with a health code violation. He opened can after can but only found water, which was being transported to make and bottle

110

the orangeade and punch. He left angry and embarrassed, because he had once again been outwitted by the de Jongs, and was unable to dump the milk.

The lease on the old milk plant in downtown Escondido was running out and Mr. Foss had given the family notice. In 1955, Karel designed the new milk processing plant, at the San Marcos Dairy, as well as the new Cash and Carry store at the same location. They finished building the new plant in 1956, just before Karel and Arie went into the Army.

The seventeen acre San Marcos dairy had approximately one hundred-twenty cows and a complete milking facility. Mr. Lievers and Tom discussed the financial details of the potential business transaction. The 17th Street dairy in Escondido had not been completely paid off; however, the payments were made on time. The revenue increased and the number of cows doubled after the de Jongs took over ownership. The family bank records also substantiated outside funds were coming in from the boys working in Los Angeles.

Pictured Tom (left) and Karel (right)

Although Arie Sr. felt very secure at the 17th Street location, he wasn't sure about tackling a business venture of this scale. He worried about who would take over the responsibility of running such an operation. He knew it was pointless to resist the optimism and forward motion of his sons when they had their minds set on an idea, and he ultimately agreed with the decision to purchase the San Marcos location.

The family had now taken on a substantial debt of $100,000, and had two dairy operations to run. The increased debt gave Arie Sr. many sleepless nights. He lost twenty pounds over a period of six weeks. By the time the first payments were made, and he saw how quickly his sons adapted to the new responsibilities, his overall anxiety decreased.

left to right: Karel de Jong, Bill Strickland, and Gerrit van Kampen

Both Pete and Elso learned the new milk routes, while Karel and John took over the milking operations. Ellie took on the responsibility of helping her mother care for their sizable family who were all home once more.

Mary remembered on one occasion how she and Jet were bottling milk when they were seven and eight years old and they ran off to watch cartoons and the bottle filler ran over, spilling milk all over the floor. They both got into serious trouble.

Compared to getting up at midnight to milk the cows, the idea of becoming a milkman was exciting for Pete. He would be able to sleep in. He was learning the trade and how to be a proper milkman from Eddie, the man he would eventually replace. The whole situation could have become terribly awkward; however, Eddie was a good mentor who was very personable and felt sorry for Pete, who was still green and very wet behind the ears.

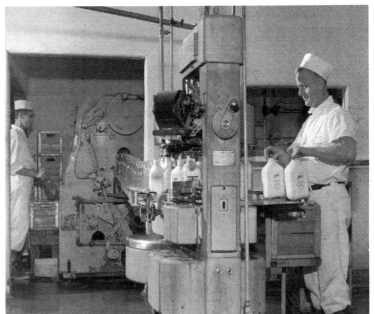

The new San Marcos processing plant 1956

He showed Pete everything he knew, instilling confidence in him with every step of his training. The realization suddenly dawned on Pete that by training him; Eddie would soon be out of a job. Kees was not green like Pete and had been busy building a route in Poway. He had taken over the route of a well positioned milkman, named Vern Hancock, who had been on his route a long time. Vern had no plans to change jobs and made it very clear he was resentful of the Dutchmen who had started to take over, and he planned to stay exactly where he was. Fortunately for Kees and the family, Vern was a man of ethics and he refused to make a mess of things. When he finally left, Vern immediately went to work for Qualitee Dairies of San Diego, who happened to have an Escondido route as well.

Kees de Jong

When this occurred, Kees came home white as a sheet, because he had lost almost half of his customers who were loyal to Mr. Hancock. Sympathetic to Hancock, those customers felt obliged to stay with Vernon out of loyalty, to the man, not the dairy. The de Jongs were very alarmed by this turn of events. If this trend continued it could be used against the family and would negatively impact the fledgling business they had started to develop.

Arden Farms was a major operator in California, with close to a one hundred retail routes in the San Diego area at that time. They also played a big role in the wholesale end and always did business with Wharton's. Hollandia received daily deliveries of buttermilk, chocolate milk, ice cream, half and half and other milk by products, from Arden Farms.

Arie de Jong

It may have been due to direct input from Mr. Lievers' that Arden Farms temporarily leant a route supervisor, Mr. Root to the Hollandia operation. Nicknamed Red, he went with Kees for 'Damage Control'. Red was well known in Escondido and was a man of solid character. It was due in large part to his input and presence that most of the lost customer base returned.

It took a while before Pete felt confident enough in his abilities to say he was a better worker than the average hired man, but felt he paled dramatically compared to both Kees and

Arie Jr. The original creamery building was owned by Mr. Foss, a nice old man, who lived across the alley, behind the plant. He liked and respected the de Jongs and felt they were a bunch of dedicated and hard working boys.

Young Arie Jr. was in school which he enjoyed, but he also had his duties and chores at home which weren't nearly as fun. Even though he was young, the family expected him to do his share. When he was fifteen, he and Karel began building a large hay barn, just off of Borden Road, which was unpaved at the time. They dug the footings by hand, which was difficult, because the earth was extremely rocky. It was a long and slow process. Everyday their brother Elso delivered cold buttermilk everyday at lunchtime. They always knew when it was lunchtime, because they could see the funnel of dust down Borden Road, created by Elso's truck.

While they worked digging the footings, Arie Jr. could see the old Richland Schoolhouse. He always wanted to go to that school and was envious of the children who did. His love of the old schoolhouse never diminished and years later, as an adult he purchased and refurbished the school in order to save and preserve it.

Arie Jr. and Karel left the house on 17th Street at 1:30 in the morning and drove to San Marcos to milk

Wholesale delivery fleet

the cows. In order to get back to Escondido in time to change clothes, eat breakfast and ride his bike to Escondido High School, Arie Jr. needed to be finished by 7am, so he could catch a ride back to Escondido with a man headed to work in San Diego. At first Arie Jr. hitchhiked back to Escondido every morning and that's how he met the man who ended up giving him a ride every day.

One morning while doing the milking Karel and Arie Jr. heard a crash. There had been a car wreck on the corner that resulted in a few injuries. They ran to see what happened and with all the excitement they completely forgot about the milking machines, until they saw the drain leading to the fields was full of milk from the overflowing cans. Arie Jr. was late getting to his pick up point and missed his ride to Escondido so he never made it to school that day.

During school holidays and vacations, Arie Jr. and his brother Karel milked twice a day; at 2am and 2pm. In between milking shifts he and Karel scraped up and bagged the dry manure. The bags were sold as fertilizer and delivered to customers in the Vista area.

Everett Pratt, a neighbor kid, was a little slow due to a mental disability, but had a kind and gentle spirit. He wanted to go along to help Arie and Karel with the milking. The boys agreed to take him along but only under the condition he was there to wake them at 1:30 in the morning by singing, "The Shack by the Road." Which he did. By 7am he was pretty much exhausted and done for the day. Everett's mother was grateful the boys took him along, because it boosted his self-esteem and made him feel important.

Everyone in the family worked. Although Jet and Mary were still very young and hadn't started school yet, they had daily work duties to perform.

Karel loved to build and create equipment. Nothing gave him more pleasure than when he created and designed a new invention that made everyone's job much safer and easier. The fact he didn't like to milk cows may have had something to do with his creative endeavors.

Karel and the fleet and maintenance staff

The town of Escondido was growing quickly and so were the size of the milk routes. When they purchased the dairy from the Whartons, the family inherited an old milkman named Buck. He ran one of the milk routes in Vista and was quite possibly the slowest delivery driver they had ever seen. Buck had known his customers for so long he'd seen their children grow into adults. He was quite fond of the customers he'd forged friendships with and he was never in the hurry to get his route done. On most evenings Buck was usually still out on his route while the other drivers had checked in and made their trucks ready for the next day. This created problems on several levels. The payments he collected needed to be tracked and processed for deposit into the bank.

Buck delivered the milk in an old truck, with leaky floorboards. This was of no surprise and nothing special. All of the trucks acquired with the Wharton purchase were old and in need of one type of repair or another.

One afternoon complaint calls were being received from customers on Buck's milk route. It was late in the day and he had failed to show up with their milk deliveries. Tom and Arie Jr. attempted to retrace his steps, in order to determine where the last delivery had been. Buck had been on the route for so many years, the actual customer addresses and order of the deliveries were not written down anywhere.

Hollandia, San Marcos retail and wholesale route drivers

With a little detective work, they traced Buck to the El Sombrero Motel in Vista. A place Buck frequented for his daily coffee stop or stayed to sleep it off when he had a little too much to drink.

When the boys arrived at the motel, they found Buck laid out across the bed and unconscious. They later discovered Buck had stopped to rest, because he wasn't feeling well. He had gone to sleep and never woke back up. They initially suspected he had a heart attack.

It was necessary for them to remove the route money collected, from Buck's wallet. Arie Jr. noticed Buck still had his un-cashed paycheck, and as tempting as it may have been...it was left behind with the wallet.

Without a printed route map or customer addresses, it was difficult, but the boys began to finish the day's milk deliveries. They received directions for the next house on the route from each customer. Because each customer wondered why they were late and wanted to hear the story regarding Buck's death, the day's deliveries were finished well into the night.

While they made deliveries, the doors of the truck remained open, so they could jump in and out to deliver the milk. On the way home, in an attempt to stay warm and stop the cold winter air, they closed the doors of the old truck, but soon began to feel dizzy, lightheaded and sick to their stomachs. Tom quickly pulled the truck over and opened the doors. They realized exhaust was coming through the leaky floorboards and suspected Buck must have died of carbon monoxide poisoning.

The town of Escondido was growing rapidly and that meant more routes and customers for the de Jongs new company as well. They learned by watching their competition and began to sell routes to independent operators. Some of the route drivers were a blessing, while others were a curse, and cost the company money and trouble. Luckily, the family was large enough to cut the fat. Whenever they got rid of a troublesome driver, one of the family members would take over the route to control the damage. This whole process was especially hard on Kees. He was exceptional at building large milk routes. Even though he knew it was necessary, it

Elso de Jong

was upsetting when the company sold his routes to an independent route driver. Many times the independents complained about business being tough, while they ran those same routes Kees had built into the ground. This practice caused the family to rebuild the routes all over again.

Kees was very gregarious. He told his route customers how the family had struggled, surviving the tragedies of war during the German occupation, before they ultimately immigrated to America. He spoke of America's greatness and the generosity of its people.

Escondido was a very small community when the de Jongs took over the dairy. Hard work and honesty were values rated highly. The community as a whole felt the de Jongs exemplified those values in every way.

 Earning the respect of the community was a key component in order for the business to grow and prosper; which it did. The entire family worked every aspect of their business. Easy going and personable, Tom was able to work well with the personnel from any plant or holdings the family acquired. Kees was doing an excellent job acquiring new customers and he was eager for the family business to grow.

Elso, worked as a route driver and foreman.

Pete was also a route driver and when he noticed his route didn't seem to be as large as when he initially took it over, he decided to hit the pavement to find new customers.

This was not as easy as it seemed. Kees encouraged Pete giving him tips on sales techniques and how to approach potential customers. They were always knocking on doors to add to their routes. For the most part it worked; the routes grew substantially.

 There was also the added problem of collections. On several occasions customers moved without paying their bill and left no forwarding address. The route driver wouldn't know they were gone until well after the fact.

Life in Escondido

Arie Jr. was the youngest of the de Jong brothers and he loved to hang out with Van Payne, a neighbor boy who lived across the street. Van's parents owned a television set, and when Arie Jr. finished his work at the dairy, at approximately 7pm, he ran across the street to watch cowboy movies, and The Lone Ranger, The Cisco Kid, Range Rider and Gene Autry TV shows.

Mrs. Payne was kind and generous. She always invited Arie Jr. to stay for dinner. As wonderful as his mother's homemade bread tasted, Arie couldn't wait to eat slice after slice, of the soft and delicious *Wonder Bread,* Mrs. Payne bought. Arie Jr. purchased the family's first television from a milk customer at a discounted price.

The de Jong kids in Poway with their 1936 Chevy

Jet was far too young when the family immigrated and has no memories or anecdotes from life in Holland or Poway. The majority of her memories revolved around dairy life and her growing up in Escondido and San Marcos. She learned how to make buttermilk from the family and continues to currently make her own lighter, sweeter version.

Everyone in the family was expected to drive the car and the tractor. Jet, like all of her brothers and sisters learned to drive the tractor when she was only five years old. Since she was too small to reach the pedals, she sat on the edge of the seat, or stood to depress the clutch, brake and gas pedals. For some of the de Jong kids, blocks were added to extend the pedals for easier reach.

In order to feed the cows, Jet drove a tractor and trailer loaded with her brothers and hay around the dairy. Her brothers, threw the hay off the back of the trailer with pitchforks, and had to be extra cautious, if Jet was driving. Whenever she drove the tractor, she popped the clutch, and they'd fall off the trailer while holding the pitchforks.

Jet had her share of accidents with the tractor and hay trailer. She hit fences, the barn and another vehicle. Fortunately none of her brothers were seriously hurt when they fell off the trailer. Her main role growing up was a combination of helping her mother inside the house and assisting with the duties around the dairy.

Mary de Jong, 1950

The men were thrown off the trailer on more than one occasion, and yelled at Jet and Mary, who were only five or six at the time, to stop popping the clutch. The girls were small and tried their best to prevent the rough starts and shifts, but they had to stand on top of the clutch in order to get it to depress. It was inevitable that the guys on the back of the trailer learned to make adjustments for the jerking. The men always felt the end of the day was a success, if no one was hurt and the cows were fed.

Jet and Mary also clipped the hay bales. Their father showed them how to fold and wrap the wire from the bales to prevent someone from having an injury. Of course, the girls were always scratched and bleeding at the end of the day, because they wore shorts and flip flops while they worked.

Arie Sr. attempted to teach Jet and Mary how to hook the suction cups of the milking machine to the cows' teats and take them back off. A flannel sock was located at the end of the pipe which led to the tank and filtered impurities out of the milk. Jet tried her best to milk,

Maartje and Arie Sr's 35th wedding anniversay, 1960

but didn't like the nasty tail hitting her in the face. She was happy when she didn't have to do any of the milking.

On Mondays and Thursdays, Jet got up at two in the morning to do the laundry for the entire family; including boarders and then hung it on the line before she started school. Her mother owned an old Maytag wringer washer, and Jet used a kitchen timer so she knew when to take the laundry out of the washer. She hand rinsed each load in cement sinks and wrung and used an electric wringer, prior to taking the basket of clothes out to the clothes line.

Because of the family's dairy life, there was always somebody home when they got home from school. Ellie took care of her two younger sisters, until she got married. Raised mainly by Ellie and their brothers, Mary and Jet rebelled at being bossed around by their siblings.

Jet enjoyed the times she could go on the garbage route with Karel, to pick up leftovers and garbage from the local restaurants for the pigs. When she went with Ellie to deliver cans of surplus milk to the Arden Creamery in San Diego, they got free ice cream.

When Mary was in her early teens, she'd sneak ice cream bars from the Cash and Carry, while she was working. Once when Pete walked in unexpectedly, she stuffed the ice cream in a drawer, and it melted all over her paperwork.

The only time Mary remembers eating dinner at a restaurant with her parents, was on their thirty-fifth wedding anniversary. When the family traveled to Visalia to see Tom and John, Mary loved it when her father stopped for hamburgers.

It was scary for Arie Sr. and Maartje because their children were exposed to so much through television, movies, and the community at large. There was a cultural clash and Mary grew up frustrated at not being able to communicate with her parents. Mary and Jet the two youngest girls, were very headstrong, they weren't allowed to go to the movies, high school sporting events, or date anyone who wasn't Dutch. The girls found it difficult to fit in, because they

Celebrating Arie Sr and Maartje's 35th wedding anniversay
At the Robin Hood Restaurant in Escondido, 1960
(pictured left to right) Karin, Tom, Maartje, Arie Sr, Rena and Pete

didn't want to accept what they felt was their parent's backwards way of thinking.

Mary states she and Jet never held their parents hard line traditional thinking and values against them. The girls would just sneak out a window and go to the movies, a school event or to meet a boy. They never felt guilty, until they got caught. Mary felt her family life was dysfunctional, because she was never really given any guidance from her mother and father. Everything was done by her older siblings.

All the de Jong boys slept in the 17th Street garage, which had no insulation. The garage was very hot, and made it more difficult to rest during the day or night. When Pete arrived from Indonesia, he added some empty paper beet pulp bags as insulation to the garage ceiling to make it more comfortable.

Over the years Arie Sr. sponsored the sons of friends and family in Holland, who came to work on the San Marcos dairy. Joseph (Jos) Rozenstraaten, the son of their blacksmith in Holland came to America to work for the de Jongs. Once he finally got out of bed, he was a good worker.

Jos had a bad habit of sleeping in, which didn't set well with the de Jong boys, and they decided to create a foolproof way of getting him out of bed. Karel and Arie Jr. paid a visit to Frank the Trader's salvage yard, on East Mission Road in Escondido, and bought an old siren from a police motorcycle. They wired it to a timer, mounted it on a board, and then hung it over Jos' bed.

He was shown and heard the siren and was given instruction on how to turn it off. The boys made sure it was always turned on before they went to bed. When the siren went off in the morning, Jos could only turn it off by going across the room to flip the switch on the ceiling. Jos was always full of excuses for being late, never was late again.

Tante Janna and Oma de Jong
At the Bar-C-Bar Ranch in Poway, 1948

Bob Shidner remembered how he took walks with his wife Dolores, and Arie Sr. called them over to have a drink. Even though he knew Bob would probably refuse, he always asked. Arie Sr.'s drink of choice was Bols, a Dutch gin. Every night the family had schnapps and Bols for happy hour.

Not long after the family moved to Escondido, in 1950, Bob Shidner got a job at Townsends Market on South Escondido Boulevard and moved his family from Poway to Escondido. They bought a house on El Rancho Drive, off East Washington in 1961. After moving close to where the de Jongs lived on 17th Street in Escondido, Bob and Dolores had five children and times were tough. Bob recalled the many occasions Arie Sr., (Papa, affectionately to Bob), would go to the freezer after butchering a cow and grab a big roast for Dolores to take home to their family. They were able to eat beef for a quite a few days. On one occasion in Escondido, Arie Sr. asked Bob if they liked pork. When Bob said yes, Arie Sr. told Dolores to go outside, pick a pig and Tony Bothof would butcher it any way she wanted.

After the family moved to America, Arie Sr.'s mother and sister Janna were very lonely in Holland and missed the family. After the family purchased the San Marcos location, Arie Sr. suggested they come to America to live on the San Marcos dairy. After they agreed, Ellie took on the responsibility of getting the house cleaned and painted for their arrival.

Ellie rode her bike early in the morning from Escondido to San Marcos with the basket full of painting supplies to get the house ready for her *Oma's* (grandmother's) arrival. The small house was located on the site of the actual dairy. Ellie cleaned and painted the house inside and out, so everything was perfect when they arrived from Holland. The two women lived in the small house in San Marcos for years.

Within three years of Arie Sr.'s family's initial exodus from Holland, his mother, sister Janna, and his brother Bouw's family followed suit in 1952 and immigrated to the San Marcos dairy.

Once they arrived in San Marcos, it was wonderful. The family would have coffee and lunch at their grandmother's house, just as they had in Holland. Their *Oma* (grandmother) would mend the family shirts and socks and tried to teach Ellie how to do the same. Their *Oma* sat on

Pictured left to right: Maartje, Arie Sr, Elso, John and Kees

the patio overlooking the dairy. Each day after work, Arie Sr. stopped at his mother's for happy hour, until she passed away from cancer, in 1955, at the age of seventy-six. For a short time, Janna continued to live in the house before she relocated to Artesia, in 1956 where she worked for her Uncle Reinier Goedhardt.

After Janna moved away, the house remained vacant until Elso and Dita moved in. They lived in the house for awhile and took in two boarders, including Cousin Rudy de Jong and Gerrit Roeloffs, Ellie's first husband. Years later, after they married, Karel and Shirley moved in and remodeled the small home. Several years went by and the family purchased a house for Karel and Shirley, close to the San Marcos Dairy from Karel's friend and neighbor, Ed Holderbaum, at 431 Mulberry Drive. Karel and Shirley continued to live there for twenty-five years, before building their dream home on Silk Mill Place.

Arie Sr.'s brother, Bouw had a Dairy Milk store in Den Haag, one of the largest cities in Holland, and the same city they now hold the world court. Immediately after World War II, the world court was held in Nuremburg, Germany, and some of the war trials against Nazi criminals were held in Den Haag.

When Bouw immigrated to America in 1952, he worked for nine months with his brothers Tom and Elso at the Cloverdale Dairy, in San Pasqual, until he purchased a dairy from the Roden family on Garden Road in Poway. Running a dairy is hard work and he was in need of good quality workers, so he approached Paultje Rozenmulder with an offer of sponsorship. Paultje accepted and immigrated to Poway in 1955. As a kid, he had worked at Bouw's milk store in Holland.

Bouw's daughters, Rena and Ellie, worked for Arie Sr's son, Karel, painting and cleaning the San Marcos barn before they moved to Poway where Bouw bought a dairy in 1953. Bouw's daughter Ellie worked at his dairy. Rena was the oldest of the cousins and was about the same age as Ellie. They became good friends.

Pictured left to right: (back) John, Elso, Pete, Tom, Kees, Karel and Arie Jr. (front) Ellie, Maartje, Arie Sr, Jet and Mary

Bill and Tom were Bouw's sons and were the same ages as Jet and Mary. While Karel worked in San Marcos he lived with his Uncle Bouw and Aunt Lena. The rest of the family still worked and lived on the original dairy in Escondido.

Rena moved in with Arie Sr.'s family on 17th Street, which is now Felicita Road. The dairy was situated across from the Fireside Restaurant and motel. It was the best and fanciest restaurant at the time. Rena worked as a cook for Mrs. Myers, baking pies and cakes.

After noticing good food being discarded, from the Fireside Restaurant Arie Sr. purchased some pigs and started picking up the food waste. The garbage collected was used to feed the pigs and hogs, in order to fatten them up for butchering. Other restaurants became aware of the de Jong's venture regarding food waste collections and put in requests to have their waste picked up as well. Arie Sr.'s pig farming business had expanded and had to be moved to the San Marcos location. The waste collections at the restaurants expanded and became a permanent garbage and food waste operation.

The two younger girls, Jet and Mary, slept in small bunk beds in one room, while Ellie and her cousin, Rena slept in the room next door. The bathroom door closed with a simple eye and hook latch and had a bathtub, but no shower. In order to take a shower, the family would have to cross the driveway to the garage, where a large shipping crate from Holland had been converted into a bathroom and shower for the boys. Arie Sr. and Maartje entered their home on 17th street from the porch, because the front door was never used. The house was small and they kept the doors and windows open for fresh air.

The floors of the house were rough cement and the small windows overlooked the dairy. The cement patio slanted the wrong way, and caused the water to run toward the house instead of away, causing problems for the de Jongs when it rained.

There was always someone visiting the de Jong family at the 17th Street dairy. Even though it could get very crowded, they always managed to make room for visitors. Some guests visiting from Holland stayed for weeks at a time or even longer. The girls worked very hard and even when there were out-of-town guests and conversations were loud, they were able to fall into a deep sleep.

When Ellie was fifteen, her mother, Maartje became mentally ill and Ellie took over the household responsibilities. For the next ten years, she cooked, took care of the house, the milking, delivering milk and washing the uniforms from 3am to 9pm. Every three years, Arie Sr. sent Ellie to Holland for three months, to let her renew her spirit and to get away from her mother's illness.

Whenever Maartje was feeling better Ellie and Rena always helped her cook. Maartje had taken care of and served people her whole life, and she always felt as though her work was never done. Arie Sr. always made time for Ellie and she adored working with her father. He wasn't picky and when it came to Ellie, he was always willing to take lots of breaks for some flavorful coffee.   Ellie was happy when her mother was feeling better, because she could do what she loved; running the milk routes and milking the cows.

In 1955, when Ellie was seventeen, her girlfriend Gien Schouten, came from Holland and lived with the family for a year. Not approving of the boy she liked, Gien's father, Leen, wanted to get her away from him and sent her to stay with the de Jongs in America. Leen and Arie Sr. became best friends during World War II in Holland, and because of their close relationship, the two girls became good friends as well. The boy Gien liked was the brother of Ellie's cousin Rudy. She went to work at the Cash and Carry in Escondido.

While Arie Jr. was in the Army he was stationed in Germany, and could drink beer. However, when he returned home at the age of nineteen, and resumed his job as a milkman he was too young to purchase alcohol. One morning while delivering milk to Mrs. Stephen, on El Valle

Opulento in Vista, he noticed 5-gallon bottles inside of her screened porch with tubes coming out of them.

Never one to mince words, he asked her what the bottles were for and why they had tubes in them. Mrs. Stephen stated very candidly, "It's my husband's project. He's making beer. If you'd like come back at 5pm, he can show you how it's done."

Arie Jr. was anxious to learn about brewing beer. When he returned that evening, Mr. Stephen showed him how to make the beer and told him all the ingredients he needed and where to purchase them. Arie Jr. traveled to San Diego to buy the supplies of malt, hops, yeast, bottle caps, and a hydrometer. He then began his beer making venture inside the shed next to the garage on 17th Street. The ingredients and water were added to old 5-gallon water bottles and left uncapped during the week long fermentation process.

After checking the alcohol level with the hydrometer, Arie Jr. would bottle the beer using old, sterilized Burgermeister quart bottles. The timing of the bottling was crucial. If bottled too late, the beer would be flat. If he bottled it too early, the fermentation would continue and the bottles would explode. He stored his bottled beer in a separate building close to the house was used as the laundry room.

Everyone enjoyed drinking the beer, which only cost a nickel a quart to make. His beer became so popular he started using a 55-gallon stainless steel vat used to pasteurize milk. After Arie Jr. finished the bottling, there were two hundred quarts of beer, stacked in cases inside the laundry room.

Without realizing it, he bottled his freshly brewed vat of beer too early, and the fermentation continued inside the newly capped bottles. While his mother was doing the laundry one of the bottles exploded, setting off a chain reaction, sending caps, beer and broken glass all over the laundry room. It sounded like bombs were going off. The incident pretty much ended his beer making venture.

In the early 60's, Rudy de Jong, the son of Maartje's cousin, came from Holland to work for the family. As a young boy, Rudy was trained in his father's freight business. While serving in the Dutch Air Force, he quickly rose to the rank of sergeant. Since there weren't any stable jobs to be found in Holland at the time, Arie Sr. and Maartje were proud to be Rudy's sponsors. The lure of a future in California attracted him and it was a good fit. He had an interest in mechanics and worked in the garage at the San Marcos dairy to attain more skills, before he became the Hollandia delivery fleet manager. He worked for the Hollandia organization over forty years, before he eventually became a partner.

The de Jong family ate dinner after the men came in from the dairy, usually between 7-7:30 pm in the evening. This included Rudy and any boarders living with them.

Education in America

After coming to the United States, Ellie was put into the 7th grade, instead of the 6th. Tom said they were more academically advanced due to the schooling they received in Holland. Because of Ellie's obligations and responsibilities to the family and dairy, she didn't make a lot of friends outside of the family. However, the friendships she made were strong and have lasted a lifetime.

Ellie had to ride her bicycle to her 8th grade graduation. None of the family was there. Arie Sr. felt there was no reason to attend, because anything to do with school was not a necessity.

She only went to school two or three days a week. When she was fifteen years old and a sophomore in high school, her father pulled her out of school to care for her mother who had become very ill. The fact she didn't graduate never bothered her. She loved to work.

When Karel was fifteen, he attended night school to learn English. The class was taught by volunteers at the old Escondido High School, located in the middle of Escondido, on the corner of 4th and Hickory. Since the old High School building was not earthquake proof, it was demolished and a new high school was built on North Broadway in 1955, where it still stands today.

Karel felt the English classes were great fun, because everyone was a teenager. Many of the tutors were sixteen-eighteen year old high school girls. Karel and several of the other boys would also socialize with the girls away from the classroom. English is a very difficult language to master and it took Karel more than a year to learn. One phrase he remembered was, "That's all that the young rat ever answered", because of the sheer repetition of the phrase in his English class.

Along with Arie Jr., the girls went to the Escondido Christian Training School, which was affiliated with the Four Square Church on West 6th Street in Escondido. Sister Thompson was the preacher and her husband was the custodian. Ellie and Arie Jr. developed many friendships that have lasted the span of a lifetime.

Arie Jr. had a number of friends in school and while attending Escondido High School he was drafted onto the wrestling team. His father only agreed to let him wrestle, because all his chores were done before 7am each day, and he had the afternoons free. Of course, since he and Karel left the house at 1:30 each morning to do the San Marcos milking. He was exhausted and many times fell asleep without eating dinner.

Young Arie hated milking the cows. During his summer vacation he worked both milk shifts with Karel. In between milking, they filled beet pulp bags with the dried manure. The bags were sold at the Cash and Carry of both dairies. They also delivered large orders to customer's homes. Selling the manure was a good money maker for the family business.

In order to participate in Escondido High School's sports programs, a student could only have so many demerits. Often Arie Jr. had trouble catching a ride back to Escondido and was forced to hitchhike, which caused him to be late for school, earning him demerits. He had to serve detention to work off the demerits so he could continue to wrestle in the 95-103 pound weight class. Arie fully enjoyed going to school, but when he turned 16 his father made him stop immediately, so he could start working for the family full-time as a milkman. That was the last day of his formal education. He immediately took over the milk route in Ramona to get away from the milking.

When Jet was fourteen and a sophomore at Escondido High School, Ellie got married. She was required to take Ellie's place assisting Etta Van der Woude with the bookkeeping duties at the Cash and Carry office. Etta and Jet's cousin, Rudy de Jong were engaged and scheduled to be married in June. Etta decided to quit working after the wedding.

When Jet asked who she was going to train to take over her job duties, Etta said, "Don't you know? You are."

Jet de Jong

Jet replied, "I can't, because I'm going to school."

Etta said with a big smile on her face, "No, you're going to quit school. You're not going back to school in September. When you get out in June, you'll be taking over the bookkeeping."

Instead of her father and brothers telling her she was going to quit school, she found out from Etta. Jet begged them to let her finish out her sophomore year, which they did. On June 21st, right after Etta and Rudy's wedding, Jet became the full-time bookkeeper.

She was only sixteen and given a great responsibility. She balanced the checkbooks for both the 17th Street and San Marcos dairies and their Cash and Carries, made the deposits, paid for shipments of grain, and was responsible for the daily receipts from both the Cash and Carry and from the drivers delivering milk. She had no computer, and all the spreadsheets were done by hand, using an old, pull handle adding machine.

On her last day of school, Jet stood on the steps of the school crying, because she would be unable to return to see her friends and finish her education. For the next two years, she worked in the Cash and Carry in Escondido, before finally going to work in the San Marcos office.

Jet states she was high-spirited and got along swimmingly with both the high school kids and other young adults. She took evening classes at Palomar College and was able to meet more young adults her age. On the days Mary came home after school, Jet was able to take afternoon college classes. She earned her GED and took accounting classes to help with her bookkeeping job at the Cash and Carry. By the age of twenty, she quit the Cash and Carry and went to work full-time in the bookkeeping office.

Mary grew up speaking both English and Dutch. She attended the Four Square Christian School on Valley Blvd., in Escondido. She loved school and enjoyed being able to ride her bike there. While in the 3rd, grade she attended Grace Lutheran on the corner of 13th and Redwood.

Mary de Jong

She was always a little embarrassed to bring any of her friends home after school, because her parents didn't speak English. Like Jet, she rode her bike to her 8th grade graduation. Only Mary, Jet and a caretaker attended the ceremony.

Mary, like her sisters, never had *"The Talk"* from her mother, regarding growing up as a young woman and the changes she could expect from her body. She started her period in the 8th grade and thought she was dying. Fortunately, Jet explained what was happening to her which helped to put her at ease.

Jet and Mary attended Escondido High School and rode the bus to school, until they were old enough to drive. Socially, high school was hard for Mary. Coming from a small Christian school, she didn't know a lot of people. Because Jet was always more outgoing, it was a much easier transition for her. Mary was shy; and just wanted to crawl inside a hole somewhere.

Mary came out of her shell her senior year of high school, and surprised everyone when she became a cheerleader. Since her parents didn't understand exactly what a cheerleader was, she told them she'd been chosen and had to go to all of the games. She failed to mention she had tried out to earn her place on the team. Since Mary had to work and couldn't attend practice at the school, everyone on her cheerleading team practiced with her at the dairy Cash and Carry, between customers.

There was an opportunity for Mary to attend a cheerleading camp at the University of Redlands, and she was very excited. She had never been able to go anywhere without the family or away from them before. After her experience at cheerleading camp, she was allowed to go to Disneyland. Her parents reluctantly began to give her a little more freedom. Even if her parents hadn't given them freedom, she and Jet were rebellious and would have taken it anyway.

Mary remembers going to school dances and being embarrassed about not knowing how to dance.

In high school Mary and Jet owned a 1964, Pontiac GTO, a fast piece of mechanical engineering. Jet wanted a fast car and Rudy found the GTO. After she convinced the family into letting her have it, cousin Rudy who was in charge of the garage, the shop and the purchasing of all the dairies vehicles reluctantly purchased the car for her.

Ellie de Jong

Before she and Jet got the GTO, she drove Ellie's car. One day when Mary was driving Ellie's Model 'A', home from school, she had a fender bender. She was terrified, unsure of how Ellie would react. Everything turned out just fine.

Mary was the only one of the ten de Jong children, who graduated from high school. Her best friend was Gayle Quade, the school superintendant's daughter. When Mr. Quade found out Arie Sr. wanted Mary to quit school, he told him that if he didn't allow her to stay in school and graduate, he would make sure they never got another milk contract from the Escondido Union High School District. That was the crowning point in the decision for Mary to remain in school.

The Quade family had a travel trailer in Solana Beach, and while in high school, Mary went with her friend on two occasions and spent the night. Her family worked all the time, so she really didn't know what having a vacation meant.

Graduation was the saddest day of her life, because it meant she would spend the rest of her life working. She was having a ball and wanted high school to last forever. She couldn't wrap her thinking around going to college. She knew she didn't need college to work at the family business. Mary graduated when she was seventeen and then went to work full-time at the Cash and Carry on 17th Street and did office work handling milk orders, billing and the delivery routes. Although she worked full-time after her graduation, working at the Cash and Carry was not new to her, she had worked there and bottled milk from the time she was five years old.

Jet and Mary both took citizenship classes at Palomar College. Once she was on campus, Mary had a strong desire to go to college, but knew her father wouldn't let it happen, so she never asked. She did however take classes in German and square dancing with Jet.

When Mary was a teenager, the family went on a short vacation to Visalia, and while there they went water skiing with the Gist family. Mary remembered how mortified she was when she saw her sixty year old father water ski in his underwear.

The de Jongs Join the Military

With the exception of Pete, all the de Jong brothers served as medics in the American Army. Respecting and loving life and the diversity of all mankind, none of the de Jongs liked to fight and didn't want to be put into a position of having to fight and possibly kill someone else. They all enlisted as conscientious objectors. Living through the hard times of the Nazi occupation in Holland taught them a great deal regarding tolerance and violence. Most of the German soldiers they met during the war were just men doing their jobs and they didn't feel good about the killing either.

Tom was drafted into the American Army in January of 1953, and served as a medic until 1955. Because Tom was a Jehovah's Witness when his number came up for the draft he didn't want to fight. He was a conscientious objector and refused to go, so he decided to leave for Canada instead of being drafted. As the time drew near for him to leave, he needed to teach Pete the ropes, but he had been too busy to show Pete the books. He knew if he was drafted or gone for an extended period of time, Pete would need to take over running the family business. A few days before he left, Tom finally found enough time to show Pete what he was doing and how to do it efficiently.

Working several years as a route driver had Pete well acquainted with the family business, and he was doing well working on his own. It was a tremendous help to be part of a family that took business so serious. He enjoyed all aspects of running the dairy; like doing the books, running the Cash and Carry or interacting with the vendors who sold merchandise and supplies. He loved working early in the morning, setting up loads for the various routes.

After he trained Pete to take over his responsibilities, Tom headed for Canada driving a 1928, Model 'A' Ford. The brakes on the car were weak and he picked up two marine hitchhikers from Camp Pendleton. The additional weight must have been too much. They had an accident in Los Angeles when the brakes failed.

While the car was being repaired, Tom stayed at the dairy of his friend Leen Verburg's, Cousin Bill. While there, he told Bill and his family the story of how because of his Jehovah Witness beliefs he was heading to Canada to avoid the draft. Tom thought it was great to have a weeklong vacation and he never gave a second thought about telling his story to Bill.

The car repairs were completed and he headed out for Canada once again. Ten days later he was apprehended by the FBI while crossing the Canadian border. They knew who he was and had been waiting for him. He was taken to jail in Bellingham, Washington.

Tom was told if he didn't do his enlistment, he would be deported back to Holland. He opted to enlist and was shipped to Fort Lewis, Washington, where he was immediately inducted into the American Army, before being shipped to Fort Ord, California and Camp Picket, Virginia for basic training. Since he was a conscientious objector, he served his military time in the medical corps as a medic. The family did not see him again until he was discharged.

At the age of twenty-nine, Tom became an American citizen in 1954 while he was stationed in Germany. He loved the United States and felt it was the right choice to make. Over fifty-six years later, he remains happy with his choice and feels it was the best decision he could have made. Being an American citizen made traveling Europe much easier.

The church in Munchweiller, Germany

While he was stationed in Germany, Tom met his first wife, Karin, the daughter of Helmut Karl Friederich, and Erna Hildegard Louise Schlueter. She was born April 13, 1938, in Brandenburg, Germany. Her father, Helmut was an Aeronautical Engineer and her mother was a tool and die maker, both parents worked at the Arado airplane factory in Brandenburg, Germany.

Karin's family moved to Prague, Czechoslovakia, in 1939, where her father worked for Albert Speer, converting peacetime factories to the manufacturing of weapons and war equipment. When Hitler took over, her father became part of the Czech occupational forces and was no longer welcome by the general public.

Her father listened to the BBC on an illegal radio he kept hidden in the hall closet. Her family escaped to the American Sector in Bavaria. Her family was given shelter in Furth/Landshut and she lived there until, when she went to live with her paternal grandmother to attend the Hildegardis Lyceum in 1948.

Her relationship with her mother was not the best and in 1954, after Karin graduated from high school, she moved to Munich, Germany where she lived with her half brother. While there she obtained a job as an apprentice with a hair design studio on the McGraw Caserne American Army Base.

Before they were allowed to work on the base, the locals were required to get a medical exam. She received her physical from Tom de Jong. Two days later he asked Karin's boss to introduce them and he did. She was very impressed with Tom, who had a car (she had never been in a car before) and he had a lot of German money. Tom always looked for ways to make money. He purchased cans of gasoline at the PX and then sold them to the German gas stations.

When they married in January of 1955, Karin was sixteen and he was thirty. She became a Jehovah's Witness just before they married. While Tom was stationed in Germany, Arie Sr. traveled home to Holland on a visit. Tom and Karin went to see him. After meeting her, Tom's father did not approve of the impending marriage. He felt his son should marry a nice Dutch girl and not a wild girl from Germany.

Tom was discharged while stationed in Germany after his tour was complete. Always strong minded, Tom went against his father's wishes and after his discharge he married Karin. The honeymoon consisted of visiting her family in Germany, followed by a five week visit to Holland. They had a good time and Karin learned how to speak Dutch very quickly. During their marriage they had three children; Mary, Arie Helmut and Tommy.

Although Pete's business and family life were good, he was beginning to feel socially disconnected. For him, something was missing. He was still trying to fit into both his new life and new country with its vastly different language and customs.

Most of the de Jong brothers were involved in religious studies. Pete states he came close to joining the Jehovah's Witness, but found he was unable to fully commit to the religion's philosophy. He was torn by previously learned religious doctrine and he reasoned that if he chose to change, the implications of that decision meant his family and the rest of the world were wrong. He was in conflict and would need more time before he could take that giant leap of faith.

In order to quench their desire to learn the truth, Kees, Elso, Karel and Pete spent one week studying with a local Jehovah's Witness family. The next week they studied with the minister of their church in San Diego, who asked the boys to look up Bible verse, Jeremiah 23:5.

'Behold I will raise unto David a righteous branch and a king shall reign and prosper and execute judgment and justice on the earth. In his days Judah will be saved and Israel shall dwell safely and this is his name whereby he shall be called: the LORD our righteousness.'

After asking if they knew who the prophecy regarded, the lesson was over and the boys were ready to make their decision.

It was the law that every American male had to register for the draft when they turned eighteen years of age. John, however, failed to register and in 1954, when he was nineteen, he was arrested by the military police and taken to Fort Ord, California, where he was automatically inducted into the Army. From there he was shipped to Fort Sam Houston, Texas, where he received his training as a medic.

During his eight weeks of basic training John gained a whopping twenty-five pounds. For the de Jongs, basic training was like a vacation. John was used to the hard physical labor, and getting up at two in the morning, so he was always up before anyone else. He felt basic training was easy and laughed at all the soldiers who complained about the hard work.

By special request and the grace of God, John served his military time in Germany. This was a great bonus for both him and the family. He served, with the 42nd Ambulance Company, in Munich, under the same commander that Tom had. When John met his commanding officer in Germany, he was surprised to learn that although the officer remembered his brother Tom, he did not speak fondly of him. This was a time of change for the family. Many of the changes were good, but the military service was more of a hindrance than helpful for the family at the time.

While stationed in Germany, John became a U.S. citizen. The ceremony was held at the U.S. Embassy in Munich. He was sad; because in order to become a U.S. citizen, he had to denounce his Dutch citizenship.

John knew when he was discharged from the Army he never wanted to work as hard as he had before. He went to the education center to get his high school diploma. He took all the tests to get his GED and passed them all. He thought if he went to college, life would be easier.

All the de Jong children were good students when their father allowed them to attend school. John had gotten very good grades while attending school in Holland and wanted to go to college. His brothers approached their father and said they wanted to send John to college. He had already picked out his college courses and he was accepted at Palomar Junior College.

When John told his father he wanted to go back to school to further his education, he was told, "We didn't come to America to get an education, and you don't need an education to milk cows." His father wouldn't allow him to go to college, because they had all promised when they emigrated, they would work toward one goal as a family; to be self-employed and self-sufficient. John thought things would be different if he was accepted to Palomar before he told his father and the family. Although the decision saddened him deeply, John was an obedient son and did as he was told.

Later, John took over the responsibility of running the dairy when Karel and Arie went into the military. John wanted to enjoy life traveling and seeing the world, like he did while he was in the military. He loved Germany and wanted to go back.

Kees and Elso went into the military service at the same time. They served their whole military service together, from their induction at Ford Ord, California, to their medic training at Fort Sam Houston, Texas. Kees was drafted and Elso volunteered. They were the only two brothers who served in Korea for a period of sixteen months.

Karel's number came up for the draft in 1954, when he was twenty. His father fought to have Karel's military service delayed. He already had three sons who were serving at the time and he needed someone to stay at home to help him run the family business. The delay was approved.

Karel (left) and Arie (right) duffle bag on their shoulders boarding the General Langford, for Germany

When John was discharged, Karel, who was twenty-three, got drafted. The family felt Karel and Arie Jr. could stay together, if Arie Jr., who was seventeen and high spirited, volunteered for the draft. The family felt Arie Jr. could have easily been steered down the wrong path without Karel's even tempered guidance. The two brothers served as medics in the American Army. Since Karel was drafted and the family forced Arie Jr. to volunteer, the brotherly duo never planned on being model soldiers. It was more of an inescapable vacation.

Tom wrote a letter to President Eisenhower at the White House, and requested he allow both Karel and Arie Jr. both be stationed in Europe, in order to retrieve their father's assets. When they received their orders, the request had been granted, they were being shipped out to Europe. The idea was to try to keep the boys together during their whole tour of duty. When they arrived at the bus station, the duo resembled vagabonds wearing old, worn out clothing. They knew the old clothes would be replaced by crisp, new military issue uniforms. Their father and Uncle Willem van Wyk drove them to the Greyhound bus terminal in Escondido. They headed straight for the back of the bus where it was much roomier and they could sleep. The bus only stopped long enough to pick up more soldiers.

After a two hour bus trip, they arrived in Los Angeles, where they spent the night. Always the pranksters, the two brothers provided entertainment to the rest of the recruits. They acted as if they were a couple of country bumpkins who had never been to a large city before. When the elevator doors opened they jumped back like they were afraid, which surprised the other new recruits, and made everyone laugh. The two boys made a lot of friends in basic training.

The next day they continued to Fort Ord, California for basic training, and then traveled by train to Fort Sam Houston, in San Antonio, Texas for their medical training. They completed twelve weeks of medical training in Texas before heading to Fort Dix, New Jersey, where after a brief layover, they boarded the troop ship; General Langford, for the Atlantic crossing to Bremer Haven, Germany.

Karel and Arie on maneuvers in Germany

Since Arie Jr. and Karel were used to the long hours and hard work involved with running a dairy, basic training was like a vacation to them. They each gained ten pounds during basic training and another ten afterwards. Their fellow soldiers and superior officers were surprised and puzzled by this turn of events. The soldiers ate in designated shifts, which both boys completely ignored when mealtime came around. They were always the first ones in and the last ones out of the mess hall. They stayed until they ate so much they were like two ticks ready to pop.

Their brother Tom told them to act like dumb Dutchmen, who didn't understand the American military system that way they wouldn't be given any orders and others would have to do the work.

Karel was feeling a little apprehensive about being drafted into the military, but knew it was too late. When Arie Jr. joined the Army, he aspired to be a regular soldier. He felt Karel just wanted to goof-off, because he had already devised a plan to get out of work.

Whenever the sergeant called on Karel to do a task, he feigned ignorance, and pretended he couldn't understand, because he was Dutch. Whenever he made mistakes, Karel acted stupid once more, so he could get out of work. The sergeant became extremely frustrated and finally stopped calling on Karel to do tasks.

One day while they were still stationed at Fort Sam Houston, in Texas, they decided to take a shortcut back to the barracks after visiting a friend off base. As they walked along the railroad tracks, they came to a fork in their path.

Karel remembered telling Arie, *"This is where the trains separate and go to different destinations. We now have a choice. You and I went into the Army together, traveling on the same bus, to the same training camp and will probably end up stationed on the same assignment. You want to be a model soldier and I*

Karel de Jong

don't. Look at the tracks, they separate here. Are we both going down the same track, or do we separate here for the next two years? Make up your mind. You are either with me you will be going alone!" Arie Jr. made up his mind right there and then to join Karel.

Karel became a United States citizen at the age of twenty-four, while stationed in San Antonio, Texas. The swearing in ceremony took place in Del Rio at the Rio Grande River. The judges made it known they didn't like conscientious objectors. Karel kept being pushed to the back of the line, and denied citizenship by the judges, while they swore in Hispanics and other nationalities.

or

Arie de Jong

139

After everyone else was sworn in, it was after five o'clock and Karel demanded to be sworn in. He showed the judge his book and stated what he wanted in no uncertain terms. The judge realized he would be in a great deal of trouble if he denied Karel his right to citizenship and swore him in even though it was after 5pm. Karel felt great that he'd won that battle and went to celebrate.

Arie while stationed in Munchweiller, Germany and his good friends

Tom, who was a Jehovah's Witness and Karel who held some of the same beliefs, were both conscientious objectors while they served in the military. Even Arie Jr, who was the maverick of the family and not very religious also served as a conscientious objector. They felt they had all seen or heard enough about war time death while living in Holland and they had experienced it first hand during the war as children.

In Munchweiller, Germany

A sea crossing didn't make Karel very happy. He still had a bad taste in his mouth regarding the nauseating boat trip he'd experienced from Holland to New York as a child. Karel swore he would never travel by ship again after that trip so many years ago, but in the military you have no say. He wasn't looking forward to hanging over the ships railings, staring at the water for days on end. Onboard the troop ship, he was sea sick during the whole Atlantic crossing.

After their ship arrived at Bremer Haven, Germany, they boarded an old, World War II, German military steam locomotive that took them to Munchweiler, where they worked as medics in a military evacuation hospital.

Before Karel went into the Army, Pete remembers him saying how much he liked the relaxation brought about by having a few drinks. Karel had always been such an intense person and was drawn into the seduction of social drinking. Pete became concerned early on regarding his brother's alcohol consumption and the eventual effects it could and did have on his health.

Karel became a social drinker during his time in the Army. This didn't change when he returned home. Social drinking was an acceptable part of the German culture and the de Jong lifestyle as well.

Although Karel drank too much, it didn't affect his ability to operate the business. He did however miss out on regular dinners with Shirley and the children. Shirley quietly accepted the situation and never complained to anyone.

Life was different in the Army. There were no personal obligations and

Karel (left) and Arie (right) helping a local German farmer harvest hay

responsibilities. By volunteering for the draft, Arie Jr. was automatically in for a two year enlistment, just like Karel who had been drafted. They felt as though they had become a form of government property.

Ellie and Karel de Jong

Arie Jr. sometimes owned four cars at a time, which he let his Army buddies in Germany borrow. Those friendships forged early in their lives have lasted a lifetime. Several of their German friends have come to America on vacation and the extended family has traveled to Germany on visits as well. He even brought a brand new Mercedes home. They visited Holland several times while stationed in Germany. They had many friends in both countries.

A book of anecdotes could be written on the Military careers of Karel and Arie while they were stationed in Germany. The two brothers always seemed to spread a great deal of goodwill wherever they went. They were the best ambassadors America could have had there.

When Karel left Germany, he returned to the states aboard ship once more. He remembered them playing, "Auf Wieder Sehen", which means, "Till we meet again" in German.

Karel choked up as he reminisced about his time in the Army, and said, "The people in the Army were very nice to us."

When Karel returned to the states, his brother, John, was taking a ski trip with his friends and invited him to go along. He tried to beg off, but John talked him into it. Once Karel managed to get up on skis, John kept issuing praise on how well he was doing. As John's group was taking off their skis at the bottom of a hill, Karel was coming down. He felt he could go straight across and didn't realize the snow was slick. His skis broke through the crust of the snow; got stuck and sent him head over heels several times, before he came to a sudden and painful stop. The ski patrol had to take him down the hill in a basket.

Karel admitted he loved all the attention. His head was in a girls lap the whole way home. He didn't go to the hospital until the next day. Karel injured his back and leg and was unable to drive. Ellie was seventeen, and had throat surgery, to remove warts on her vocal cords. After her surgery, she had to drive to San Diego for six months of voice lessons. The long drive scared Ellie; because she made the trip alone and sometimes fell asleep at the wheel. Since she was unable to talk, and Karel couldn't drive, they helped each other out. She did the driving and he kept her company and did all the talking. He ended up having back surgery years later. He had two separate surgeries and it took over two months for him to fully recover.

Tom Breaks Away From the Family Business

The family was happy to receive the news; Tom was coming home from Germany, with his new bride. Having him home would be a big help to the family business. For Pete, having Tom back would take a great burden off his shoulders. Tom was more positive and dynamic when it came to dealing with people and Pete was anxious to turn the reigns over to him. Tom's bride, Karin was very young and after the joys of a romantic honeymoon in Holland, the reality of immigration to America hit her hard and the marriage was under great stress.

Tom returned to California first and Karin, who was already pregnant, followed shortly after. Karin felt Tom had changed after his return home, and felt as though she had lost her husband and was living with a stranger. He had ascribed to the Wareland Theory about diet and health and she rarely saw him. She felt alone in hostile territory. Tom's father made it very clear he was not happy about the union between his son and Karin.

Karin never received prenatal care while she was pregnant, because Tom felt it was unimportant. When she went into labor with Mary (Maartje), who was born on October 13, 1955, Karin drove herself to the hospital, because Tom was gone. Later, when he called to see what she had and found out the baby was a girl, he said, "Only a girl. Better luck next time."

Karin's mother came to visit when Mary was born. Her mother disliked Tom, as much as Arie Sr. disliked her. The visit was a complete nightmare. Karin began to feel the marriage was one of convenience and that Tom didn't love her.

Three months after giving birth to Mary, she was pregnant again. When she was eight months along, Arie Sr. asked what she was going to name the baby. She said, "Arie."

Arie Sr. made it very clear, that no son of hers would ever be called Arie. While Tom sat in silence, Pete piped up and said he would be honored if she named the baby after him. Karin felt Tom never came to her defense.

She also felt making money was all that ever mattered to Arie Sr. and that it was not his father, but really Tom who had all of the ideas and knew how to deal with people.

When she went into labor with her second child, she drove herself to the hospital again. The baby, a boy, was breech. Because she was still underage, and Tom could not be located, they used forceps to deliver the baby. Since Tom was unavailable, Karin filled out the birth certificate, and named the baby Helmut.

Tom had a conversation with his father and three days after the baby was born, Arie Sr. begged Karin to forgive him and change the baby's name to Arie. Tom was able to retrieve the birth certificate in time and the baby's name was changed to Arie Helmut.

On 17th Street, with two small babies to care for, Karin also helped Maartje out with the cleaning and cooking. She bore witness as Maartje was having psychotic episodes with more and more frequency. On one occasion Maartje had failed to care for or keep an eye on baby Arie. Luckily, Karin came home just in time. Her episodes became so bad, she was boarded up in her room and only Arie Sr. could go in. Soon after that she was admitted into a local hospital for medical management. With all her flaws, Karin loved Maartje and realized the woman was just mentally fragile.

Karin felt abandoned by Tom after suffering a miscarriage and ran away to Red Bluff with friends, only to discover she was pregnant again. Tom brought her back and they moved to San Marcos. When she went into labor with Tommy, one of the milkers drove her to the hospital, because Tom was gone once again. Three months after Tommy's birth, she tried to commit suicide. When Tom came home and found her, he told her how stupid she was.

That's when the family decided to send her home to Germany for a visit. The three small children stayed with Pete and Rena while she was gone. As she left, Maartje was sad and said she hoped Karin would not come back.

After a few years of living in the states and having a rocky marriage, Karin wanted Tom to leave the family business and go into business for himself. He obliged and bought the "City Edge Guernsey Farm," a dairy in the city of Fresno, located in California's central valley in October of 1958. The dairy was not located in the best area of town. The dairy, Tom renamed "The Milky Way," could not offer a smooth path for the rocky road the marriage continually found itself on.

When Karin returned from Germany, Tom had already purchased the dairy in Fresno. She had high hopes they could settle down and be a family since they'd be away from his father and brothers.

Tom felt going into business on his own was a good idea. If the marriage did end in divorce, the family and Hollandia Dairy would be left out of the mess. If it was just him and Karin, it would be a lot less complicated for everyone involved.

Moving away was a very painful and difficult decision for Tom to make, because he loved his family deeply. Arie Sr. felt the move would be the best course of action for both Tom and the family business. Tom had taken a few Dutch boys with him to Fresno to help work the dairy. The Golden State Freeway had not been built yet, and the trip to Fresno took over five hours by car. He knew the family would want to take many trips back to San Marcos to visit Hollandia Dairy and decided to buy an airplane.

He purchased a four person Piper Cub Airplane for $5,000 and it was decided Herman Van Zonneveld would take flying lessons and become the pilot. In March of 1959, they flew to San Marcos to surprise Maartje for her birthday. Herman had not received his pilot's license yet, and was not allowed to carry passengers. It was a beautiful morning; they had no flight plan and no insurance on the plane, so of course they flew to San Marcos, with Paultje Rozenmulder tagging along. They felt like heroes when they landed. The trip only took two hours by plane.

Tom thought it might be a good idea to purchase insurance on the plane before the return flight home. He called his insurance agent and they were insured in time for the return trip to Fresno. However, they had no onboard radio and would not have known how to operate it even if they did. There was a terrible storm and Karin called to warn them not to leave. They had been in the air for almost an hour and never received her message.

As they reached the mountains, Herman said, "Tom something is terribly wrong. We're only going thirty miles an hour."

They looked out the window at the freeway traffic, and both of them realized they were being pushed backwards by the force of the wind. It was one giant dust cloud, as far as they could see. They had not been able to read, or use the instrument panel. Luckily, Tom had brought binoculars with him, which allowed them to follow the path of the 99 freeway and read the freeway signs to gauge their location.

Herman tried to turn the plane around, but the force of the wind was too great and he lost control. The up draft carried them up the side of the mountain and Tom felt they would be ok if they could reach the valley on the other side. Before they knew what was happening, the plane was quickly caught by a strong vacuum that pulled them back down the slope, smashing them into a huge oak tree. Most of the plane was scattered across snow over a foot deep.

Fortunately, the only injury was to Herman, who hit his head on the steering wheel of the plane. Luckily, it was not a serious injury. They walked down the slope to the freeway before they hitch-hiked the rest of the way back to Fresno. Karin was happy and relieved when they arrived home safely. The plane was a total loss, but the insurance paid off the loss. At four o'clock the next morning they all got up and went to work as usual, as if nothing had happened.

Karin met someone while she was in Germany and had an affair. She still wasn't happy, but felt she had to atone for her sin, and confessed her indiscretion to Tom. They tried to overcome her transgression and make it work. Karin milked, and cleaned the equipment before the kids got up in the morning. The house was a dilapidated mess, but she tried to keep it clean. There were no celebrations, entertainment, dinners out and no affection. They continued to grow apart. She had been unfaithful and he now thought of her as damaged goods.

Tom's dairy was located in Fresno on the corner of Church and Elm, a mainly black area and not the best of locations. She was nineteen, had three children and wanted to be free. Tom purchased the dairy farm in October of 1958 and less than six months later, a month after the near fatal plane trip, Karin left the family, and pursued her new life by starting college. The children were still very young, just one, two, and three years old at the time. Tommy, the youngest, grew up without having the benefit of knowing his mother. Tom had taken on the role of both parents.

Tom wanted to make the divorce as easy as possible for them both. Instead of giving money to attorneys, he felt he would just give it to Karin. He made her a deal; if she gave him the kids, he'd give her all the money. She would have no way of supporting the children and she agreed. In essence she felt she'd traded her children for an education that would insure the financial security of her future. She was twenty and her mistake determined the path of her unstable future. Tom gave her the car and $10,000, which was a lot of money at the time. It was all the money he had. He figured he could always make more money, but not necessarily more kids. After the divorce Karin hardly ever visited the children, and they never seemed to miss their mother.

She went on with her life, was married two more times, and excommunicated by her religion. No decent man wanted a woman who had abandoned her children. She became a Jehovah's Witness once again. She will be forever grateful to Tom and Ome Rienus for introducing her to what she felt was *the Truth*. She was eventually married in the Lord and found a truly loving and giving husband and stated her marriage to him had been the best thirty years of her life. She has a daughter, Kathy, by her third husband.

Tom chose to raise his three children on his own. He promised Karin he would remain single and celibate for the next twenty-five years, and he was determined to never get married again. He felt the obsession people had regarding sex was mainly in their heads. Tom wouldn't even date, because he wanted to raise his children morally. Many women made advances towards him regarding dating and sex, but he just turned them down nicely. He wanted to set a good example for his children.

To avoid further temptation, he wouldn't allow any women to work for him helping around the house. He only hired men whenever he needed domestic help. He employed recently released ex-cons for a dollar a day and housed two or three of them at a time, as boarders. He felt the ex-cons were good young men who needed a new beginning and if possible Tom wanted to give them every opportunity to start over again with a clean slate.

Hiring the ex-cons came about in an unusual way. Tom had hired a man who took him to court and lost. The judge presiding over the case was German and he told Tom he sometimes got boys that were good and didn't belong in jail. It was agreed Tom would help give them a second chance at life, by giving them a job.

Tom felt honored to be given an opportunity to help these men and agreed to the terms the judge stated. The conditions were such that the men could not leave Tom's home as long as they were on probation. The probation officer would be allowed to come and check the property to evaluate the working and living conditions. Tom would supply room and board, pay them a dollar a day and fill out a monthly probation report. If at any time the men failed to uphold the conditions of their probation they would return to jail.

Tom's neighbors were afraid of the ex-cons and didn't want them around their children. However, Tom felt his children learned a lot from them about making the wrong choices and the consequences of making those decisions. He gives the ex-cons credit for helping to deter his children from crime. His family still remains in contact with several of those men.

Living conditions were very tight and cramped with the addition of the boarders in the house. Tom and his children slept together in one bedroom. Although he didn't share his neighbors' prejudices against the ex-cons, he felt it was better he take this precaution, and kept his children close to him. Better safe than sorry.

To help add more sleeping area for him and the children, he turned the bed sideways, placed two milk cases at the end, then added a strong board across the top and covered it all with a blanket. Each night before bed, he and the children would pray, and sing songs before going to sleep. The nightly ritual brought them closer as a family.

Another ritual was reading letters from the family. It was important to Tom that the family in Fresno and San Marcos remain close, even if only through written correspondence. The family wrote his children many letters and cards, which he read several times. Of course, he embellished the letters at times to make them more interesting.

To create a swimming pool, Tom dug a hole in the ground; cut an old water tank in half, placed it into the hole and filled it with water. It was approximately fifteen feet across and five feet deep. At night before they went to bed, they jumped into the water and played for a while. When it was hot they slept outside, with the beds ten feet from the pool.

At any given time their yard was home to over one hundred rabbits, some chickens and roosters. Orange trees and pine trees offered shade, while an electric fence surrounded the house to keep dogs and cats out.

There were times when rabbits got in the house. One occasion when Mary was doing laundry she noticed socks were missing and told Tom. Later the socks were found under the sofa. A rabbit had made a nest and given birth to six babies.

Tom was fond of multi-tasking as a father. Instead of feeding the children, then giving them baths, to save time he did both. He put all three in the tub and fed them dinner while they washed up. His children never had a babysitter. He preferred to pay someone to run his business, instead of paying them to care for his children. He hired enough people so he wouldn't have to work, and could watch them himself.

His daughter Mary helped around the house, cleaning, answering phones and helping with her two younger brothers. Since she was needed at home, Mary didn't start school until she was seven, when both boys were old enough to attend too. Arie Helmut was six and Tommy was five at the time.

Before they started school, Tom started their education by reading to them as much as possible every day. Mary started her education in the first grade, but was immediately moved into the second grade with other children her age.

Arie Helmut didn't like the fact that Mary left him behind in the first grade, so he studied her books until he could do the work and was advanced to her grade as well. Like his father, he had a thirst for knowledge and was driven to succeed. He was promoted a few more times. By the time he was eleven, he had already been advanced to the eighth grade level.

One Mother's day, when Mary's class made cards for their mothers, Mary expressed to her teacher she was making a card for her father and asked if it was alright, since she didn't have a mother. The teacher had no idea or indication Tom was raising them on his own until Mary said something. He never had any regrets or complaints about being a single father. His children were always with him. He loved it and thought he would never remarry.

Tom and his children continued to live on the dairy farm in Fresno, from 1958-68. Then Tom's agricultural teacher, Hans de Jong (no relation) came to visit from Holland. He expressed to Tom how important it was for his children to finish their education in Holland. This would allow them to see where the family came from and give them a stronger understanding of the family's customs, roots and culture. Tom agreed.

Pete and Rena

Pete felt driving a milk route taught a person about human nature and gave great insight about how other families lived. He wondered what would happen when he eventually married. How would he find a wife who would be faithful and he could enjoy the future with. Pete realized one of the girls from the church, Rena Dragt, was something special. The more he learned about her, the more he liked what he saw. She was the daughter of a Friesian family who immigrated to America in 1950. Rena was also from a large family of ten kids.

When Pete and Rena decided to get married, Karel and Arie were at Fort Ord, California, where they were inducted into the army. The wedding was on January 30, 1957, the same day the boys were to leave Fort Ord on a train headed to San Antonio, Texas. Once they arrived in San Antonio, they would be transported to Fort Sam Houston to report for duty. However, the boys decided to get off the train in Oceanside to attend their brother Pete's wedding. They stayed several days before re-boarding a train headed for San Antonio.

The family was excited to have them at the wedding and they were treated like uniformed celebrities. The whole family was busy celebrating the wedding and hadn't a care in the world regarding the boys being AWOL.

Three days later, when Karel and Arie finally arrived in San Antonio, Texas, a special envoy was sent to pick them up at the train station. They had missed the training with their group and had to be placed in the following group for their training as medics.

Tom knew how hard the family all worked as a team and how they rarely took time off for vacations. He was also very aware Pete hadn't taken any time off for seven years. He told Pete to go to Holland for their honeymoon and not to come back until they were both good and ready. The newlyweds stayed away for three months, and traveled all over Holland, Belgium, France, Italy, Austria, and Germany.

Pete and Rena wanted a large family. Between the years 1957 to 1968, they were blessed with seven children, four boys and three girls.

Kees and Helia

When Kees got out of the Army, he wanted to get married and went to Holland with his father in order to find a good wife. A few girls were interested in him, but he chose Helia. When they met, he was twenty-seven, and she was nineteen. They were introduced by his cousin Ellie Reyneveld at her birthday celebration. Helia lived in town and he escorted her home, pedaling her bike with her holding on behind him.

Helia went to night school to study English. One evening as she left class, Kees was waiting outside for her. He was in possession of a car Karel and Arie Jr. had purchased while stationed in Germany.

They took a ride, went for coffee and then to the beach. The chemistry between them was perfect; they were smitten with each other. Arie Sr. and Helia's mother had been in the same class in school.

Helia, Kees and baby Maartje

Helia stated she was in love after the first date. She admired and liked his strength of character. Kees said he loved the naughty look in her eyes and how she was so high spirited.

He was in Holland for four weeks. During that time he and Helia went on group dates with friends and cousins before he returned to California. They wrote each other letters every week for almost a year.

Helia said, "The letters were so nice. I shared them with my family and they always enjoyed them. He wrote in such an old fashioned way.

Ellie and Elso went to Holland for a visit and when they returned, Helia came with them. She was given a job working at the Cash and Carry for nine months. She and Kees wanted to become engaged, but her father wanted her to return to Holland, and give it more thought. She was so in love, and wasn't homesick any longer.

Helia loved being around the fun loving de Jong family. There was always something going on. She loved the good humored way Ellie embarrassed her and the boys. They were all very hard workers and there was always harmony.

Kees was a very hard worker and it was difficult for them to spend a lot of time together. They went out together in groups, or at church outings. Helia stayed at Pete and Rena's home and Kees stayed at his parents. Since they weren't married they weren't allowed to stay under the same roof. The only time they spent time alone together was when he walked her home around the horse corral. There were times they would sit on the hay to have deep and meaningful conversations. Helia returned to Holland once more to take care of her aunt and her aunt's two children. They wrote each other at least once a week, sometimes more often.

After five months, Kees returned to Holland and asked Helia's father for her hand in marriage. They had no formal engagement and were married in Holland on August 20, 1959. Her father was the town *Secretaris* (secretary), an office similar to that of a city manager and he performed the wedding ceremony. They honeymooned in Germany, Italy and Switzerland. After they returned stateside, the newlyweds moved to the Dairy on 17th Street and lived in the small play house for four months. Helia worked at the Cash and Carry.

The Hepner Ranch in Reedly, California was for sale and was a beautiful place. The local farmers used the location for picnics and social gatherings. An offer was made and after the purchase was finalized, the newlyweds went into business for themselves. Cows were cheaper than in Escondido, so they started with sixty. Kees was very happy to start a life on his own with Helia. It was also wonderful to have his brother Tom nearby.

In December 1959, the couple drove a Model 'A' Ford, with no windows, and a pick-up truck to their new home in Reedly. While waiting for the previous owners to move, they slept on concrete floors in a garage for four months. The only furniture they had were the seats from the car. The couple quickly moved into the house as soon as the previous owners relocated.

On the day their first child, Maartje was born, Helia was out cleaning the barn and milking the cows when Buster Blyleven, an important businessman from the creamery came by the dairy. He took one look at Helia and told her to stop milking. Kees took her to the hospital immediately. The baby was born soon after their arrival.

There was a lot of balance to the relationship between Kees and Helia. When she was weak, he was strong and when he was weak, she was strong. Building up a business can be difficult, especially when there are children involved.

They always worked so much, they never went out, but Kees wouldn't allow anyone, including the children to complain about work, or while they worked. Helia held Kees in high regard, because he was such a good provider, a hard worker and an excellent father to the children.

Kees was a good father and never had a problem caring for his children, or changing a diaper. When the children were older he taught them how to drive the tractor, and took them with him on the hay trailer as he fed the cows. Over the years their marriage was fraught with many challenges and at times tragedy.

One tragic episode that put their relationship to the test was in Woodville, when they lost their eighteen month old daughter, Ellie in a tractor accident. She'd been playing with the other children and stopped to follow her father, who was on the tractor. Kees was unaware of her presence as he backed up. Ellie was hit by the tractor and her injuries proved fatal. It was a very sad and tough time for the couple and their young family. They received full family support. Everyone was there to give them help and comfort.

In 1965, Kees purchased a large parcel of land from Joe Branco in Visalia, where he and Helia eventually built a new home and two dairies. After Kees passed away his children took over the daily operations of the dairies, and his wife Helia stills resides in the family home.

In 1977, Kees won an award for the *Dairy Family of the Year,* a reward given by the California Dairy Institute (CDI), for most success in family and business.

Kees said he respected Tom's position as his elder brother and always strove to be obedient to him. He saw Tom led a life style that he felt was important to him and his children and Kees admired that.

Arie Jr. remembers how Kees was a tough boss and not easy to work for at the Escondido dairy on 17th Street. He always admired Kees for his work ethic and loyalty.

Tom lived in Fresno and in 1961; he found and made a down payment on a dairy John bought in Riverdale. Several years later there was a big flood in 1969. Everything on Kees' dairy was in deep water, including the cows. Mary, Richard and John helped Kees and Helia pull the cows and calves out of the water to save them. Dairy life can be very hard and takes the combined effort of the whole family unit.

For several Christmases, their daughter Henrietta kept asking for monkeys. In an effort to surprise her, Kees took his son Bertje deep into Mexico in 1992, to purchase two monkeys. They traveled 2000 miles in ten days. The monkeys were smuggled across the border under Bertje's coat. The children knew Kees had gone to get the monkeys and when he returned there was a large sign which said, "NEXT TIME A GIRAFFE."

The monkeys were always in the house, hanging on the curtains and light fixtures. They adored Kees and sat on his lap and slept with him. When he rode his bike, a monkey was on his back to keep him company. Kees liked a little chaos, but Helia hated it.

While living in Visalia, whenever they had people over for coffee, the children played with the monkeys. On one particular Sunday, a child was bitten. The mother who was concerned and began asking questions regarding whether the monkeys had rabies shots, filed a formal complaint.

The authorities were notified, and inquired about the monkeys. Kees told them they were descendants of the Hollandia Dairy monkeys and his father's dairy had had the monkeys for over 30 years.

Kees relaxing with his monkeys

The trial was held at the Federal Courthouse in San Diego, California. Since the monkeys' point of origin was Mexico and the authorities had been told the monkeys were descended from the Hollandia Dairy, in San Marcos, the trial had to be held in San Diego County. Tom, had committed himself to testify on Kees' behalf, but changed his mind. He would have to swear to tell the truth on a bible and was not willing to perjure himself.

Arie Jr. told Kees, "No problem. I'll take care of it and testify on your behalf."

He went to court and gave testimony the monkeys had indeed been the descendants of the original Hollandia Dairy monkeys, and that Kees owned the only remaining monkeys from the original bloodline. The judge was satisfied. After the verdict, there was a family celebration at the San Marcos Dairy.

The child who was bitten underwent a series of rabies shots, which did not make the mother happy at all. Though very old now, the monkeys are still at Kees' home in Visalia. For many years they received busloads of tourists from all over the country, Europe and Asia wanting to see the dairy, the Dutch family lifestyle and the monkeys. Kees got on a loud speaker and Helia would furnish homemade Dutch cookies and fresh coffee. The tourists usually stayed from 9am until 12 noon. Helia prepared them a lunch of home-made bread, soup, Dutch cheese and fresh milk from their dairy.

A good storyteller, Kees loved history and gave tours until the day he died. Every afternoon he had a cup of tea and a piece of chocolate with his grandchildren.

During the last years of his life, Kees, who was always used to being in control, began to suffer from the same illness as his mother Maartje that caused a loss of emotional control. It was very difficult for him and the whole family to adjust to the changes and challenges brought on by his illness. His children were grown and no longer lived at home and he didn't work in the business any longer. The family strove to keep him actively involved in their lives. The boys met with him daily, for advice and counsel. The whole family gave him errands to help keep him busy.

On December 24, 2007, Kees was very upset due to the restrictions his family imposed on him due to his illness. He had been trying to get some tools from his workshop on the dairy. Someone had locked it and he became extremely angry and frustrated. When he was unable to open the door to get his tools he had a massive heart attack. One of his workers found him, but it was too late. It was a very sad event. It was discovered after his death, that he suffered from atherosclerosis, which hardened his arteries and attributed to is heart attack and death.

His whole family had come home to celebrate the Christmas holiday, but instead they had to attend his funeral. The service was held on Monday, December 31st, and was the largest funeral ever held at his church.

Elso and Dita

Elso was fortunate to have found himself a good wife, in Dita Vroegop. She was the daughter of a Dutch family that grew flowers in the coastal region of Lisse, in Northern Holland. Her family emigrated from Holland to North Carolina, where her father was in the flower business. She had a boyfriend in Holland and was homesick. Her father's business was losing a lot of money and he decided to make a move; they would either move to Mexico, or to California.

Dita's family had a friend, Bill Boekee, a sales rep for a Dutch tulip grower that knew the de Jongs and had written them a letter. The letter stated the Vroegop family had one son and three daughters. In his usual manner when reading, Tom of course embellished the story, telling his brothers there were thirteen daughters. All the boys were excited, because they wanted to marry good Dutch girls.

Dita's family moved to California and took up temporary housing in a motel. They were invited to attend tea at the de Jongs. Before she knew it, a Pontiac pulled up outside the motel room full of the de Jong boys, who wanted to take Dita who was still in her pajamas and her sisters for a ride.

Although Kees was looking for a girl to marry and took a liking to Dita, he had already purchased his plane ticket for Holland. His father would accompany him on his quest to find a wife.

Dita's family moved to Redlands not long afterward, and they lost touch with the family for several months, until the de Jong boys were heading to Big Bear to go skiing and saw Dita's sister, Leni, walking down the street. They called out to her, and went to Dita's home for afternoon tea.

Now that Elso knew where Dita's family lived, he traveled the eighty miles from Escondido to Redlands to visit her. Although she was impressed by this, she wasn't taken with him right away, because he came to call wearing a suit he had purchased from the Goodwill and the sleeves of the jacket were at least four inches too short. They began to date, but broke up twice.

After they broke up for the third time, Dita was at the beach in Oceanside with one of her sisters. Elso showed up. He stated, she was wearing a blue swimsuit and once he saw the way the sun played on her curly hair, he thought she was beautiful and had a good figure. This time he showed Dita his more serious side and talked to her about the Bible. She thought, "Maybe he's not so bad after all." They started dating again. They got engaged right away, and were married a year later on April 27, 1960.

They were married in Redlands and moved into the original small ranch house on the dairy in San Marcos for a short time, where they took in two boarders; Gerrit Roeloffs, Ellie's future husband and Rudy de Jong, a cousin from Holland. The boarders had cocktail parties every night which were a nuisance since Elso got up early to deliver milk.

A few years later, Elso and Dita began their family. Their son Arie was born April 8, 1962. Their daughter Nellie was born a year later, on April 9, 1963. Elso always felt his parenting skills were modeled more after his mother than his father.

Elso stated he was a little selfish, because he didn't work as hard as Arie Jr. and John. He worked and stayed more on the sidelines. He worked a milk route and became the sales manager after Kees moved to Reedley.

Dita, Arie Elso, and Elso

Elso and Dita lived in Escondido on Rock Springs Road for ten years, not far from the San Marcos dairy, where he worked for the family from 1949 until 1968, when he bought a small dairy in Bonanza, Oregon near Klamath Falls. By this time his brother, Kees and Helia were already in Visalia, and his sister Mary and her husband Richard were working for his brother, John in Hanford.

When Arie Jr. decided he was tired of the dairy business and wanted to venture out on his own, his father became very upset by the whole proposition. He would have been content to keep everyone home and actively involved in the family business. Elso remembers how it took some persuasion to turn around his father's way of thinking, but it was a much easier task once he realized how successful Arie Jr. and his ideas were.

Around 1990, Elso's son, Arie Elso, took over the daily dairy operations in Bonanza. In addition to the family's traditional dairy, Arie Elso started an organic dairy as well. The two dairies operate within five miles of each other.

Due to Elso's failing health, his daughter Nellie traveled to Bonanza, Oregon to see her father. He collapsed two days later on June 23, 2013 and was revived by his son Arie Elso. The two shared a beer together and then Arie Elso returned to his home.

Elso's health continued to fail and the caretakers from hospice arrived on June 25th, the day he passed away. Dita stated that Elso sat up in bed, yawned, closed his eyes and never woke up. At the time of his death, 6:45pm, the regulator clock in the kitchen stopped working.

The Davenport Chapel Service removed his body and his service was held at the Bonanza Community Church, with his brothers and sisters in attendance. Elso was laid to rest at the Lost River Cemetery. His tombstone faces his Bonanza View Dairy, where he watches over his family. Elso was at peace with God and ready to go.

John Buys a Dairy in Riverdale

As time went on, Arie Sr. became more and more interested in the Dutch owned dairy connection in and around the Fresno area. True to his nature, Tom typically shared information with fellow Dutch dairymen. One of whom was Leen Verburg who had been a de Jong neighbor in Alphen aan de Rhine, in Holland. Leen was a good dairyman. He and his sons had a nine hundred cow milking operation in Riverdale, a town not far from Hanford and approximately thirty miles South-West of Fresno.

Leen told Tom he was tired of the business, because his sons were not easy to manage regarding the dairy operation, which placed more of the responsibilities on him. Tom told the family they could take over the lease on the dairy and purchase the herd of cows outright, which would keep the initial investment output low. Karel and John had lengthy discussions regarding who should go to Riverdale to take over and run the family's new acquisition.

The dairy in Riverdale had no houses on the dairy property and was purchased for $162,500. The cows were purchased for $325 each, which was a lot of money at that time. It was a little pricey, but unlike their neighbors, they had good milk contracts.

Even though Karel didn't have a girlfriend, it was hard for him, like Ellie, to leave Escondido and the family. He had always been a real home-body. After a thorough discussion between the two, it was decided that the opportunity could not be passed over and John was the logical choice to go. Though very persuasive in his own right, John can be swayed once he takes in the scope of the big picture. Though Karel was also very persuasive, he usually could not be moved.

John had no intention of ever getting married, at least not for a long time. All that changed when he met Willie Brouwer, who worked as both a cashier and receptionist at the cash and carry in San Marcos. She was very shy about answering the phones, because she couldn't speak English very well. She eventually became his wife.

They both attended the Christian Reformed Church, in Escondido. John and Willie's first interaction away from work and from formal church functions, when they attended a beach party with a group of immigrant children who attended their church. They took a walk away from the group and talked for hours. Afterwards, they went horse-back riding on a weekly basis.

Once they started dating, John made up his mind they were going to get married. Although they were engaged John told Willie's parents they would postpone the wedding, because they needed her income for her siblings schooling.

John and his girlfriend Willie were about to be married. Karel thought the wedding should wait, because John was the best one to run the dairy. The wedding was postponed from May to June. Understandably, John was concerned that if he relocated to Riverdale before the marriage, it would not set well with his future in-laws. The dairy operation in Riverdale was for sale, but not the land and it was a good deal. John leased the Riverdale dairy for $400 a month from Frank Borba, a Portuguese farmer.

The rent at the Riverdale location was paid for with the income made from selling the local farmers the manure, so they could fertilize their crops. It was a very lucrative arrangement. The timing was everything when harvesting the manure, especially when the rainy season was approaching.

John had the best understanding of cows and how to run a dairy, so he went to Riverdale to get everything up and running. He moved to the Riverdale in April of 1961. At the time he was 25 and engaged to Willie and wrote to her every day for two months until they were married.

Gerrit Roeloffs originally worked in the Artesia/Bellflower area, before he was recruited to work for Hollandia. When John relocated to Riverdale, he requested Gerrit be allowed to go as well. He needed the experience and the work ethic that Gerrit brought to the table, to ensure the dairy's success. He was nervous regarding the daunting task of running a dairy alone, and that's why he enlisted Gerrit's help, who quit his job to help John manage the dairy.

John received the news regarding the Riverdale dairy purchase, at Willie's birthday party and he and Gerrit left the next day. There was only a barn, corrals and the feeding troughs. The only house located on the property belonged to the farmers renting them the dairy and there was no house available on the property for them to live in. The whole process of renting the dairy and taking possession happened very quickly, so the Verburgs were still living in the only home associated with the property.

There was also no money to build a house, so after John and Gerrit finished their chores in the early morning hours, they went to sleep in the Verburgs bed after they got up to start their work day. They did the sleeping rotation around each other's work schedules, until John found a little house to rent close by. At $65 a month, the house was a bit pricey.

Once the dairy was up and running, Arie Sr. and Gerrit told John to go ahead and get married, and they would take care of the daily operations of running the dairy while he and Willie were on their honeymoon. They got married on June 28, 1961, and traveled to Europe for their honeymoon. Fortunately, Tom was running a dairy nearby in Fresno and offered to help with the accounting and payroll in their absence.

While on their honeymoon in Holland, John and Willie reconnected with Anneke. The two young women had been good friends growing up in Holland. Anneke had just finished her teaching degree and they suggested she come to the states. She agreed, but life in Riverdale with the newlyweds was tough and Ellie suggested she relocate to the house on 17th Street in Escondido. That's when she met Arie Jr.

On one level, Arie Sr. and Gerrit did well in John's absence watching over the dairy operation and managing the workers. However, the bills had not been paid while he was gone and although John had left plenty of money in the bank, the vendors were getting very concerned.

After John returned from his honeymoon, Arie Sr. greeted him and said, "We have plenty of money from the milking."

The reason for the surplus of cash was because no one was paid for the hay, or the feed. Arie Sr. simply told all of John's creditors he would be back in July. The couple returned from their honeymoon rested and happy, but found the creditors at their doorstep wanting to be paid right away. Before he could even come up for air John had to do damage control.

John and Willie's first home as a married couple was a rundown house located near the dairy. Willie fixed the house up by painting, making curtains and turning it into a home. Though John managed everything at Riverdale, Gerrit helped on many levels and they had a great working relationship. Gerrit was a boarder for six months before he married Ellie, and became part of the de Jong family. After Gerrit and Ellie were married they relocated to Mesa, Arizona.

The Riverdale location exceeded all expectations. Willie was not only a homemaker and cook; she was also the accountant for the dairy operation. They leased the dairy and bought six-hundred-thirty cows.

On June 19, 1962, their daughter Christina was born and named after Willie's maternal grandmother. There were only two doctors in the area at that time. One was a dairyman and the other was in the farm community.

On the day Willie had Christina; she had just seen the doctor who thought she was having false labor. The pains began to get worse and her contractions kept coming. They called the landlords wife who came over immediately. She suggested they go back to the doctor at once. As they got out of the car at the doctor's office, Willie's contractions were so painful she collapsed on the lawn.

Dr. Hunt had been heading to a wedding and came out in a tux. He said, "We can't let her have the baby in the yard. Put her in my Cadillac, I'm taking her to the hospital in Fresno."

As soon as Willie was in the car, the doctor took off in a flash leaving John in a cloud of dust. John hopped in the truck and headed to Fresno. He arrived twenty minutes after the baby was born.

Marietta, who was named after Mary and Jet, was born on November 7, 1963. John was never good about changing diapers. He'd take the dirty diaper off and hose the baby down and just let them run around naked. He thought it was an easier way to deal with the matter.

During this time, as more and more of their children moved to the Fresno, Hanford area, Arie Sr. and Maartje took several trips in their pick-up truck to see their children and new grandchildren. Maartje always packed lunches of cheese, bread and hard boilded eggs to eat along the way. Before each trip Maartje gathered eggs from the fields and boiled them. She had no way of knowing how old the eggs were, or if any were bad when she cooked them.

On one occassion, while driving to Northern California, Arie Sr. picked up two hitchhikers. When it came time to for lunch, he offered some eggs to the men riding in the back of the truck. They gave him a nod 'yes' and he passed them eggs while driving. No one realized any of the eggs were bad, until an hour after the hitchhikers had eaten them and the men were hanging over the side of the truck, throwing up. Arie Sr and Maartje had no negative effects. Over the years they had built up an immunity to eating the older eggs.

John was blessed and fortunate to be able to sell the dairy milk to a creamery in Los Angeles. Safeway owned the creamery and processing plant bottling for the Lucerne label that was sold and marketed in their stores. The Safeway plant in Hanford manufactured cottage cheese. About a year and a half later, Safeway approached John with a proposition. There was a local dairy for sale and they were able to control who made the purchase. They wanted to continue to be supplied with the superior quality of milk they received from John, and gave him the first shot at purchasing the dairy from Joe Branco, located in Tulare.

By this time the family had almost paid off the bank. The banker jumped at the chance to finance the new dairy venture for John and the family. John began running both dairies at the same time, traveling thirty miles back and forth every day.

John employed a good steady crew of workers to assist with the heavy workload. In the 1960's there were a lot of Oakies, and Portuguese, searching for work in the San Joaquin Valley. John had mostly Portuguese immigrants working on his dairies, who later became independent businessmen themselves.

A cow is typically milked for ten months out of the year. For two months prior to the birthing of a calf the milking process stops and the cow goes dry. Then two months later the cow is inseminated again. The new calves are born nine months and ten days later. They are allowed to suckle for only a few days to get the colostrums, then they are taken away and bottle fed.

They owned the cows, but leased the dairy in Riverdale. Approximately six years later, they purchased the property in Hanford, California. Karel was actively involved in designing and building the new dairy. John ended up with the real estate and the cows in Hanford. It was during the building phase of the new construction when Karel first came up with his design to slope the dirt of the dairy corrals.

Willie holding Marietta, John and Christina

Neighboring dairymen and farmers couldn't understand why the de Jongs were spending so much time and money on grading the area. When all was said and done, they were able to see the logic in the design and began to implement the idea on their dairies as well.

Karel's biggest accomplishment in dairy design was a simple sloping of the corrals. This common sense design element prevented the cows from standing in their own feces during the rains and simplified the cleaning of the corrals as well. Prior to this, the corrals would get flooded out during the rains and also the cows become sickly. Karel's idea helped to keep the cows from standing in their own waste and kept the cows healthier.

When the health department did an inspection at the dairy and saw Karel's design, they changed the regulations regarding dairy design, and no longer allowed flat corrals on dairies. The health department officials believed, *"If the de Jongs can make it this way, we want everyone to do it this way, for the health of the cows and the quality of the milk products."*

At the cow washing area, the cows were washed down using clean water from a sprinkler system. This water served the dairy on many levels. First the water was used to prep the cows for milking by washing them and the recaptured water was used to wash any feces from the concrete milking stalls.

In 1967, another of Karel's designs was implemented at the San Marcos and Central Valley location. Karel created a means to pump the water from the cow washing area, into two manmade ponds, along with the manure to form a rich liquid fertilizer, which would be pumped through an aluminum pipe four inches wide, back through the fields to water the grasses. He also strategically added dikes around the dairy, redirecting storm waters to the ponds during the rainy season. Karel, thirty-three at the time, had never received an engineering degree, or taken any formal engineering training. He only took a drafting class in Holland. Design and engineering were skills that came naturally to him.

Having John take over the new dairy was the right move. John was the best when it came to business dynamics and working with the cows. He became a powerful force in Hollandia Dairy's history. The production and processing of milk are completely different ends of the milk business.

When the processing side is profitable, the big factor is low milk-cost, so production suffers economically. John was instrumental in keeping a balance between the two. He was by far the best dairyman in the family and remained an integral part of Hollandia Dairy.

One of the main reasons for Hollandia's staying-power has been the favorable balance between cows and milk-plants. Of the over fifty milk processing plants that were in the San Diego County, there was only one left: *HOLLANDIA*.

The Arden Farms franchise had close to a one hundred retail milk routes in San Diego County, and numerous wholesale routes within California and other States. Hollandia was purchasing milk by products from them, including whip cream, half and half, buttermilk, chocolate milk, cottage cheese, butter and ice cream. Hage's was a large creamery located in San Diego County. The local dairy co-op in San Diego County was *Qualitee/Carnation* and had a beautiful processing plant located in San Diego. The co-op had a number of producing dairy members in the San Pasqual Valley and Pala areas, as well as, retail and wholesale members throughout the County.

Challenge Creamery and Butter Association was another dairy co-op. Arie Sr's younger brother, Bouw was a member of that group and had a dairy next to the family in San Marcos. The Challenge co-op also had a milk plant with wholesale, resale and retail operations in the Mission Valley area, of San Diego County, where the Interstate 15 and the 8 Freeways intersect today.

Dairy Mart in San Ysidro and Golden Arrow in San Diego were mainly home delivery dairies with about one hundred retail routes each around the county. At its highest mark, the number of Hollandia home delivery routes had increased to twenty.

For a variety of differing factors all of these dairies were sold, moved or went out of business. One of the main reasons was the lack of owning their own herds and subsequent milk supply. Today, Hollandia is the last man standing and the only one left in San Diego County.

While John worked his magic at the Riverdale location the family pursued the business at home. Arie Jr. was no longer in school and became a home delivery man. He was trained by Chuck Lothspeich, who had been a top performer at Dairy Mart Farms. Chuck knew how to make the sale. The pairing of Arie with Chuck was a good fit.

Around the same time, Tom left for Fresno, where he bought City Edge Guernsey Farms, located on the corner of Church and Elm from Mr. Johnson. Mr. Johnson decided to sell, because his son did not want to live the life of a dairyman. Typical of his style, Tom made some fast moves and purchased the dairy. He changed the name to *The Milky Way Dairy*. He also changed to modern bottles and added a filling system that was more efficient. All Tom's changes were done to make and perfect his own brand.

Pete admits he was envious of Tom's opportunity to replace his old bottling equipment with something new. The family's bottling operation was still using cellophane covers over wide-neck bottles, and they were afraid to invest the amount of money needed to modernize.

Like all the de Jongs, John happened to be an excellent businessman. After running the Riverdale dairy successfully, John bought a dairy in Tulare a year and a half later after his lease expired. They bought the property and the inventory with over one hundred-sixty acres of land and four hundred-fifty cows. It was bought as a family business with everyone investing except for Tom and Kees who were operating independently of the family at the time.

After improving the Tulare facility, John was in a position to build the Hanford Dairy, just off the Highway 198. In February of 1968, they stopped leasing the Riverdale dairy and sold the dairy in Tulare as well. This enabled him to purchase the two-hundred-seventy acres of unfarmed land just off the 198, in Hanford. They had the huge undertaking of not only building two homes, the dairy barns and milking sheds, but moving the 2000 cows. Every move John made was an improvement. Karel was instrumental in the design and regarding quite a few of the improvements made.

John and Willie felt good to be on a dairy that was more up to date and modern. It was also the first new home they had lived in since the beginning of their marriage. Willie was in charge of where and how the new home was to be built. She also continued to do all the bookkeeping for the dairy.

Over time, John's job became more managerial and less hands on dairy work. Since he didn't have to drive back and forth between several locations each day, he had more time to spend with his growing family.

Their fourth daughter, Ellie Mae was born August 31, 1969. She was named after Ellie and Willie's sister-in-law, Mae. A year later on August 20, 1970, Arie Jan was born, named after John and his father Arie Sr. He finally had his son.

They probably took business a little too seriously, because when Willie went into labor, John took her to the hospital, but the nurse said it would be a while, so he went back home to work. While he was working, his brother-in-law Richard approached and said, "John I want to congratulate you, you had a son."

Jack was born July 24, 1973, and named after Willie's father. Willemina was born July 31, 1974. Karel, their last and youngest child was born on October 14, 1975. He was named after Karel and Ellie's late husband Gerrit. When he was 8 years old, he was swinging from a rope off the top of a twenty foot pile of cotton seed, and lost his grip and fell, hitting the back of his head on the concrete floor. Because of the broken blood vessels and trauma, his head began to swell. Thankfully he was still breathing. Nettie and her girlfriends who were only fourteen or fifteen at the time, knew how to drive, but didn't have a driver's license. They put Karel in the car and rushed him to the hospital. Later that evening he was taken off life support and passed away. John said although they did lose Karel, his family has been very blessed with good health and good fortune.

John gradually retired in his 60's, after the children were married and gone. He had always been lucky enough to have good managers. After working so hard all his life, he found it was a lot easier to adapt to retirement than he anticipated.

Karel not only aided in the design, but the construction as well, of many of the buildings on his sibling's Kees and Ellie's dairies throughout the California, Central Valley. He also helped to set up the milking machines. Ellie and Gerrit's dairy was located in Mesa, Arizona in 1962.

Though he had moved away, John stayed an active part of the family business for a long time; however, with his growing family and business, he realized it was necessary to buy himself out of Hollandia.

After Ellie's husband, Gerrit passed away, the family bought into her dairy in Mesa, Arizona. The family took over the controlling interest and became responsible for every aspect of its success or failure. John took over managing the dairy for her. Whenever John traveled to Mesa, Arie Sr. would go along to help with the daily operations. Gerrit's death was very hard on both Jet and Mary as well.

John had always been a good businessman. When it came time to make the sale of the Mesa Dairy, John made the family a nice profit. The dairy operation, cows, etc, but not the land was sold to Dennis Taylor, the man who had been managing the dairy. Later, Dennis relocated his dairy operation to Tucson. The land was sold to the City of Mesa for future development of homes and a school.

John bought himself out of the family business, just like his brother Arie had. They went to the accountants in December and by the first of January they had both broken off from the family business. Instead of one corporation, they now became three: Hollandia, John de Jong, and Arie Jr.'s various business interests.

With the help of the company accountants and Bruce White, the family attorney, the value of each family member's portion of Hollandia was decided. This was extremely important to John, who needed to come up with a value for the part he played in the running of the family business and the properties he had managed. Hilltop Group is an investment of Arie Jr.'s, which was created after the split, to oversee all the holdings for his newly established corporation.

With his red books, Arie Jr. is the family historian and has kept the most accurate account of the family's history and legacy.

Arie and Anneke

Anneke had just graduated from college with her teaching credentials and her father gave her the trip of her choice as a graduation gift. She was a nice girl from a good family that

resided in Gelderland, a province of central Holland. John's wife Willie was also from Gelderland and she and Anneke were friends. While on their honeymoon John and Willie ran into Anneke and suggested she take a trip to California. Her father agreed and when they returned from their honeymoon, Anneke came with them on a visitor's visa.

Pictured left to right: Alice van Kampen, Coby Wildenburg and Anneke Verkuil (de Jong)

The newlyweds returned to Escondido, packed the wedding gifts into the car and drove to their new home in Riverdale and Anneke went with

them. Although she and Willie were good friends, Anneke felt like a third wheel with the newly married couple. Ellie, who was dating Gerrit at the time, went to Riverdale on a visit and told

Anneke she would have more fun with the family and suggested she relocate to Escondido for the duration of her six month vacation, which she did.

At the Rose Parade in Pasadena, California in the early 1960's
Pictured left to right: Rudy de Jong, Etta van der Woude, Anneke Verkuil (de Jong), Karel de Jong, Shirley de Haan, Alice van Kampen, and Paul van Elderen

She helped out at the 17th Street, Cash and Carry and she did odd jobs to

earn money. She and Ellie became close friends and did everything together. It wasn't until the end of her vacation that Arie started to really take notice of how special she was. He drove her to the airport and when she returned to Holland, they wrote to each other regularly.

In 1963, Arie went to Holland on a vacation. He had pre-ordered a new Volkswagen and went to Germany to take possession of his new car. His cousin Joop Roeloffs had gone to

Holland before him and met Arie in Hanover, Germany. They traveled to Wolfsburg, where they took a tour of the Volkswagen factory before they picked up their new vehicles. Joop returned to Holland, but Arie elected to visit Munchweiller to see the German friends he made while he was in the Army and stationed there.

He only planned to spend the weekend and while he was driving back to Holland, he had an accident. He ended up borrowing a bicycle just to get back to Munchweiller, where he stayed while his car was being repaired. What started off as a quick visit, ended up as a week layover in Germany.

So she could spend time with Arie, Anneke had scheduled a vacation. By the time he returned to Holland, most of her vacation was over. She wasn't happy and when he arrived at her home, her parents were there to meet him. The reunion didn't get off to a very good start. It was rocky at best. To give them time alone as a couple, Anneke's family went into the kitchen and left them in the parlor. This only lasted about five minutes. Arie wanted the interaction of the group, so they joined her family in the kitchen. He told them humorous stories about his car wreck and wild adventures while he was in Germany. Her family is very dignified and proper, compared to Arie's relaxed and free spirited family. Anneke was culture, while Arie was agriculture.

Anneke Verkuil (de Jong)

Since Anneke had to return to work a few days later, they didn't have much time to spend together as a couple, so when she went back to work, he went to Den Haag to party with his cousin, Joop. Before he left Holland, Arie went back to Woudenberg to see her once more. Anneke wasn't happy about the way things had gone, and although they continued to correspond when he returned home, it wasn't quite the same.

The following year, Anneke returned to California on another six month vacation. By this time Ellie and Gerrit were married and living in Arizona. Arie rented a mobile home across from the dairy on 17th Street, so Anneke could have her own place and more privacy than she could staying with his family. His cousin Maryann de Jong, Rudy's sister, shared the trailer with her and they both did house cleaning to earn money. When they weren't working, the couple spent their spare time going to the movies, dancing, swimming, having picnics or just sitting and talking.

Unlike western culture and customs where a man drops to one knee and asks a woman to marry him, it's customary in Holland for a couple to discuss marriage at length before making the decision to actually get engaged and married. After having many long discussions about their future Arie and Anneke decided to get married. They traveled to Jessup's Jewelry store in San Diego and bought each other engagement rings, and on March 7, 1964, they exchanged the rings at the old teepee on San Pasqual Rd. It was important to the couple that the family be witnesses to help celebrate the engagement.

Everyone came from Oregon, Northern California and Arizona for Maartje's birthday, so two days after becoming engaged, and a party was held on his mother Maartje's 61st birthday. It was a dual celebration, and perfect...everyone was home.

Anneke returned to Holland and they were married there on December 18, 1964. All of her family, and his relatives living in Holland attended. Because Anneke didn't know how to snow ski, they decided to spend their honeymoon in Paris. They returned to Holland to have Christmas with the family, before returning to the states.

When the newlyweds returned to California, they moved to San Diego so Arie could take over the retail delivery routes there. Their first home as a married couple was an apartment on Claremont Mesa Boulevard where they lived for a few months before moving to 4512 Kamloop Avenue in the Claremont area. The retail business in San Diego had become, a proverbial, *"pain in the neck."* Pete was amazed at how Arie handled a difficult set of circumstances with such ease.

In 1966, Arie and Anneke rented the house located at 1270 Nordahl Rd. in Escondido, for $75 a month. He bought the house from his landlady, Mrs. Whitmore two years later for $19,500. In 1968, Elso and Dita purchased a dairy in Bonanza, Oregon and when they moved Arie took over all the retail business operations for Hollandia.

He and Anneke have four children; two sons and two daughters. Eric, their oldest son is married to Silva and they have three children. Eric assisted his father with the running of his operations around North San Diego County, before he started his own business ventures. He owns Diamond Environmental, a portable toilet company covering all of southern California. He also owns and operates Palomar Water and has been very successful at whatever he has attempted.

Their son Johnny is married to Anneke and they have four children. Johnny currently runs a 2500 cow dairy, a goat dairy and a facility that bottles goat milk in Hanford, California. He supplies goat milk to the Trader Joes stores in California, Oregon, and Washington states. In the past he has operated a large hog ranch/food waste recycling operation in Ontario, California.

Their oldest daughter Dorinda is married to Ned Vander Pol, the assistant fire chief in Vista, California. They have four children.

Their youngest daughter Serena is married to Mike Carlson, who owns and operates a family dental practice in Escondido. They have three children.

Several of their children's business ventures were inspired by Arie and supported by both parents.

On December 20, 2014, there was a large celebration in honor of Arie and Anneke's 50th wedding anniversary, held at their Melrose Ranch home in Escondido, California.

Ellie and Gerrit Meet and Marry

The family members and the dairy were like magnets attracting a multitude of young Dutch immigrants. Arie Sr. was very charismatic and Maartje was almost too hospitable and couldn't turn anyone away. For her, the door was always open.

After the family's immigration to Poway, Arie Sr. continued to have strong ties with family

and friends in Holland. Their California home served as a vacation/entertainment revolving door for the comings and goings of extended family and friends, stateside and abroad.

Gerrit Roeloffs and Paul Van Elderen had emigrated from Holland and were working in the Artesia/Bellflower area. The first time she met Gerrit, who was twenty-eight at the time; Ellie was ice skating in Paramount, California, not far from Los Angeles. She thought he was a show off and didn't care for that quality and liked another boy. Her father and brothers all thought she was far too picky and wanted her to get married. They didn't want her to become an old maid like her mother's sister Mag. Like Ellie, her aunt Mag was smart and beautiful, but had lofty goals when it came to matrimony.

Unfortunately, they were too lofty and Mag ended up marrying at the age of thirty-five settling for a farmhand returning from Argentina. He had a son, named Otto, from a previous marriage and over time Mag suffered from mental illness. They didn't want Ellie's life to end that way.

She met Gerrit again when she attended a party in Covina. He tried to kiss her, but she turned her head into his chest to avoid the kiss. She kept reminding herself of what Tom told her, "Don't let any guy touch you."

Gerrit could get any girl he wanted and was not used to being rejected. Since Ellie had rejected him twice, he was intrigued. Gerrit's Aunt, Aagt Roeloffs had dated Arie Sr. in Holland and knew the family very well. She told Gerrit, if he married Ellie he'd be getting a good girl.

Gerrit visited the family in San Marcos. He was persistent and never gave up. Once after bragging about how much he could drink, Ellie rejected him again. She didn't like drinking and after that Gerrit stopped his bragging and tempered how much he drank.

It was a hardworking and busy life for everyone.   During the transition of life in the 60's, Gerrit Roeloffs, joined the ranks of the Dutch working for the family. He was a very personable guy and in time he made a romantic connection with Ellie. With so many young and eligible Dutch men working for the family, Ellie had ample opportunity to find the right man. The family, especially Arie Sr. was looking for the right type of man for Ellie, who had good connections both personally and in business. That happened to be Gerrit.

Ellie, Gerrit, Arie, Willemina and Johnny

Ellie always had the respect of her brothers and father, because she worked as hard as a man, but behaved like a lady. She has been a very moral person of strong character her whole life, peppered with a positive and cheerful attitude.

By the time Ellie and Gerrit were married, the family as a whole had increased their dairy holdings substantially. They owned several other dairies, besides Hollandia, which were all capable of showing a profit. The business opportunity in America had grown for the family in Escondido, and San Marcos, due to the children moving away after marriage, to find new opportunities.

Ellie was afraid to leave the family and broke off her engagement to Gerrit. They got back together again, but when she began to think about how marriage could take her away from the family, she broke off the engagement once more. He became frustrated and threatened to move away, and because she didn't want to lose him she decided to marry him. He came back December 21st, her birthday and they were married that day. Maartje, who was suffering from a bout of depression, was unable to attend.

Gerrit started looking for a dairy to purchase, and began searching out of state and found one in Mesa, Arizona. He heard about Adolf Weinburg, a Jewish grain dealer, who financed hard working immigrants, allowing them to purchase a dairy. Most were immigrants who had trouble getting a traditional loan to start a dairy business. Adolf was a shrewd businessman and would only finance hard workers, to ensure a guaranteed return on his investment.

Gerrit was financed and made monthly payments on his Mesa dairy to Mr. Weinburg, who also made arrangements to sell Gerrit the feed and hay he needed. The newlyweds moved to Mesa, Arizona in 1962, where they owned and milked over two hundred cows.

Even though it was 115 degrees and she worked hard the whole time, they had a good life while in Mesa and had three children; Willemina, Johnnie and Arie. Ellie never gained a pound her first pregnancy. She actually lost weight, which concerned Gerrit.

Arie Sr. became concerned, afraid she would suffer from the same type of mental illness her mother had been plagued with after having a baby, so he visited a lot. He loved Gerrit and the two of them would talk until the wee hours of the morning.

Ellie loved being a mom, but was very homesick and missed her brothers. Since she wouldn't visit the family without Gerrit, they only went home twice a year, once in March for Maartje's birthday, and again in May for Arie Sr's.

They began attending church in Scottsdale and were very social. The couple always worked together or played with the children. They were never apart. Ellie continued to be homesick until she met and became friends with Mrs. Vriesekoop, who they called *Buurvrouw,* which means neighbor lady.

Gerrit had suffered from a sore back for a while and thought he had cracked a rib in his upper chest. The doctors were unable to find anything wrong. After a month his pain had gotten so bad, they did exploratory surgery and that's when they found an egg sized lump. It contained teeth and hair and he was told it was his undeveloped twin.

The doctor also stated he had a fast growing cancer and only had three months to live. Gerrit was never sick and they were shocked by the news. Ellie never truly realized how severe his pain was. Knowing he would face her wrath, he would have a few drinks to help ease the pain. The cancer moved quickly and had spread throughout his whole body and spine.

Gerrit was a highly moral man. Ellie said he tried to make a lady out of her, but she felt he never succeeded, saying, "I never became a real lady and I was thankful he didn't leave me for another woman."

The children were five, four and two when he passed away. The two boys don't remember him, but Willemina missed him terribly. While he was ill, she stayed at her father's bedside for hours. She just stood there holding his hand.

Gerrit was only thirty-four when he died. Ellie, thirty, stayed to run the Mesa dairy for six months, before she moved back to California with her three young children. She moved back on the San Marcos Dairy, and lived in the remodeled old dairy barn. Later, Ellie and the family built a new house for her young family on top of the hill. She and John traveled to Mesa once a month to oversee the dairy operation.

By the time he died, Gerrit had increased the herd size to four-hundred-fifty cows. From his hospital bed he coordinated the construction of new corrals and a barn with the contractors. He refused to talk about his dying with Ellie. They traveled to Mexico, so Gerrit could be treated by Dr. Contreras. He wanted to die without pain. He would be able to receive laetrile for the pain, which had not been approved by the FDA in the United States. When they left for Mexico, he said good-bye to his children for the last time. The children stayed with Arie and Anneke during the three weeks their parents were gone. The doctor was right. He only lived three months.

Gerrit passed away on July 13, 1967. As always, Ellie was at his side.

Gerrit Passes Away

Ellie's first husband Gerrit died, from a combination of congenital heart disease and lung cancer in 1968, at the age of thirty-four. The family wanted to keep their Mesa dairy, but Ellie wanted to move out of Arizona, so John agreed to manage her dairy in the Phoenix/Mesa area for the family.

Gerrit's death was very hard on her. She relocated her young family back to California and moved into one of the houses on the dairy in San Marcos. John managed the two dairies, traveling back and forth between his home and Mesa, Arizona.

Gerrit's foreman Bill Boyle was a very reliable and capable onsite manager who oversaw the dairy in John's absence. John flew in once a month to check on the operation, and managed the dairy for over twenty-five years. Because he had a very good manager onsite, he went less and less often. It was a good partnership between him and Ellie.

Ellie hated Arizona and when Gerrit died, the family built a house on the dairy in San Marcos and she moved back on the ranch with her children. Arie and Anneke had four kids and Ellie had three.

 Ellie didn't think it was a woman's place to run a dairy farm, but was more than capable of doing the job. She sold John partial interest in the dairy. During the next four years, Arie and Anneke helped her quite a bit. He was like a father to her children. Ellie felt it was unfair, because he treated her better than he did his wife Anneke, who was wonderful and never showed any jealousy and never complained either in that time. The two combined families were as one.

After Gerrit passed away Ellie didn't work. She just raised the children and took in boarders from Holland. She needed to be busy and enjoyed cooking for more than just the children, so she always made sure she had plenty of boarders lined up.

To ensure they wouldn't approach her, she only took in boarders who were married. One boarder from Holland was single. His first name was Gerrit, the same as her late husband and though they became friends, she didn't think he was for her.

Karel and Shirley's Seven Year Courtship and Marriage

When Karel first saw Shirley, it was during the service at the Escondido Christian Reformed Church on 6th Street in Escondido. She was fifteen and he was twenty-two. Karel looked handsome and sharp in his Army uniform. It was customary for the young members of the church congregation to attend church and social functions together.   The teenagers got together after church as a group to socialize, sing and talk. Karel and Shirley were able to spend time getting to know each other better during those occasions.

Shirley began working at the Cash and Carry in San Marcos and Karel remembered watching her through the window of the cooler box, where they stored the milk.

"I liked what I saw and that kept me going," said Karel.

She had Wednesday afternoons off and they went on dates. Once he brought her home around 10pm and her mother was furious. Sometimes they kissed in the hay shed, or stole an occasional kiss in the cold case of the Cash and Carry.

They continued to date for a year and a half, and then on Valentine's Day in 1960, Karel broke off the relationship. He was afraid of commitment and he felt Shirley was still too young for marriage. Three years later they got back together. Karel, was so smitten, he kept looking through the window at Shirley. He was still attracted to her and felt the fires of his love rekindle once more. They started to date again and periodically talked about marriage, but Karel never moved forward.

Shirley's sister Coby met Bert Ton and they decided to wed quickly. Karel hated to make decisions and was a procrastinator when it came to romance and making emotional commitments. He loved Shirley and decided if he was going to make a move toward matrimony he better do it, or risk losing her forever. The two couples were engaged on September 30, 1966. The double wedding ceremony was performed on December 9, 1966.

 Karel laughingly commented that it took Bert seven months to propose to Coby and it took him seven years.

There were over 400 guests in attendance at the wedding. The brides wore matching wedding gowns, and held father's arms as he escorted them down the aisle toward their future. The minister went back and forth between couples during the exchange of vows. Coby was the eldest sister. There were four bridesmaids in attendance and one fainted during the ceremony.

Karel and Shirley went to San Francisco for their honeymoon, with a stopover at the Hilton in Los Angeles. When Shirley signed in at the desk, Karel said he'd have his secretary handle the paperwork. The desk clerk misunderstood, thinking Karel was requesting a room for him and his secretary. Shirley was unaware of what the clerk was implying and didn't correct him. It never dawned on her that people took their secretaries to hotels for a rendezvous.

As he recalled all the special details of his wedding day Karel had a smile on his face and a glimmer in his eye. Speaking of how beautiful Shirley was then and how she's continued to remain so beautiful all these years.

KAREL AND SHIRLEY AT KNOTT'S BERRY FARM

"Yes," he sighed. "I truly lost my heart in San Francisco, and lucky for me Shirley was there to capture it and keep it all these years."

While on their honeymoon, the old ranch house was renovated. When they returned, there was no electricity, or working bathroom. When they were lucky enough to have electricity, it would go out a lot and the roof leaked. Shirley said, "It was a lovely house, but it had a lot of problems. While living on the dairy we ate lots of dust and there were lots of flies."

When Karel was thirty-two, two years after they married, their first child Brenda, was born, on March 19, 1970, at 2:34am. All of the children were born while Karel and Shirley lived in the old ranch house.

Fathers weren't allowed in the delivery room, so Karel was unable to be with Shirley during the birth. They named the baby after her maternal grandmother Boukje, which means Barbara in Dutch, just to keep the letter "B" going. Karel and Shirley preferred to call her Brenda instead. She was a very bright and sweet child, with a stubborn and independent streak, always wanting to keep up with the latest fashions. She could never be seen without a necklace.

On December 16, 1972, they were blessed with their second daughter, named after Karel's mother Maartje, to keep the letter "M" going. Her American name is Marianne. There were complications with the birth, so once again Karel was not allowed in the delivery room. Marianne was an easy going baby, with a sweet and gentle nature like Karel.

Five years later on February 26, 1977, they were blessed with the birth of a son. Eric John, or EJ, was named after his paternal grandfather Arie Sr., which is Dutch for Eric and his maternal grandfather Jan, which is Dutch for John. Karel remembered how EJ cried during the circumcision. This time Karel was in the delivery room. After two girls, they were both happy to have a son.

The children grew fast and Karel remembered riding around Hollandia on a bicycle with EJ laughing, while he rode in a milk crate that Karel attached to the bike. Karel was a loving and devoted father. He always tried to take the time to play with his children and laughed as he gave them piggyback rides, or walked with them standing on his feet. It was quite comical to watch. He always tried to be in a good mood, and he never got mad, so the children would have happy memories of their father. He was the good time Charlie, leaving the discipline for Shirley to take care of.

In 1979, Karel moved his family to 431 Mulberry Drive, in San Marcos, where they continued to live for the next twenty-five years. That land is now the location of the Mission Hills Church, an affiliation of the Emmanuel Faith Church in Escondido.

After the San Marcos Dairy land was sold to Mission Hills High School, the brothers bought all of the property which is now known as Silk Mill Place, to build their new homes.

Pete was the first to build his new home there. Two years later construction started on Karel's house. The new house was over 5000 square feet, included a large office upstairs for Karel and an elevator.

In January 2007, when Karel was seventy-three, he and Shirley rented a house at 487 Borden Circle, in San Marcos, while they waited for their house to be built. There was a factory close by, where silk parachutes were made during World War II, from the surrounding Mulberry trees. They moved into their new home almost two years later, in December of 2008, just in time for Christmas and their 42nd wedding anniversary.

During construction, they stopped to check the progress on the house. The elevator opened and they felt a slight shock. Unworried Karel went into the elevator to give it a test run. Luckily Shirley waited outside, because the elevator went up one floor and refused to either move or open the door. They had no cell phone with them and Shirley quickly ran to the nearby home of their daughter and son-in-law John, who was the building contractor. The elevator supplier was called and Karel was out within thirty minutes time. Karel says he was never worried. There were plenty of resources available to free him.

December 9, 2012 Karel and Shirley celebrated their 46th wedding anniversary.

On February 12, 2013, Karel, Shirley, Arie, Anneke, Tom, Hinke, Klaas and Joan de Haan, traveled to Tulare, California, in a motor home, to visit their children and attend the annual "Farm Equipment Show." The next morning, on February 13th, the brothers attended the farm show seminars and exhibits. Karel was driven to the show by his son EJ. Soon after he stepped out of the truck, Karel collapsed in the farm show parking lot. He was cradled in EJ's arms, and passed away while waiting for the paramedics to arrive. The paramedics were unable to revive him, and transported him to the closest hospital where he was pronounced dead on arrival. Karel died doing what he loved, surrounded by the ones he loved. He did not suffer and is now in his Savior's arms.

"Absent from the body, present with the Lord." 2 Corinthians 5:8

Tom Moves Back to Holland

Hans de Jong, the Ag teacher in Holland, asked Tom if he was in a good enough financial position to retire early. Hans said if Tom were able to move back to Holland, he would buy a house for his family to live in. Tom thought it over very carefully and checked his financial situation. He took an early retirement from the dairy at the age of forty-two and traveled back to Holland to live for the next four years. His children who were twelve, eleven and ten looked forward to the adventure. They spent one week of their journey crossing the Atlantic, aboard the "New Amsterdam".

Once they pulled into the dock, he realized how much the country had changed. Holland had become so industrialized it was the largest port in the world, even larger than New York. It wasn't what he or the children were expecting. The children thought Holland looked and smelled like Los Angeles.

This trip to Holland was for his children. He wanted it to be the most extravagant and enjoyable time of their lives. They spent three days and nights on a train, with a one night layover in New York. When they woke the next morning in New York, they had to look straight up to see the sky.

The train trip started off a little rocky. The children had gotten small pox vaccinations two days before and all three were having bad reactions. They had no appetite since receiving the vaccine. Tom decided to take about fifty pounds of Thompson seedless grapes to eat on the train.

He felt the vitamin "C" and sugar would help the children feel better. He used the grapes to help keep their fluid levels up. On the last two days of the train ride, other passengers were trading their food with the children, wanting the sweet juicy grapes.

The children had the time of their lives on the boat ride across the Atlantic. There was so much food of such variety and it was all so delicious. One person in particular the family befriended was a gentleman by the name of Ed Rehil. Ed visited Tom and the children several times while they were in Holland. They've continued to write or call him every year.

After twelve days of traveling by car, train and boat, the children knew Holland was a long way from California. Tom really wanted to impress this fact on them. He wanted them to understand the distance would make it impossible to see their grandparents, uncles, aunts, cousins or friends for a long time.

When they arrived in Holland, Tom moved his family into the house Hans purchased. The farmhouse called *"het tolhuis"*, which means the toll house, was situated right on the side of the road, and sported a side door, that had been used to collect the toll from anyone traveling to the next city.

The *"tolhuis"* was built in the 1700's and used to house Napoleon and his troops after he seized the Nederlands in 1806. Napoleon later appointed his brother, Louis, King of Holland. The toll road was the only well-maintained and travelable road from Alphen a/d Rijn to Gouda at the time. There was a fire in the early 1900's and the house burned down. It was later rebuilt in 1915, as it stands today.

Tom raised the children on his own in Holland. He did gardening and gave the extra vegetables he grew to friends. The children rode their bikes to school.

The children spoke a little Dutch, but were unable to read the language. With the help of Tom and the school, the children began to read, and speak Dutch fluently. Tom reinforced what they were learning by having them read, write and speak Dutch at home.

Although they were adolescents, the children drank from baby bottles until they went to Holland. Tom had become very health conscious, and he gave the children a mixture of honey, juice and tea mixed into their milk. He thought it was important to stay hydrated and the children would drink more from bottles, because it was easier and they liked it.

While he lived in Holland, Tom returned to the States for two months every winter and stayed with his brothers and sisters. The children stayed in Holland with family while he was gone. The family in Holland had a hard time watching over such independent, mature, strong willed and carefree children.

One winter, Tom left the children in the care of his twenty-two year old cousin Kees de Jong, who thought it would be great fun to take care of such lively children. Arie Sr. was on a visit from California. He and Tom traveled to several locations around Holland and were gone approximately one week. Tom thought it was a good idea to have a test run with Kees. When they returned, the children, ages ten, eleven and twelve were alone. Kees just couldn't handle them and had left.

Since the majority of Tom's family in Holland were either dead, or had previously immigrated to the United States, Tom decided to employ a non-related, elderly couple to care for the children every winter while he was gone.

He hired, Rienus and Mien Fase, the same couple that had been arrested during the war for being Jehovah's Witnesses. Arrangements were made for them to move in with the children.

The couple did not want any compensation for caring for the children. In exchange for their help, Tom taught Rienus how to drive and purchased him a car. They would be in charge of the safety and well being of his children during the winter and would need reliable transportation.

The couple did their utmost to teach Tom's children from the Bible and Watchtower publications. Tom felt they did a great job teaching the children, because all three of the children followed the religious teachings faithfully. For Mary, it was nice to have Rienus' wife Mien, as a substitute mother. The children referred to them as Uncle Rienus and Aunt Mien.

In 1972, Tom's boys went back to the United States, a year before their father and sister returned. Mary met her future husband in Holland and she returned in 1976, to be married at the age of twenty-one. The newlyweds moved to Visalia, where her husband Joep Rijlaarsdam worked on her Uncle Kees' dairy. There was no need for Joep to have a sponsor when he and Mary returned to the states, because Mary was an American citizen.

Arie Breaks Away From the Family Business

Always on top of his game, no funny business ever got by Arie Jr. He worked day and night if he had to, rather than let any monkey-business happen. It was in his blood and nature. If asked, he would probably say some of his fondest memories are of the customers and events on his milk delivery days.

Concerning business and politics, Arie continued to prove what a first class tactician he was and is. He hired the right people, fought whatever battle was necessary and made peace where he could.

He settled out his loan from the family and from that time on his ability to receive credit has come to him on the strength of his own business. Of course, Hollandia was always there and always will be part of his legacy as a businessman.

Arie sold his trash and recycling operation at the right time, for an incredibly large amount of money. His family was flabbergasted. Then Arie did something which only increased his goodwill and his reputation. One-hundred-sixty-eight of his employees received bonuses totaling a million dollars. The money was divided among them according to their position and time of employment and presented at a party thrown at the Old Richland Schoolhouse in San Marcos. Everyone had a good time.

From that time on, Arie has never been short of money except for the times he took on a new business venture.

Arie delivered milk to Green Oak Ranch Boys Camp in 1958-59, when it was an alcohol and drug rehabilitation center; a non-profit organization, owned by the Los Angeles Rescue Mission. He later purchased the property in 1997, after he sold Coast Waste Management in Carlsbad. When he first took over the non-profit, there was so much deferred maintenance, it was a money losing proposition, but after four years it finally broke even.

Because he was only ten when the family came to California, Arie was the only brother who grew up the American way. He has always been success oriented and never did or accepted half hearted work, demanding the best of himself and those around him. When he was sixteen he obtained a driver's license and became a milk route salesman for the dairy.

Arie has forever been a Maverick, preferring to do things his way, instead of by the book. This practice has gotten him into trouble on more than one occasion.

His very nature kept him brimming with ideas to make Hollandia grow and the family's financial holdings stronger. There were times he felt trapped and stagnated by the resistance of his older brothers and wanted to break out. Karel was always the tough one and by his nature Pete was complicit.   At a point when he couldn't take it anymore, Arie looked for a separate business venture of his own.

In regards to business, Karel was still the older brother and could not be swayed or moved by Arie or anyone else. Many of his good ideas fell dormant, stranded by Karel's deliberate and stubborn nature. Karel did not welcome or embrace change, it made him uncomfortable. Karel made efforts to recruit Pete to be on his team, to ensure nothing was done unless he was consulted first and considered it. Pete found this situation difficult to accept, because he was the older brother. However, peace was more important to him than power and he knuckled under for the rest of his business-life.

Though it was hard for Pete, it gave him a lot more freedom. Pete and Rena had a growing family and they used the freedom to travel and see more of the U.S. Pete and Rena always wanted a large family. From 1957 to 1968 they were blessed with seven children, four boys and three girls.

Reflecting back, Pete says, "If at that time I would have realized how good Arie was going to be as a businessman, I might have sided with him, but that's quarterbacking after the game is over and not helpful." It hurt Arie terribly to say goodbye to the family business. The roots of the family tree grow deep and he still sees himself as 'Hollandia,' and always will.

Arie felt the dairy wasn't presenting him with enough of a challenge, and he wanted to get away from both the animals and perishable products. He was hungering for a career change. Of course, the family strongly disagreed; running a dairy for them was the only way. Arie looked at several businesses and decided on the trash business. He found out that although two trash companies could operate in an area, there was currently only one in each area.   He applied for a permit, but was denied.

He submitted a written appeal which was also denied. George Stevens, the chief of staff for county supervisor Jim Bates, was sympathetic to Arie's plight and tried to help. The board of supervisors' election was coming soon and Arie wanted his appeal to be put on the agenda before anyone new was on the board. Arie was put on the agenda at the last board meeting of the calendar year. His appeal could finally be heard. His permit was granted and also to allow for competition the county opened it up so anyone could apply to get a permit to start a trash company. The whole process took a year and a half. That's how Arie ended up going into the trash business on his own. He started North County Disposal and started with two trucks, two brooms and two shovels.

In 1977, Arie came across a business opportunity he felt was too good to resist. He found out about a trash business in Carlsbad that went into receivership after the owners; the Van Orts were killed in a plane crash. The bank took possession and put the business up for auction. Tom went to the courthouse with Arie and during the auction they sat across the room from all the other business owners and accountants. Arie needed a lot of capital to make the deal.

Arie bought the business at the auction held in the judge's chambers at the Vista courthouse. The judge stipulated the terms of the auction and the bidding began. It came down to Arie and a bidder from Chicago. The Chicago offer was for a higher price, but Arie was offering more cash up front. The judge was very familiar with the de Jongs and their business savvy. He called for a recess and met with the bankers and accountants for Van Ort Enterprises and the decision was made to sell to the de Jong brothers, (Arie). After the acquisition he renamed the company Coast Waste Management.

After the auction, Arie broke the news to the family. He went directly to Karel's house to tell him first, because he was the biggest opposition and would take it the hardest. Karel felt Arie was very instrumental in making positive changes at Hollandia and never wanted him to leave the family business. He didn't take the news very well and was livid. Arie saw the opportunity and told Karel he was sorry, but if given the chance he would do it again. By going with him, Tom had gone rogue and spoke up on Arie's behalf, and stated he should be given the opportunity to try.

Pete who was striving to keep the family's Hollandia finances in order was very unhappy. After a lot of coaxing, Arie and Tom got their father on his side. Although Arie Sr. wasn't happy, he could see the potential and understood why Arie had pursued the purchase. His father then got the family to agree to help Arie out in his new venture.

From there Arie's business ventures have grown exponentially. He has Hilltop Group Property Management, Green Oak Ranch and his newly opened RV storage facility was completed and opened in Vista in 2011.

Later on, Arie wanted to hire Tom's son, Arie Helmut, however, he was unavailable and his brother Tommy went to work for him instead. The trash business took a lot of personnel and overseeing and Tommy was selected for the job. Arie's keen business sense was proven to be right. Under his tireless leadership, the business flourished.

It took a great deal of cash to purchase the business. Arie's only real source of credit was the family and the family loaned him the money. He repaid the loan, in a record amount of time.

Arie has an incredible knack for and a love of business-politics and has developed quite a name and reputation for himself in the local communities of San Diego County. In this regard he is a great deal like his Father, whose leadership and guidance was very productive as well as lucrative.   All the children wanted to follow his example. For Arie it all just came naturally.

Across the street from the dairy, located at 807 East Mission Road, in San Marcos, where Diamond Environmental and Hilltop Group stand today, Arie owned a twelve-acre parcel of land. The property was in the flood zone and he wanted to fill it in, so he could have the area rezoned for industrial use, in order to build.

In the meantime, the city of San Marcos had purchased the Wilgenburg Dairy to build an industrial park. The abandoned dairy located across the creek from Arie's land, sat on a hilltop which the city had begun to level. Arie noticed the dump-trucks full of dirt and paid the contractor to bring them to his parcel of land. He found out the company, "Dirt King" was being paid by both him and the city for the same loads of dirt. The city paid to have the dirt removed and Arie paid for the dirt to be delivered.   He thought it was a pretty good business venture, so he formed a partnership with the owners George Monte and Greg Whillock.

Not long after he became partial owner, Dirt King was awarded the contract to grade a large parcel of land in San Ysidro next to the Mexican border. The land was being graded in preparation for the construction of a sizeable residential sub-division. Arie's father-in-law and mother-in-law were visiting from Holland and he suggested they all take a field trip in the motor-home, so they could see his new business venture firsthand. Arie Sr., Maartje, Arie's mother and father-in-law, Tom, Karel and Arie took off for San Ysidro. When they arrived they noticed they were right next to the Mexican border. All that separated them from Tijuana was a chain-link fence topped with barbed wire.

When the three brothers got out of the motor-home, Arie noticed the opening to a huge, uncovered storm drain. Since they were so close to the border they became curious if they could use the storm drain to cross over into Mexico. They told the family what their intentions were and then the three brothers began their trek through the storm drain, leaving behind the rest of the family who could not speak English. After walking several hundred yards they came across a man-hole cover above them and used it to climb out into a residential area of Tijuana. When they walked over to the fence and saw the motor-home they waved so the family could see they made it.

They inadvertently caught the attention of the border patrol who thought they were coyotes, or drug runners and they headed to the motor-home to investigate. The brothers were unaware of the border patrol and flagged down a man driving by, who took them to the main street in Tijuana, Avenue Revolution, to get some tacos and margaritas. While they were having a good time and getting a little tipsy, the family was in the motor-home being visited by the border patrol.

No one could speak English or had taken their passports or any other form of identification along. Since they were unable to communicate with the officers, they couldn't tell them the situation. The officers were at a loss after they checked the vehicle and only found a small group of elderly Dutch people. Arie Sr. tried his best to explain in his limited English. The officers finally gave up and left. Arie's in-laws were very cultured and proper and not used to his family's unorthodox way of doing things. Needless to say, hours later when the brothers finally returned to the motor-home, the family was pretty heated. It was a very uncomfortable and quiet ride back to San Marcos.

Arie tried his hand running the wholesale side of the family business for awhile, but felt he was better suited for retail. Since the overall sales go at a much slower pace, the wholesale side of business could be somewhat frustrating at times, especially because the family was up against some major players who were a lot more powerful. He feels that even though he may be viewed by some as unorthodox, he's a decent man with a kind heart. His family means everything in the world to him.

Arie was instrumental in restoring the Richland Schoolhouse in San Marcos. He wanted to attend school there, but was unable to when he was a child. The schoolhouse was built in 1889, by the San Marcos School District. He acquired the property in 1995. He decided to convert the schoolhouse into a place where weddings or other social events could be held. In order to do so, he felt he needed to build a deck at the site in order to house a larger number of guests more comfortably. Without receiving preapproval or permits from the city, Arie and his crew built the deck over a weekend after city hall had closed.

Since he had circumvented city hall many times in the past, they realized a fine would be just a slap on the wrist to Arie and he was ordered to do community service instead. He viewed community service as cleaning windows or some other menial service. Instead he was told he needed to do other forms of community service. The city manager called and told Arie he needed to give back to the community.

The city owned an old building that Arie and his construction crew remodeled in order to complete his community service. Always the maverick, he of course worked without getting the proper permits. In 1997, after the Alzheimer's Daycare Center project was completed, he received a city enhancement award from the San Marcos city council. The center was later closed and turned into a daycare center for Cal State University San Marcos.

Arie built a new blacksmith shop in Grape Day Park for the City of Escondido, and was also involved in the relocation of a small historic church on Pico Avenue in San Marcos. The church was moved from downtown San Marcos to its new location next to the San Marcos Cemetery, an appropriate new home.

He was also instrumental in moving the "Fred and Francis Williams, "Red Barn Dance Hall," to its new home located at Walnut Grove Park, in San Marcos. The city of San Marcos originally wanted to demolish the barn, but at Arie's insistence the building was saved. Through his connection to the Parks Historical Community Center, Arie has also been involved in the relocation, restoration and preservation of several other historical buildings.

Mary and Richard

Mary and Jet were always pressured by the family to date Dutch men, and, because everyone in the family was so insistent it was very stressful. Richard was an independent trucker and owned two trucks. One hauled milk and the other hauled hay for different dairies throughout the Chino, Artesia/Bellflower areas. One of the dairies he hauled milk for belonged to Cor and Aagt van Beek, Ellie's husband's aunt and uncle.

An initial meeting was arranged between Jet, Mary and Richard, for tea at Gerrit's aunt Aagt's house in Chino. Both Jet and Mary didn't think much about it when they met Richard, because he was twenty-two at the time. Two years later, his Aunt Aagt pressed for Richard to take the girls out.

Another meeting was arranged, this time over dinner. Ellie, Jet and Mary met Richard and his friend at the home of Gerrit's aunt.

Mary and Richard gravitated to each other from the beginning. He preferred quiet women and told his friend, "I get the dark haired one and you get the blond." When Mary was nineteen, they began to date and that was it, they never dated anyone else and eventually married.

There was a family meeting consisting of all her siblings, but not her parents. Ellie and Karel were instrumental in making the final decision. She and Richard were married on March 29, 1969. She really didn't want to get married. She wanted to go out, live it up and enjoy her life. She wanted to go to San Francisco with Jet and her friends, but the family had a meeting and convinced her to get married.

The first years of marriage were simple. There weren't a lot of changes or adjustments. John's wife, Willie, taught her how to cook, because she always worked at home, and never learned how. As a newly married woman, cooking was a skill Mary needed to acquire. The first time she tried to cook for Richard, the meat was tough as nails.

Because he was gone all the time, Mary didn't like the idea of Richard working as a trucker. John didn't either, so he offered Richard the foreman's job on his dairy. At first Richard turned him down, but in time he went to work for John. Mary didn't want to move to Hanford, because of the heat and the mosquitoes. However, it wasn't long before they eventually moved next door to John on his new dairy.

Mary did John's bookkeeping for $30 a month and Richard made $25 a day. She also fed the calves and did a lot of yard work. She was used to working and so John did his best to find things to keep her busy.

Mary grew tired of taking care of all her nieces, nephews and everyone else's children, so they decided to have children of their own right away. When she was twenty-one she gave birth to their first child, John Diderick, who was named after Richard's father.

The birth of her children came regularly after that. Mary and Richard only planned on having six children, but had a total of eight: John Diderick, 6-3-1970, Eric Thomas, 7-31-1971, Melissa 2-14-1973, Tineka Evelyn, 9-14-1974, Richard Klaas, 2-9-1978, Marietta Ellie, 9-20-1979, Katrina, 6-9-1983 and Daniel Karl, 4-28-1985.

Tom felt buttermilk made from raw milk was much healthier than processed milk. He taught Mary how to make her own buttermilk, so they wouldn't have to purchase it at the store, because it was expensive. She taught her children how when they became old enough.

In April of 1976, when Mary was twenty-seven, she and Richard purchased their own dairy and house in Tulare. The house needed lots of work, so they weren't able to fully operate for two months. They were excited to have a home and dairy of their own. She kept busy doing projects around the house and dairy, like pouring cement, feeding the calves and doing the book-keeping.

In the beginning, they didn't have enough money to operate and purchase the feed and grain they needed. John gave them grain, until they could afford to buy their own. Life in Tulare was extremely quiet. It took a while for Richard to get used to the change, although he did enjoy all the commotion and noise when they had coffee at John's.

They moved to their current home in 1982. The new home was very large. Their previous house was very small. Everyone had always been on top of each other and there had been no breathing room. The children found all the room in the new house to be quite an adjustment.

When Johnnie, their oldest son was eighteen, he was riding around the dairy on a dune buggy which was used for irrigation. Daniel Karl, their three year old was riding on the back and the buggy turned over. The three year old fell off and the wheel ran over him, taking off hair and scalp as it tore across his head. He suffered a concussion and twelve stitches.

Mary remembered how Johnnie ran to the house crying, as he carried his blood covered brother in his arms. He gently laid his brother on the cement, before hosing him off to see how bad his injuries were, and how he sang, *Jesus Loves Me,* as they drove to the hospital.

Her children attended "Central Valley Christian School" and because the church elders didn't believe in dancing, and wouldn't allow dances to be held at the school, she held all the dances at her home.

At first the dances weren't sanctioned by the church elders, until the teachers began to chaperone. Mary was instrumental in the implementation of dances for prom, homecoming, graduation, vice versa, and Sadie Hawkins. She held all of the dances at her home for six years, before the school finally allowed them to be held on campus.

Coffee time at Mary's is 11am, and there are usually around thirteen adults and twenty-one children on any given day. She serves homemade bread, ham, Gouda cheese, peanut butter and jam.

Mary has eight children and twenty-seven grandchildren. She feels very fortunate, because her home is the central point of four dairies run by their children. Like her mother, Maartje, she keeps a family tradition of everyone coming for morning coffee and lunch. In Holland coffee was at ten, but eleven works out much better for her family. There's always plenty of coffee, bread, fruit and cheese for anyone who shows up.

Jet and John Get Married

When Jet met John Jenson, an attorney in Escondido, he was graduating from officer's training school in San Luis Obispo and he invited her to his graduation. She agreed and attended with a group. That was when she met John's best friend, John Gailey, who was also graduating from officer's training school. Both men would be 2nd Lieutenants in the National Guard.

They had enlisted for six years in the Guard and took the officer training to prevent taking a tour in Vietnam. John Gailey was an only child. His father Willis Gailey absolutely forbade him from going to Vietnam and told him to get out of it anyway he could. John's father had been a Captain during World War II, and fought in the *Battle of the Bulge.* He refused to talk about the death and carnage he saw during the war, and he never wanted his son to experience it either.

As a war veteran his father realized the stress and horrors soldiers experienced. He didn't want John to face hatred from his fellow countrymen during the Vietnam era, instead of the celebrations the soldiers of WWII met on their homecoming.

The graduation ceremony was beautiful and the celebration dinner was held at the Madonna Inn. Of course, because they were best friends, Jet sat at the table with both Johns. Afterward, she returned to Escondido and didn't give the matter a second thought. One afternoon while shopping at the Escondido Fedmart, she ran into John Gailey. His family rented space there for their camera store and they also owned a camera shop in downtown Escondido.

John fished around trying to find out if Jet was in a relationship with John Jenson or anyone else. He knew John had gone away to college after their graduation. When she said she wasn't seeing anyone, he jumped at the opportunity and asked her out. Jet admits she didn't want to say yes, because he was such a nerd with his black rim glasses, but he was such a nice guy she decided to say yes. When he asked where she wanted to go to dinner she told him San Diego, so no one would see them together. She was shocked when he took her to the Charthouse on Shelter Island. They had a wonderful time. He was out going, friendly and fun with a great personality.

They went out again, but as friends and continued to date over the next two years, but nothing serious. If either of them needed a date for an event, they simply called each other up. He was a member of the Optimist Club and the Jr. Chamber of Commerce. His grandfather, Andy Andreason, was a judge, the Mayor of Escondido and the Chief of Police.

Jet felt she needed to find a good Dutch dairyman, someone who belonged to her church. That wasn't to be the case. One night John took her to dinner at Anthony's Star of the Sea Room; the nicest restaurant in San Diego at the time. Men couldn't get in without a coat and tie and women had to wear formal dinner wear as well.

While having dinner John casually said, "You know I'm going to marry you someday."

Jet protested back, "No we're only friends. I'm going to marry a Dutch dairyman."

"No, you like this life too much. You're going to marry me."

She thought the conversation was strange, since nothing had passed between them except for a platonic peck on the cheek.

"John, you have to love each other to get married."

He replied, "Well, I do love you Jet."

She did a lot of soul searching and even called it all off a few times, stating how she wasn't going to get married, and even tried to convince herself to date other people to try and find "Mr. Right." She always found herself thinking about John and how much she cared for him.

John was an only child, who was outgoing, personable and was the love of her life, but he was also spoiled, lazy, and drank too much. Jet says she never noticed those things at first. She was young, high spirited and having a good time. She didn't worry about those things. She felt when the time came he would knuckle down, settle in and get to work. She didn't realize some people just never settle down and John was one of those people. She now admits she didn't have a clue at the time.

Jet did the bookkeeping at the San Marcos Dairy. She continued to work long hours, and at times she got up as early as 2am. Her brother, Arie was always at the office by the time she arrived. As they worked together processing the paperwork, the two continued to have lengthy and serious discussions. Arie kept advising her not to marry John. Sometimes the conversations lasted until the other women arrived at 8am. This pattern continued at least two or three days a week. Of course, she stopped working long hours after she had children.

Her other brothers also cautioned her not to marry John, and advised her to find a good Dutch guy instead. Karel was elected the spokesman for the family. He was supposed go to John and Jet and talk them out of getting married. That never happened because John and Karel had become drinking buddies. Jet held her ground and said she didn't care for any of the good Dutch guys, she loved John. Due to John's persistence they became engaged.

Jet and John were married September 18, 1971, at the Christian Reform Church in Escondido. The church held 500 people and was packed to the rafters. While on their honeymoon in the Caribbean, John rented a sailboat and they floated from island to island.

She had two children right away. Johnny was born in January 1974 and Eric was born in November of 1975. After he was born, Eric spent the first four months of his life in the hospital due to his illness. When it was time for Eric to come home, John said, "He's not coming home. You are not going to bring him in our house."

The rift between the two escalated after that point. Jet was surprised when her father, Tom, Kees and Karel all sided with John and said, "Don't worry about it. The kid's not ok. Just leave him in a home."

Several other family members didn't agree with them and sided with Jet. It was a common practice at the time for disabled children to be placed in an institution. It was only around the time of Eric's birth that children with disabilities went home with their parents. Sending Eric away was very hard on their marriage. The couple had three more children, Karel, Matthew, and she was pregnant with Mark when they separated.

John had been raised in an environment where he was exposed to a lot of alcohol and drinking and he became a very heavy drinker. Jet was naïve concerning alcoholism and she thought he would out grow it and settle down. During that time, drinking, like cigarette smoking, was the norm. It was very common place for people to have drinks at lunch, hit the bars after work, or have happy hour at home. John was also a heavy smoker. After fifteen years, they split up and eventually got a divorce.

After John and Jet got married, Arie sold them the house he owned, located at 1270 Nordahl Road, Escondido, California. Arie had purchased the house from his landlady Mrs. Whitmore, in 1966, for the sum of $19,500 and sold it to them for the same price he originally paid. However, at the time of their divorce, Jet discovered John had forged her signature and borrowed a large sum of money against the house to support his lifestyle.

Hollandia Continues to Grow and Prosper

With everyone on their own dairy, the family was so busy, that at times it was hard to notice just how much everything was changing. Financing for each step toward growth was provided on the strength of Hollandia. The quantities of cows were increased by great numbers. Fortunately for Hollandia, John remained an integral part and was the best operator of all the de Jong brothers.

In the 1960's, as a unit, the family milked sixteen-hundred cows a day. Hollandia milked four hundred cows. John milked seven hundred in Riverdale. Tom milked one hundred in Fresno, and Kees milked two hundred in Reedley. While Gerrit and Ellie milked two hundred in Mesa, Arizona.

Karel de Jong

The de Jongs' cousin, Rudy de Jong proved to be ambitious. He suggested the family needed to take care of the light maintenance of the growing fleet of trucks. Over the years he proved to be a strong fleet manager and handled personnel well.

Although Elso was a good and charismatic salesman, no one could match the speed and efficiency of Arie, who was also very ambitious. He really showed his strength in retail; it was easy to tell he loved to sell and loved his customers.

Arie Sr. provided his wisdom, experience and encouragement. Karel was responsible for the production plant and creamery. Elso and Arie were responsible for maintaining the existing milk routes, as well as, the building and development of a new and extended customer base. Pete was in charge of Public Relations, Marketing and Administration. By utilizing everyone's strengths, the family had an enthusiastic team in place.

Titles were never important to the family and were only given out of necessity concerning documents. Far more importance was placed on positions. It was very key and instrumental that all primary positions within the company were filled with family members. This helped to insure the prosperity and growth of the company.

Karel became the president of Hollandia dairy in 1979, at the age of forty-five. Being a very humble person he was never after titles or glory. Like his brothers, he just believed in doing a job to the best of his ability, to achieve overall success.

Karel was forever on the go, he oversaw the milk plant, the milkers, and the plant maintenance. He was ever steady, and steered the course, he got up early and went to bed early as well. He was a creature of habit, even when it came to his wardrobe. He could easily be spotted by his blue jeans and light blue shirt. He ate an apple and an orange everyday and squeezed fresh orange juice in the morning for his family.

Karel designed the Cash and Carry, at both the San Marcos and Escondido locations and he did the design for the milk plant in San Marcos.

John worked at the San Marcos location until 1961, when he moved to Riverdale (near Hanford) after the family purchased a dairy from the Verburgs, who had been neighbors of the de Jong family while living in Holland. The family began selling milk in cartons and it looked like the local schools would be the best place to try their luck at expansion. Naturally there was a

good amount of politics involved with the whole process, because the schools wanted to help the growth of local companies.

Hollandia was lucky to be the hometown dairy for both Escondido and San Marcos.

Initial decisions of who to purchase milk from were made by the school business manager, but the school board had the final say. A few of the local markets had gracious managers who took a chance on Hollandia and began to sell their products as well.

Pete was running a wholesale route. He faced the difficulty of filling the truck, even though he had a few of the local schools, restaurants and stores as clients. Over time, several people besides Pete ran the same wholesale, route including his brothers John and Arie, Gerrit Roeloffs, their cousin Rudy de Jong and Klaas de Haan.

Elso was the perfect choice to make and keep the customers happy. He was careful to spend

Does city ♥ sign?

time with all the key people, and made sure he referenced the success achieved in the schools who were already customers. Growth was slow at first, but it was growth none the less and the family prospered. The biggest obstacle and stiffest competition was Golden Arrow, who had TV advertising and Johnny Downs. It was fortunate for the family that Elso was wily in obtaining the school business and his brother Arie was an unstoppable powerhouse on the retail side. Pete was Elso's sales team partner. Elso used a sympathetic, charismatic approach, while Pete went in to seal the deal. Karel, Rudy and Arie were well acquainted with the politics involved in obtaining and keeping the school contracts and they attended school board meetings as the eyes, ears and voice of Hollandia.

Golden Arrow was Hollandia's main opponent and in spite of brilliant presentations by Don Calorie (a Cal Poly graduate), the de Jong boys were often surprised how the family was given contracts instead of Golden Arrow. They knew it was due to all of Elso's fine work. Years later, Golden Arrow obtained another aggressive salesman by the name of John Keeley, who set his sights on the prize and did not expect to lose. By coincidence his personal friend Bruce Ruppenthal, just happened to be the superintendent/business manager of the San Marcos School District. Elso found out about this connection and he went to see the school board members personally, to gain their sympathy. The contract was awarded to Hollandia and remained there. Many years later John Keeley came to work for Hollandia and recounted how shrewd Elso was in his business dealings. Having Keeley work for the family was great, because he was highly respected by his customer base and his employers. He strove to have the company live up to all the promises he made to the customers.

Rudy de Jong was highly respected for his willingness to take on any situation. He was a hard worker and a strong boss. More and more of the automotive work were being done 'in house,' because of his mechanical ability. Outside mechanics were only hired for work his team was unable to perform. If there was a problem with any other aspect of the business, Rudy was always available to help. As the business continued to grow, Rudy became more powerful. Karel, who was laidback and easy going by nature, took care of production and the processing plant. Pete was busy with the financial and administration side of the business. Arie broadened his view of the business and came up with ideas for growth and efficiency.

In 1982, the San Marcos milk plant was processing greater volumes of milk. They had outgrown their existing milk storage capacity and the dairy needed a larger tank to keep up with its ever increasing milk production. The de Jongs heard the Roger Jessup dairy in the San Fernando Valley was closing, and the cows and equipment were being auctioned off. Karel, Arie and Rudy de Jong attended the auction, it was there they purchased a 55 foot milk silo, which holds 33,000 gallons of milk and had it shipped to the dairy in San Marcos.

Arie commissioned Larry Onan, of Onan Sign Painting, to paint "We Love San Marcos, Hollandia Dairy," on the side of the massive silo. Saturday was the slowest day at the milk processing plant, so they rented a large crane and erected the silo on a Saturday morning.

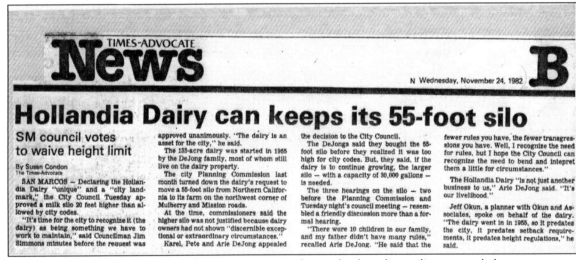

However, a week after the silo was put into place, the brothers discovered there was a height ordinance in San Marcos, and the silo was too tall, and there was a sign ordinance as well. The dairy was in violation of both. Darrell Gentry, the Planning Director in San Marcos went to see Arie regarding the matter. The silo was twenty feet taller than the city code allowed for.

Councilman Jim Simmons went to bat for the de Jongs. He stated the 138 acre dairy had been in existence since 1952, and it predated the city codes and setback requirements. He also argued the silo should be allowed to stand, stating the dairy was an asset to the city. After long discussions and three hearings, the city council took a vote and unanimously agreed to allow the silo to be kept in place, but they were unsure if they would allow the sign to remain.

Arie purposely had "We Love San Marcos" painted on the silo to help thwart any opposition from the city council. The council agreed to let the sign, which could be seen from the 78 Freeway to remain in place.

Elso wanted to start a dairy of his own and after looking in Oregon, found a place in Bonanza, Klamath Valley.

Karel and Rudy enjoyed the challenge of keeping the fleet and dairy operation going as economically as possible. Pete admitted he would not have been able to handle the stress and demands involved in maintaining the operational side of the fleet and dairy and felt the company was extremely fortunate to have had the natural abilities and resources of Karel and Rudy.

Pete always felt more comfortable in his office and stated it was his good fortune when Karel convinced him to hire his brother-in-law, Klaas de Haan to do the actual office duty work. Klaas was a veteran and had earned a purple heart when he was wounded in Vietnam. He was not only a faithful and loyal person, but he had a degree in both financing and accounting.

Having Klaas on board with Hollandia took a great deal of stress off Pete. If any problem arose in the sizable administration, it now became Klaas's problem. In addition to Klaas, Karel foresaw the need to have someone on board who knew the milk business and movements in greater depth than anyone else in the company. Both Pete and Klaas were highly critical of this idea.

At Karel's insistence the family finally agreed to hire Lee Hodge, a partner of the former Golden Arrow Dairy. He was just the man the family needed to handle milk pricing and the State of California milk pooling reports.

In 1970, at the annual company party, held at Felicita Park, it was announced that Pat Farrill, the first non-family employee ever hired by Hollandia, and his wife Edith were being given a trip to Holland. They would accompany Tom de Jong and his daughter Mary, who would be their tour guides. Pat was hired in 1952, and although he had officially retired from Hollandia, he went to work for Arie doing collections for the company. It was at Arie's insistence that his father agreed the family business, Hollandia, would pay for Pat's trip to Holland.

The time for the trip was rapidly approaching, and although Edith had gotten her passport, Pat still didn't have his. There was confusion on where he was born and Arie finally found out from one of Pat's children, he was born in New York City, but there was no birth certificate on file there. They knew the name of the Catholic Church Pat had attended as a child and Arie called to see if there was a baptismal certificate on record. He spoke to an Irish nun and found out Pat was really Italian and not Irish as he had originally thought, and he was two years older.

His birth name was Fiorrillo.   Arie obtained a copy of the birth certificate, and Pat was able to get his passport at the last minute.

It was the trip of a lifetime for Pat, who had never been out of the country before. He and Edith spent three weeks seeing the sights. Tom took them to Switzerland, Austria, Belgium, and throughout Germany, including the Dom Cathedral, in Cologne.

On Thursday, September 14th while getting ready for the return flight to California, Tom sent Mary to Pat and Edith's room, because they thought Pat was sleeping in. The de Jongs were unaware that Pat had suffered from heart problems for years and while in Holland he had not been taking his medication. When Mary went into the room, Pat was still in bed, and stated he wasn't feeling well. She sat down next to him and he died in her arms of a massive heart attack. Funeral arrangements had to be made in America and Edith needed to obtain a death certificate before Pat's body could be shipped back home.

It was a very sad homecoming for everyone, especially Edith and Arie, who had been instrumental in sending them on their trip to Holland. Pat was a very good story teller and Arie had been looking forward to hearing all about their adventures while on their trip.

The following week Arie and Anneke picked up Pat's body and Edith from the airport and the funeral was held two days later. Arie, Pat's three sons and two of his grandchildren were the pall bearers.

Ellie Meets Willem

When Ellie was thirty-three she went to Holland with her father, mother, sister Jet and her friend Nancy. Everyone in Holland told Ellie she needed to marry again. The Ag teacher, Mr. de Jong, repeatedly introduced her to boys ready to immigrate to America; however, she wasn't interested in any of them.

Gerrit Griffioen, one of Ellie's boarders suggested she look up his cousin, Willem Griffioen, a dairyman and also a good man of strong character. When she arrived at Willem's home, Ellie felt uncomfortable and pretended to be looking for the home of Gerrit's parents instead.

She was invited in and met Willem, who, eventually became her second husband. She enjoyed his company a great deal more than she did any other potential suitor she'd met while in Holland. Tom set up a double date for them and they all went to the beach. Even though they had a marvelous time, he didn't call again. She decided to make a clean break with all the guys she'd met, because she was returning to the U.S. anyway.

Willem really wasn't sure about a widow with three small children or leaving his home in Holland. He prayed about it and went to find her at a going away party for the family. They talked at the party and exchanged contact information.

Ellie returned to California and they wrote weekly letters for the next three months. He asked her to come to Holland. Ellie admits she was miffed at the invitation, because he failed to visit her while she was there. She told him in no uncertain terms, she had three children and wasn't going to Holland. If anyone was going to make the next move it had to be him.

Willem came to the states for two weeks at Christmas and Arie Sr. liked him immensely. He went to work on the family dairy in San Marcos. When Ellie went to Holland on vacation, she stayed with the family of Arie Sr.'s best friend, Leen Schouten, the father of her best friend Gien. She and Willem liked and appreciated each other a great deal, but she was hesitant because she felt he was disorganized and not as thorough in his work ethic. Even so they eventually became engaged.

Gien's father, Leen Schouten held an engagement party at Avifauna in Holland, which is a bird sanctuary and restaurant in Holland. Her children were six, eight and nine and they loved Willem. They were married on April 2, 1971, and lived in San Marcos for the first year, before they moved to Tulare in 1972.

The first few years were a tough adjustment. Willem didn't know English and was no longer his own boss. He was working with Ellie's brothers and doing a little bit of everything on the farm.

Willem wasn't very precise and Ellie and her brothers were very exact in how they wanted things done regarding how a dairy should be operated. She admits she was hard to live with. Ellie was also used to the way Gerrit had been in his approach to work. Although Willem had a hard time with the American way of business, they had a nice farm and things were good.

He only milked twenty-eight cows in Holland but milked eight-hundred in the U.S. It was much more physically demanding and difficult for him to be told what to do by his wife. She was too clean and he was too easy going. They had to find a middle ground.

After they got married, Ellie and Willem eventually built a new dairy in Tulare. They had three more daughters, Wendy, Maartje, and Sophia. Ellie felt Tulare was great because her brother Kees lived in Visalia with his wife, Helia and ten children. John lived in Hanford with his wife Willie, and eight children. Mary lived in Tulare with her husband Richard and eight children. They all traveled together and had family picnics and swam at the lake. Everyone worked hard and played hard. The thirty-seven children always had fun together and have remained close.

Ellie enjoyed having her children and all of her nieces and nephews around her. She wanted more children, but her doctor told her she wouldn't be able to, because of scar tissue. After the birth of her first three children Ellie suffered from a collapsed bladder and her last three daughters were delivered by C-section. She felt she was a good mom, but wasn't always an easy wife.

As a young girl, Ellie told their family minister, Harry Dykstra she would take care of him when he was an old man if he ever needed help. In 1976, he moved to Tulare several years after his wife passed away and he had remarried. He was a missionary in China and was well renowned in Christian reformed circles. He had also been a chaplain at Camp Pendleton. He had been on his way to Ripon to look at a retirement home, and stopped to visit Ellie.

When she and Willem learned he was going into a senior home, she decided to fulfill her promise. They put a mobile home on their farm close to their house for Reverend Dykstra and his new wife, Winifred to move there. Ellie took care of them for the next twelve years, until he passed away and Winifred relocated to Grand Rapids, Michigan. Part of their social life was through Reverend Harry Dykstra, because everyone connected with the reformed church in California knew him. She and Wim traveled in a motor home with him all over America.

In 1989, when Ellie was fifty, her girlfriend Gien came to visit from Holland. They planned a trip to the Grand Canyon, but before they left on vacation, Ellie felt a lump in the lymph node under her arm. Gien's husband a doctor, said it needed to come out before they went on the trip. The procedure was done in her doctor's office.

They were gone for five days and when they returned, the doctor's office called and asked her to come in. When he told her the results of the biopsy, she was in shock. He told her the words she had heard before.

"You have cancer. It's a fast growing form."

Ellie said she thought to herself, "How can that be?"

Her younger children were in high school at the time and had a hard time with the news. The older children had lost their father to cancer and were afraid. They thought they were about to lose their mother as well.

In Tulare, the doctor was unable to locate the specific area where the cancer originated. With the help of her friend Willy Diepersloot, Ellie went to San Francisco to see the doctors at Stanford. That's where they discovered the main source of the cancer was in her left breast and had spread to her lymph nodes. They did a mastectomy and removed the lymph nodes under her arm as well.

After undergoing chemo for six months, she lost some hair, turned yellow with jaundice, and lost fifteen pounds. Ellie had always weighed about one-hundred-thirty pounds, but people began saying she looked really rough. Usually very gregarious, she didn't want visitors and began to shut herself off from people. She didn't want anyone to feel sorry for her and wanted to work it out for herself. She even drove herself to her chemo therapy until the day she pulled over in an orchard and fell asleep before she got home.

Reverend Dykstra's wife, Winifred, (referred to as, Tante Wini), was worried Ellie had no one to take care of her, and she took Ellie to her family in Michigan. Ellie knew she would survive the cancer. She never accepted Gerrit's death from cancer and she was not going to accept her own illness. She finished the chemo treatments, and was back to her old self. It's been more than twenty years and her cancer has remained in remission.

At sixty, she and Wim moved to Sierra Village, an over fifty retirement community comprised of members of Christian churches. Their daughter, Wendy and husband, Mike took over the dairy operation in Tulare. It was an easy move and they didn't miss the dairy. After retirement, the marriage was a lot better. They have traveled more and use their free time to help babysit the grandchildren, do yard work, socialize and entertain members of their neighborhood.

Father Arie Passes Away

On one occasion in 1984 Tom, Kees, Karel, Arie and Rudy went to Arie Sr.'s for happy hour. Arie Jr. was late, and before he arrived, his father told the other boys he was having trouble breathing. Kees was putting his father to bed, but once Arie, who had asthma problems, saw him, he knew they needed to get their father to the hospital right away. It took some convincing, but Arie emphasized the fact their father wouldn't make it through the night, if they didn't get him to the hospital. His brothers finally agreed.

They rushed him to Tri-City Hospital. He was immediately taken to the intensive care unit and given a tracheotomy. He stayed in the hospital for a week. Arie Sr. was used to being active and hated the hospital, the confinement and the all tubes. His hands were strapped down to prevent him from pulling out the tracheotomy tube. If the boys had not taken him to the hospital he would have died, instead he lived five more years.

Arie Sr. was a big man, excessively overweight and smoked. This contributed to his respiratory problems. In 1989, he was ill with respiratory issues again, and although he was suffering from emphysema, he died of a heart attack a week later.

Arie Sr. loved pigs, and kept forty to fifty at all times between the years 1950 to 1980. He would go to the Chino auction once a month to sell his larger pigs and purchase young ones to take their place. His son Arie owned two large, garbage fed hog ranches in Ontario, California. His father loved to check out the hog ranch operation. One hog ranch was a converted, vacant dairy and housed over 8,500 pigs.

Arie Jr's father wasn't feeling well and was unable to go to the hog ranch in Ontario, California with him and John Keely. When they stopped to visit him when they returned that night, Arie noticed his father's swollen and infected finger. Arie sent John to the pharmacy to get some Epsom salt, and he soaked his father's finger in the hot salty water to drain the pus and alleviate the swelling. There was no indication anything was wrong other than his finger during their visit and after having happy hour, Arie and John left. He died the next day.

On the night he died, he had been sleeping on his side and he woke asking Maartje for the time. She responded that it was 2am. He said it was too early and they should go back to sleep. An hour later he was dead. It was shortly after three o'clock in the morning when he had rolled out of bed and died.

Maartje tried to get him up, but when he didn't move or speak, she realized he was dead and covered him with a blanket, and went back to sleep. The next morning, she went to the

Cash and Carry to get Chris. He ran the house and found Arie Sr. on the floor. He passed away in 1989, at the age of 88. Arie Sr.'s father, Teun, died of a stroke at the early age of 59.

When Arie Sr. found out Ellie had cancer, it hit him really hard. She had her surgery on May 26, 1989 and her father passed away seven days later, on June 2, 1989. At the time of his death, Arie Sr. and his wife Maartje had produced a wondrous living legacy. They had a total of twelve children, fifty-four grandchildren and thirty-six great-grandchildren.

His funeral service was held at the Escondido Christian Reformed Church, the Reverend Andrew Cammenga officiated. He died peacefully in his sleep, and was interned at the Oak Hill Memorial Park.

A Bicentenial Horatio Alger Tale

by COURTNEY SWENSEN

HOLLANDIA Dairy

Enterprising Independents: Hollandia's working owners, the de Jong brothers and cousin. Left to right, Arie, Karel, cousin Rudy de Jong, Pete, and Tom, who founded the dairy and is now retired.

Hollandia Dairy, the small, independent producer and processor in San Diego County, California, is living proof that the Three Musketeers, the Rover Boys, Tom Swift and Horatio Alger exist outside the pages of fiction.

Hollandia, which is celebrating its 25th birthday from May to December, is the accomplishment of a family of 12, plus assorted relatives, who emigrated from Holland to Southern California, and in the process proved America is still the land of opportunity and rewards those who toil diligently, intelligently and honestly.

Tom de Jong, the oldest son, came to San Diego County to live with an aunt and uncle soon after World War II. The rest of the de Jong family followed eventually after Tom's enthusiastic reports about the New World. In 1950 he bought Ratlief's Dairy in Escondido, complete with one milk route.

Aided by other members of the family, he bought Wharton's Dairy in Escondido and its ranch in San Marcos in 1952. By 1956 the ranch in San Marcos became the headquarters of the dairy business and has remained so except for occasional additions. The first purchase brought 28 cows into the new Hollandia Dairy. The second added 110. With the start of 138 cows it had already come a long way since Father de Jong had a dairy with 30 cows near Amsterdam.

Today three brothers and a cousin run the operation that employs 70 people, converts 60,000 gallons of raw milk weekly into fluid milk products and keeps 18 routemen in business within a 30-mile radius, serving an estimated urban center of 150,000 people.

Pete, Karel, Arie de Jong and their cousin Rudy de Jong handle all aspects of the business, each having his specialty. Tom, who founded the dairy, is 50 and has been retired for seven years but is available for consultation any time he is home. Another brother John runs a dairy in Hanford in the San Joaquin Valley. The head of the family, a young 72, still has a specialty. He trims the cattle's feet when this operation is necessary.

How can a small independent survive today's competition? Pete, the office manager, said, "We go after that segment of business that big creameries can't or won't handle for various reasons. We supply 50 schools and hospitals in north San Diego County. We also deliver to Camp Pendleton, the Marine base at Oceanside, and often to the Naval Training Center." These two customers buy about 25,000 gallons weekly, a big percentage of Hollandia's output.

Home delivery is franchised, and the 18 drivers own their own trucks. This operation distributes about 12,000 gallons of milk each week. For those with nostalgia, homogenized milk is available in glass bottles, quarts and half gallons, as well as the customary cartons. And who wants milk home delivered when it is more expensive than at the markets?

"These are customers who can't or won't go to the market every day to buy milk," says Arie de Jong, who is in charge of production and sales. The oth-

The Changing Face of Hollandia

There were a lot of big changes at the dairy farm while Tom was gone. In 1968, when he left the price of a cow was $450. After he returned in 1976, a cow sold for three times as much. His boys wanted to go into the family business when they returned to America. Arie Helmut, fifteen, was upset, because his father had retired from the dairy and the children didn't have a family business to jump back into. They were by far the poorest of all the de Jong families. Tom didn't even have ten percent of what his brothers and sisters did. Tom was close to his brother Karel, the main owner of Hollandia, so he stayed at the dairy, while his boys worked there.

Arie Helmut worked feeding, milking and managing the cows. Though he was an excellent worker, he wasn't very flexible. He and his uncle Karel disagreed. Arie Helmut felt he was in charge and would tell his uncle to get lost. He was a little kid with an inflated ego and a big chip on his shoulder. He wanted to feel important and valuable. However, his gross lack of respect was a big problem for the family. To show everyone how important he was he bought a new, bright yellow Porsche when he was sixteen and he still owns the car. At that time it was the most expensive car in the de Jong family.

After his Uncle Arie took over the dairy operation in 1973, they began butting heads. Arie Helmut continued to act as though he was in charge and a foreman at the dairy. He and his brother Tommy decided to go to join their father in Holland, Tom who vacationed in Holland for two months every summer. Arie Helmut left without his Uncle Arie's permission. When Tom and the boys returned from Holland, Arie Helmut found himself out of a job. Because he had left without permission, he was terminated by his Uncle Arie for abandoning his job.

Tommy still worked for the dairy feeding the cows and calves and he hired his Uncle Arie's sons, Eric and Johnny to be his helpers. He also had a crop of marijuana plants growing behind the old equipment shed by the dairy's junkyard. None of the adults realized what was going on, because the scent of the plants was disguised by the smell of the pigs, calves and machinery. Not only was his Uncle Arie unaware of his illegal crop activity, but he was also unaware Tommy paid his sons, Eric and Johnny to water the plants. When his sons began coming home late for dinner, Arie confronted them, Eric and Johnny said they were late because they had been taking care of Tommy's plants.

When Arie pressed them for answers, they admitted the plants they had been caring for were marijuana plants. The next day Arie and the kids went to have a look at Tommy's crop. That's when he discovered all of the kids knew Tommy was growing pot. He had a "Come to

Jesus" meeting with his children and all of his nieces, nephews and Tommy's friends. When he asked how much longer before he could harvest his crop, Tommy said he needed three more weeks before they would be ready. Arie agreed to let Tommy harvest his crop, but then everything including the seeds would be destroyed. Tommy also agreed not to grow anymore and neither would anyone else. Problem resolved.

When Tom returned from Holland, he had no place to live. He had to live in a travel trailer with a drug addicted woman his brother Arie was trying to help. Tom didn't judge her; especially since his own son Tommy was smoking pot he grew on the ranch. He felt sharing an outside toilet with twenty-five people who worked the dairy ranch was more difficult than sharing the small trailer.

Karel was in charge of Hollandia's maintenance, including the creamery. Karel hired Arie Helmut immediately. It was a wonderful learning opportunity for him. He already knew a lot about cows, but fell short when it came to the other diverse and vast aspects of running a dairy. He was paired to work with Ed Holderbaum, a very capable man who loved Arie Helmut a great deal. Arie Helmut acquired knowledge regarding maintenance, welding, trucking, processing, and mechanical fundamentals.

Ed had no children and always dreamt of having a son of his own to teach and pass his knowledge to. The father and son style partnership worked out tremendously. After he retired, Ed Holderbaum and his brother, from Detroit, traveled to Arizona with their wives and helped Arie Helmut on his dairy. A practice he continued until he passed away. Ed even loaned all the money he could to Arie Helmut, who was able to finally pay it all back to Ed's wife Mary, several years after Ed passed away.

Tommy had a job working at the San Marcos dairy, but unlike his older brother Arie Helmut he was more into socializing with his friends, smoking pot, drinking and going to the desert to ride motorcycles. During one of their excursions to the desert, two of Tommy's friends were riding under the influence, and while going up a hill, crashed into each other. Neither boy survived the accident.

Tom was very surprised, when Tommy focused his reaction on the loss of the bikes, instead of the tragic loss of his friends. Tom was very afraid something might happen to Tommy on one of his desert excursions, so he made him buy the best protective equipment available. Despite the equipment and what happened to his friends, Tommy continued to ride under the influence. He crashed on one outing, fracturing his ribs and breaking his collar bone in three places. He was in the Palomar Hospital for ten days. Tom was upset with Tommy and refused to visit him, even though he drove by the hospital several times a day.

The Humvee Incident of 1995

On May 17th, Shawn Timothy Nelson, thirty-five, an unemployed U.S. Army veteran of San Diego, had stolen a 57-ton M60A3 Patton tank from the United States National Guard Armory in Kearny Mesa. He went on a destructive rampage and fortunately, the tank was not armed at the time. The top speed for the M60A3 is thirty miles per hour and he took the police on a slow chase through San Diego neighborhoods as he destroyed cars, fire hydrants and recreational vehicles.

He attempted to topple a bridge by running into the supports and when that failed, he tried to cross the concrete median of State Route 163, where the tank became lodged. This allowed the police to climb onto the tank, open the hatch, and then Nelson was fatally shot by San Diego Police officer Paul Paxton, a gunnery sergeant with the Marine Corps reserve.

In the early part of 1995, Arie attended the new car show at the San Diego Convention Center with his sons and nephews. While there, he remarked about how much he loved Hummers and would love to own one just like the California Governor at the time, Arnold Schwarzenegger. After they left the car show he never gave his statement a second thought.

Arie's daughter Serena was married a few months later, on June 16, 1995, at the California Center for the Arts in Escondido. The next day, a brunch was held for the family at the Old Richland Schoolhouse, on Richland Road in San Marcos. There was a partial keg of beer left over and Arie gave it to his nephews, who quickly loaded the keg into a Suburban and took off for parts unknown.

They headed north on the 15 Freeway and headed west. They stopped at an abandoned dairy that was owned by the Whealan family in Oceanside and bordered Camp Pendleton. With a few more beers under their belts, they took off, driving through some fields off of Old River Road, before stopping at the back end of Camp Pendleton.

They could see a fleet of Humvees on the tarmac staged and ready to ship out for the Persian Gulf. They remembered how much their Uncle Arie loved Hummers and the boys decided to get him one and quickly found a way in through the fence. They boldly drove up to the line of Humvees, picked one out and took off with the Suburban riding shotgun. They used back roads and went straight to their Uncle Arie's house on the San Marcos dairy.

The boys were all pumped up and proudly announced they had a present for him. He had been taking a nap at the time, and was surprised to see the Humvee. They drove around the dairy and tested its climbing ability on the large manure piles. The vehicle needed to be refueled and the boys wanted to take it to the 7-11 on the corner. Arie cautioned them not to drive the Humvee anywhere to get fuel and then he went back home. In order to refuel the Humvee, they took 5-gallon cans to the station and filled them up.

Later that evening, Greta, Rudy de Jong's daughter and her husband Robert had a block party. The boys decided to take the Humvee to show everyone. As they drove up, their Uncle Karel, who had been drinking, was standing in the gun turret. They achieved celebrity status because of the Humvee and gave rides to everyone at the party. After the party ended all the boys went home and left the vehicle on the dairy. Early the next morning they buried it under a pile of loose cottonseed.

Concerned about how taking the vehicle was a federal offense and the consequences of the boys taking it, Arie got up early and searched the dairy for the Humvee. When he was unable to locate it and he went to see if his brother Tom knew where it was. They both searched the dairy again, but were still unable to find it. They gave up the search so that Arie could attend the late morning service at his church. That's where he ran into his brother, Pete's, sons who told him everything was taken care of, the vehicle was hidden and not to worry.

Tom, Karel and Arie had a meeting with all of the boys involved. It was decided they would return the Humvee to Camp Pendleton. Jet's son, Johnny was driving the Humvee and one of Pete's sons followed him in the Suburban. The plan was to take the Old 395 all the way to Fallbrook and go in the back way, like they did the night they originally took it.

However, when Johnny got to Rainbow and saw police cars he got nervous. He called his Uncle Arie for guidance. He told his Uncle he was close to the Rainbow Fire Station. Arie told him to leave it at the firehouse instead of going any further and to call the authorities to tell them where it was and to hang up quickly. The news story broke the next day, with a request for anyone who had information to come forward. The FBI showed up at the dairy a few days later, with a list of names. It is believed that someone from the block party called, because most of the names on the list were Pete's sons.

The family sought legal council from Bruce White, an attorney who met with the FBI and the military police. Someone needed to take the fall and once again the family had a meeting with all of the boys involved. It was decided they would draw lots and whoever got the short straw would take the rap. Tom's son Tommy drew the short straw, but after he talked to his wife Sue about it, she became infuriated because they're Jehovah's Witnesses. She forced him to go back to the group and told them he couldn't take the fall. His decision didn't set well with his cousins, especially due to the fact; he was the primary instigator in the whole matter. His brother, Arie Helmut, wasn't even involved in the whole episode took the fall instead.

The incident was a federal offense and Arie Helmut went before the judge, who showed him leniency, because he was an upstanding citizen, business owner and family man who had never had problems with the law in the past. He was fined an undisclosed amount and given three years probation. The judge told him if he ever got into trouble of any kind in the future, he would not get off so easy and would be sent to prison.

If the military hadn't already had egg on its face due to the stolen tank incident a month earlier, he probably wouldn't have been shown as much leniency.

Maartje Becomes Ill and Passes Away

Maartje's depression was actually connected directly with her hormones. When she was sixteen years old she was put in an institution for six months and again after Teun was born. She lived her life generally happy and was a loving, hardworking person. She worked all the time, sixteen hour days and was never sick and maintained a healthy appetite. After Arie Sr. passed away, she continued to live at the house on 17th Street for three more months.

Every Sunday after church the whole family continued the tradition of having coffee and lunch at Arie Sr. and Maartje's home, at the old homestead on 17th Street in Escondido. The family continued to carry on the Sunday tradition after their father passed away. The boys tried to encourage their mother to relocate to San Marcos, but she refused. Because of her refusal, one Sunday they decided no one would go to her house for coffee and lunch.

Pictured left to right: Arie, John, Karel, Elso, Kees, Pete and Tom

The very next Sunday after church, while they had coffee, Arie asked whether she would consider relocating to the San Marcos Ranch. She surprised everyone by saying she was ready to go right then and there and only needed her purse, some flowers and a few other personal possessions. The family had already completely furnished and prepared a home for her. When they finished coffee she was taken to her new home before she could change her mind. A short time later, the boys took her other possessions to her new home. Once she relocated to San Marcos, she was very happy. The family tradition of having coffee and lunch at her home after church continued.

Before and after Maartje moved to the San Marcos ranch, Jet and Hinke did the shopping, so nothing was ever lacking after she became ill. There was beer, whiskey, and apricot brandy for

213

happy hour, and snacks, coffee, cookies and books. Many older Dutch acquaintances would also visit her during the week. There was a cleaning lady who came in one day a week as well.

Hinke made a nice hot meal for her every night which Tom delivered to her at 6pm. Afterwards they prayed together and Tom tucked her in on the couch and covered her with a blanket. She didn't want to sleep in the bed where Arie Sr. died and she elected to sleep in her dress.

One night when Tom arrived with her meal, she said, "Teun it's enough. I don't want to eat anymore. I want to die. I'm almost gone. It's enough."

He tucked her in and took the food to the Hollandia Dairy office, and told the story to Arie, Karel and Rudy. They ate the food and decided to go over to their mother's to continue happy hour, say good-bye and wish her a good journey. They all had a good time; a few extra drinks, and kissed her good-bye.

Usually, at 10am, they had coffee prepared by either Anneke or Hinke. On that particular day Anneke had prepared coffee for the family. On the way, Tom stopped to check on his mother and was surprised to find her doing well.

When he told her he was going to Arie and Anneke's for coffee, she said, "I want some coffee too. I'm coming with you."

There was to be no mention of the night before. Similar episodes happened off and on for almost a year. There were times that Arie was the only one present when she said her time was up. He would gently and lovingly tuck her in, kiss her and say good-bye. The next morning he would stop to check on her and she would be sitting up in good health and spirits, like nothing had happened.

Arie remembered asking her, "Mom, is that you? What happened?"

She would smile and say, "Oh child, God just wasn't quite ready for me yet."

On one occasion when Maartje was feeling like her old self, Arie and Mike Sams stopped to have happy hour with her when they returned from a day at the hog ranch in Ontario. They brought her a baby pig to take care of. She was delighted. The pig was placed in a small pen outside of her home and two weeks later when they stopped again for happy hour, they asked her where the little pig was.

She smiled and said, "He needed his freedom, so I let him go."

They never did find the pig.

Every summer, Tom and Hinke left on their annual trip to Holland, and would be gone for two months. This was a problem for Maartje, who had become very ill and was unable to care for herself. Ellie traveled to San Marcos to pick up her mother and took her home to Tulare. Maartje stayed with Eliie for a few months.

Ellie's sister, Mary had a large home in Tulare, a big family and a loving husband, Richard, to help take care of her mother. She seemed very happy to be around so many of her grandchildren during the last years of her life Maartje began living with them in 1993 and Mary cared for her mother for the next six years, until she passed away at the age of 96, on November 13, 1999. Her mother may not have always had the best mental health, but she was always physically strong.

Maartje didn't mind Mary taking care of her and the two of them always got along famously. It was a very busy and tough time for Mary, but she felt it was a good experience, especially for her children and grandchildren. They learned to be patient and have a lot of respect for the elderly. The last three years of her life when Maartje became bound to a wheelchair, it proved to be quite challenging, but Mary persevered and rose to the task.

Maartje experienced a series of mini strokes. She recovered well from each one, except for the last. After her last stroke, she had trouble eating, swallowing and talking. She wasn't afraid to die and had accepted death. The family prayed the Lord would take her and end her pain.

Maartje had to rely on the use of a wheelchair due to her strokes, and became more and more dependent on the assistance of others. She was lucid for the most part and after her passing, the family received quite an abundance of letters of condolence from many people who admired her. Maartje was very low key, but extremely hospitable.

Tom sent his sister, Mary and her family a message after Maartje's passing, saying, "It is much less work for all you now that mother is gone. I must say it was a loving sacrifice for all of you to take care of her from the age of 90-96 years old. Wow!"

Mary replied, "Tom we considered it a privilege and honor to be able to do this for mom. She cared for all of us her whole life."

Mary remembers her mother saying, "I'm going to live with you until 2000." She almost made it.

The de Jong Grandchildren Branch Out

Although he had retired, Tom remained involved with the dairy, giving visitor tours and mentoring his sons. The boys lived with him until they both married in 1980 at the ages of twenty-two and twenty-three. In the summer of 1979, just before Arie Helmut was married, he purchased a dairy in Arizona. Tom went with Arie Helmut to help get his new venture off to a good and solid start. Tommy stayed behind and continued to work with his Uncle Arie at Coast Waste Management.

When Tom and Arie Helmut arrived in Arizona, the dairy was a virtual mess, and they set about doing a total remodel right away. They bought four hundred cows and began milking in three shifts: 3-11am, 11am-7pm and 7pm-3am. The cows were milked in a double four herringbone.

There were three homes on the dairy. One was still occupied by the previous owners, who rented the house they lived in until their new home was completed. It would be almost a year before they left the dairy. Tom and his son Arie Helmut stayed in the house that resembled more of a shack. As soon as they vacated the property, Tom and Arie Helmut began remodeling the home to suit their needs and make it their own.

The Arizona heat was unbearably oppressive; and when Arie Helmut's fiancée, Nina Petrovich came to visit, they were forced to sleep outside on the lawn. After Arie Helmut and Nina were wed, the three of them moved into the largest house, which had been remodeled. Tom continued to stay in Arizona for a year to help get the business established. With the help of Ed Holderbaum, it took six months for Tom and Arie Helmut to rebuild and get the dairy cleaned up.

They continued the tough, back breaking work, until the job was completed. The days were long. Ed was an independent heavy equipment contractor, and he drove the earth moving equipment and he did a lot of work for Hollandia. He worked with Arie Helmut in Arizona for a couple of years. He was semi-retired, family friend and had relocated to Michigan. He stayed and worked in Arizona for as long as he was needed and then returned to Michigan.

Tom returned to California and lived with his son Tommy who had been working for his uncle Arie at the trash business since he was seventeen. Due to health issues, Arie was struggling with his trash business and originally wanted Arie Helmut to work for him. Arie Helmut suggested he hire Tommy instead, because he was relocating to Arizona.

When Tommy and Sue, got married, they moved in with Tom on the dairy, in San Marcos and continued to live with him until his marriage to Hinke. Tom waited twenty-five years after his divorce to finally remarry. He wanted to make sure his children were grown and had families of their own first. He remembered quietly celebrating his 25th year of being a single parent.

Tom's daughter Mary and her husband, Joep Rijlaarsdam currently have a dairy in Mesa, Arizona. They also own acreage in Visalia where Joep was given a start by working for her Uncle Kees.

His oldest son, Arie Helmut ran a dairy in Chandler, Arizona. Rumors circulated that he owed massive amounts of money and he would go broke. However, he has always been a smart operator who made it and prospered as he went.

Tom's youngest son, Tommy, has a dairy of his own in Buckeye, Arizona, and an additional dairy approximately twenty miles west of Buckeye, which is also very efficient.

Pete's oldest daughter Jeanne married Theo de Haan and they live in Hanford where they built a heifer ranch for Hollandia. His oldest son, Arie is a dairyman in Visalia. His middle son Gerrit is a dairyman in Waukena, near Hanford. Pete's daughter Margie and her husband Gil Den Dulk live in Indiana. His son, Peter married Ingrid Ton. Peter is well liked and has a good head for business. He has been very instrumental in growing the Hollandia interests around Hanford and for getting the whole family more focused on dairying and farming. Pete's youngest daughter, Elsie, and her husband Mark, ran her uncle Arie's hog ranch in Ontario, now, raise hogs for medical research in Ramona.   His youngest son, William, married Sandra van Die. They had five children. William later died at the age of thirty-six from lymphoma cancer.

Kees' children also operate dairy ventures in the California Central Valley area, except for his son Bastiaan, and oldest daughter Maartje who own dairies in Michigan and his daughter Marenta who has a dairy in Sunnyside, Washington.

Elso's son, Arie Elso runs an organic dairy and his father's dairy in Bonanza, Oregon. His daughter Nellie has a dairy in Lakeside, California.

Karel's son E.J. and his daughter Maryann both have dairy operations in Hanford, California.

John's son Jack operates two dairies in Hanford, California. His daughter Marietta owns several dairies in Michigan and Indiana. His son, Arie Jan also owns a dairy in Indiana.

All of Ellie's children own dairies in California, except for her son Arie who owns a dairy in Idaho. In addition to owning a dairy, her daughter Wendy who also owns a pen fed calf and cattle feed lot operation in Madera, California.

Arie's sons Eric and Johnny are partners in a dairy operation in Fairoaks, Indiana.

Jet's son, Johnny manages his cousin, Arie Helmut's dairy in Visalia, California. Her son Matthew owns a dairy in the Fresno area of California and manages the pen fed beef lot for his cousin Wendy.

All of Mary's children own dairies in California, except for her oldest son Johnny, who owns a dairy in Iowa.

The total number of animals in the family's combined dairy operations are far too numerous to count.

At one point John owned a dairy on the island of Oahu. It was the largest dairy in Hawaii and was managed by two local Hawaiian girls. He owned the dairy for approximately ten years before he sold the operation. The distance from the mainland proved to be too much of a headache and he decided it was time to sell.

Tom and Hinke

Tom met his current wife Hinke in 1978, when he was fifty-two and she was thirty-two. Hinke's brother worked in Hanford, at John's dairy as a foreman. When they met she was in the states visiting her brother as she did each summer, taking time off from her job as a clothing store manager in Holland.

When Tom first saw Hinke, she was at the pool in a bikini. She was so beautiful; the usually talkative Tom was at a complete loss for words. He was visiting his brother John for only two or three days. After his divorce from Karin while his children were small, he had never even given women a second thought; except for the short time he had dated a girl named Jannie in Holland. Meeting Hinke changed all that. He said it was like watching fireworks.....she took his breath away.

Tom knew she wouldn't be in the states for long, so he asked her to join him and his relatives on a trip to Tijuana, Mexico. She went along and they traveled from Hanford, to his home in San Marcos, before heading south to Mexico. Two days later, while walking down the streets of Tijuana, Tom proposed to Hinke. He had seen a wedding ad that stated, 'Get Married Here' and so he began to think, "Why not? Why waste time?"

Although Tom wanted to waste no time and suggested they get married right away, that is exactly what he did, he wasted time. It would be six more years before they got married. Both boys were still living at home when they met. Tom felt the boys would be gone soon, like their sister Mary.

Hinke returned to Holland and waited patiently, but her patience began to wane as time dragged on and he dragged his feet. Tom managed to keep the relationship going, and helped it slowly grow. He wrote her long letters about his love for her, the family and his plans for their future.

The next few years they hardly saw each other. Like two ships passing in the night, she came to the states during the summer, as he was going to Holland. They only saw each other once or twice during the first three years of their courtship. Then in 1980, Hinke immigrated to America, and settled in Hanford with her brother.

Tom and Hinke's families spent time traveling to San Felipe, Mexico for vacations spent camping at the beach. An activity they enjoyed every year until the criminal activity became so prevalent, making it unsafe to vacation there in recent years. Suddenly all eyes were on them. They were inseparable, and spent every waking moment together, when possible. Then to

Hinke's dismay there was a period of almost two years they didn't make any progress on their wedding plans and spent very little time together.

Tom was very involved with Arie Helmut and was spending a lot of time in Arizona, while Hinke did quite a bit of work for Arie Sr. and Maartje in Escondido.

Hinke had never been married, so it was a long time for her to wait. At times she felt discouraged, because some of Tom's family told her he would never go through with it, he had been single far too long. While he was still living at home with Tommy and Sue, Tom felt he couldn't marry Hinke. For him, his children had always been his number one priority.

Tom felt some of his relatives didn't want him to marry either. He had always been so accessible around the dairy and they believed this would change if he married. A few tried to sabotage the relationship by telling Hinke it would be a disaster if they married, because his first marriage had ended so badly, plus he had three children who were set in their ways.

Hinke felt nothing was going to happen between them, regarding marriage, especially when they had not been spending time together and she told Tom she was moving back to Holland. It was the sudden realization he could lose her forever that sprung Tom into action.

After reaffirming his love for her and his intentions, they were married five weeks later. The wedding took place at his sister Mary's home, witnessed by one hundred guests comprised of family and friends. The ceremony was performed by a chaplain, because of the differences in their religions, Hinke belongs to the Dutch Reformed religion and Tom is a member of the Jehovah's Witness.

Everyone was surprised. It had been such a long expanse of time no one believed the marriage would ever take place, especially since Tom was now fifty-eight and his bride thirty-eight. After six long years of waiting, the couple was finally able to begin their journey together as man and wife. They both say their life together has been good. They celebrated their twenty-fifth wedding anniversary in 2008.

During their courtship, Hinke worked as a nanny. She also lived with and cared for Tom's mother Maartje, who continued to suffer from depression. After Arie Sr. died in 1989, Maartje moved from the original dairy on 17th Street in Escondido, to the ranch in San Marcos. After the marriage, Hinke continued to care for Maartje before she went to live with Mary. There were quite a few days Maartje wouldn't get out of bed or eat, because she wanted to die.

In 1982, Tommy deserted his job at his uncle Arie's trash business when he left on a trip to Oregon without permission from his uncle. When he returned he was terminated. He then went to work with his father, making and selling cheese. Their small, one thousand square foot cheese making operation didn't require a great deal of capital to get started, and was located at the Hollandia Dairy in San Marcos. Tommy and his father had developed a reputation as a cheese maker, building a customer base from all over.

The Golden Door Spa of San Marcos, located not far from the Hollandia Dairy, frequents a list of wealthy clientele who come for a weight loss regime. The diet is so restrictive; the clients would periodically go in search of food with more sustenance. On one such occasion, a friend of the family, Conley Wolfswinkel was at the Golden Door and met Lee Iacocca who had grown tired of yoga and the skimpy diet. He was dying for adventure and something to eat. Tommy remembered when Lee Iacocca and Conley Wolfswinkel came rolling up to the small dairy house in a Rolls Royce to sample his cheese.

After three years of running his Arizona dairy, Arie Helmut was making a good living. He purchased a second dairy, for his brother in law, Joep to run. Two years later he rented another, much larger dairy located in Buckeye, fifteen miles south/west of Phoenix. The dairy was rented from Bob Luke. Tommy initially took charge of the daily operations and would later purchase the property from Bob's wife, Diana. That's when Tom took over the cheese manufacturing at the San Marcos location from Tommy and continued making cheese until in 1990 when he was sixty-five.

Karel who had begun drinking a lot and Tom spent a lot of time caring for his brother. Karel began drinking in the Army while he was stationed in Germany in 1957-58. Drinking was never frowned upon within the de Jong family. They were generally good social drinkers and his father considered it to be very macho if someone could drink a lot.

In Germany, drinking is an acceptable part of the culture. In the 1950's when Karel and Arie served there, if you ordered a beer, you were given a liter, which is a little more than a quart. Many of the locals and soldiers drank several beers during their night out visiting the town's bars.

In some bars, the inebriated, beer drinking patrons sang:
In heaven there is no beer, therefore we drink it here.

Karel and Arie Have Health Concerns

Tom was always very health conscious regarding diet and exercise, and he helped his brother Arie with nutritional guidance, to help with his stress, asthma and weight. In the years from 1977-79, by following Tom's outline for exercise and nutrition, Arie was able to lose weight and saw an improvement in his asthma. In 1975-1977, Arie was not only running North County Disposal, his new trash business, but he was still working long hours at the San Marcos dairy as well. He ran the Cash and Carry, and oversaw the milking and dairy operation.

Arie continued to work the long grueling hours at both locations for almost four years. The long hours finally took their toll on him and he collapsed, his asthma had been aggravated immensely.

His respiratory problems initially began in the very cold winter of January of 1939, five days after he was born. His mother had undressed him to change him and had left the room forgetting all about him. When she eventually returned, he was blue and barely breathing. That was the beginning of his asthma and respiratory problems.

Though retired, Tom always wanted to be there for his brothers and children. Being the senior family figure, he was continuously involved with what the family was doing on one level or another.

Karel had been a pretty steady and heavy drinker for most of his adult life. Now in his late 60's he was faced with going to alcohol detox for the first time. The original facility was located in Visalia. At the advice of a doctor, he was moved to a rehabilitation center in Phoenix, Arizona, called, "Calvary," for an additional four weeks. The family had done an intervention, out of concern for Karel's health.

The intervention was spearheaded by Mary's husband, Richard Westra. Richard's friend Tom de Groot was a former alcoholic who had gone through rehab and had been clean and sober for years. Mary, Richard, her brother Tom, and Tom de Groot, took Karel to a Christian rehabilitation center in Phoenix, Arizona. Karel had been there a month and was doing very well. Tom felt Karel was doing well enough to return home and went to Phoenix in the motor-home to pick him up. It was the one and only time Karel went to rehab and it was a bust. Once he returned home, he started to drink again.

Retirement was very hard on Karel. He always needs to be busy and challenged. The transition was not easy. He had to shift his focus and spent time in his home office reading, going through old photos, visits with family and friends, or just hanging out with his brothers, having a drink and reminiscing about the old times.

Karel had developed sclerosis of the liver due to his excessive drinking over the years, which took its toll on his overall health.

In 2006, Karel once again found himself in a rehabilitation facility. Although this time it was for only a week. When Karel was released he was very weak and unsteady. He had to use a walker to have mobility. In 2008, Karel had to cut way down on his drinking to prolong his life.

Phil Kiesler/The Times Advocate

The 1,000 cows now grazing on Hollandia's San Marcos land will probably be moved to other DeJong family dairies.

Hollandia Dairy may moooooove soon

By Wayne Halberg
Times-Advocate Staff Writer

SAN MARCOS — San Marcos' claim to fame as the only city in the area with a downtown dairy could be just a memory in a few years.

The acres of cows and rolling grasslands that announce entry into San Marcos from the east will probably give way in three to 10 years to shops, houses and apartments.

The Hollandia Dairy is the largest working ____ in San Diego County. But it will have to ____ way for progress, said Arie DeJong Jr., who runs the operation with two of his seven brothers.

The family has hired a planning consultant to map out possibilities for the 130-acre dairy and took some preliminary ideas to the city Thursday to be reviewed.

The cost of maintaining a rural enterprise such as a dairy in an increasingly urban area is taking its toll, DeJong said last week. Within the next few years, the 1,000 cows now grazing there will probably be moved off their valuable land and onto other DeJong family dairies in the San Joaquin Valley.

"It's probably not even all that economical now, but we kind of like living here," he said. "But the kids are all grown and it may be time to change things."

Thirty-nine years ago, Arie DeJong Sr., started his family's empire with a 30-cow operation on 5 acres in Escondido. Two years later the Dutch immigrant bought the San Marcos dairy that he would turn into one of the largest in Southern California.

Most of Arie Sr.'s 10 kids have moved on to run other dairies around the western United States. But Arie, now 87, and his wife, Maardja, 85, still live on the old Escondido homestead on Felicita Avenue with a few company cows. That land, too, probably will be sold eventually, Arie DeJong Jr. said.

DeJong said he and his brothers and their families will probably stay in the area, as will the milk-processing plant, which homogenizes and distributes milk from dairies all over Southern California.

"It will be hard (to sell the dairy)," he said. "We've been here a long time. But the economics are better (in the San Joaquin Valley). The property is less expensive and the feed is less expensive."

Early plans for the property include shopping centers along Mission Road, with apartments, condominiums and single-family homes farther north. A school and a park also figure to be part of the plan. DeJong said efforts will be made to preserve the historic schoolhouse on their land, but the ranch house on the hill overlooking the pastures isn't likely to survive.

San Marcos eyes dairy for park

By John Berhman
Staff Writer

SAN MARCOS — The City Council would like a piece of the 130-acre Hollandia Dairy for a city park.

A pretty big piece, in fact — perhaps as large as 50 acres, or about twice as big as the city's largest park, Walnut Grove.

The council Nov. 27 went into a closed session to discuss the possible purchase, and then directed City Manager Rick Gittings to begin negotiations on the acquisition with the DeJong family, which has owned Hollandia Dairy for almost 40 years.

The DeJongs intend to sell the dairy, because of the encroaching development in the area, and move operations and 1,000 cows to property they own in the San Joaquin Valley.

The council discussed the matter at another closed session Tuesday and heard a progress report from Gittings, who has met once with the DeJongs.

"One parcel we are looking at is 48 acres, and it would make a beautiful spot for a park," Councilman F.H. "Corky" Smith said yesterday. "It's up Rock Springs Road and over the hill and offers a beautiful view."

Earlier this year the DeJong family hired a firm to devise a development plan for their property. The plan included 288 single-family homes, 419 apartment and condominium units, and a 16-acre neighborhood shopping center.

It included an elementary school site and a 7.5-acre park, although the city's parks master plan calls for at least one 15-acre park on the property.

Smith said the city would like the family's plans for the property to include some commercial development along Mission Road, on which the dairy fronts.

The council would have to approve any plans that the DeJongs present for their property.

San Diego Union 11/13 90

SAN DIEGO BUSINESS JO

VOLUME 11   NUMBER 2

WEEK OF JANUARY 8 - 14, 1990

Hollandia Dairy plans 700 homes at San Marcos site

By SUSAN C. SCHENA

A 40-year-old dairy in San Marcos requested approval late last week to convert its 80 acres of pasture and surrounding land to a site for about 300 homes, 400 apartments, an elementary school and parkland.

With suburban development closing in on Hollandia Dairy, which once had the hilly Mission Road area to itself, its owners have decided to relocate their herd and milking operations and sell their pasture land to developers.

"It's something they've been facing for a while," said Doug Boyd, principal of Turrini & Brink, Santa Ana-based planning consultants. "They've seen the urbanization approaching them. It's difficult to operate a dairy in an urban environment."

Side effects of dairy farming — the flies and the odor — would eventually become

The cows may be leaving the Hollandia Dairy to make room for homes.

Will M. Lipman

a nuisance to growing numbers of nearby residents, he said. Boyd said the dairy owners hired his firm last year to begin preliminary plans for the 80 acres plus 20 acres of surrounding property.

Anticipating that the property would soon be for sale, several developers have

contacted the Hollandia owners, said Boyd. He declined to identify them, and he was unwilling to discuss the land's value or possible selling price.

Owners of the dairy farm, the de Jong family, are securing development

Please turn to page 36

Hollandia Dairy welcomes city's proposal for park

■ PLANNING: *Owner Arie De Jong still plans to have houses and apartments as well*

MICHAEL FISHER/*Times Advocate*

SAN MARCOS — Hollandia Dairy owners are open to a city proposal to create a 43-acre park at the dairy after the rural landmark closes, according to co-owner Arie De Jong.

De Jong, part-owner of the 39-year-old family operation, said the city is proposing to buy 43 acres of the 130-acre Mission Road dairy to build a park. The park proposal includes a grassy knoll, a valley behind the knoll that stretches to Borden Road and the house where De Jong no lives.

"We're not averse to setting aside open space," De Jong said. "We just got the city's appraisal (Thursday) and we are evaluatin it now to decide the position we should take."

He declined to say how much the appraisal totaled.

In a closed meeting held on Tuesday, San Marcos City Coun cil members instructed staff to

Please see **DAIRY**, B2 ▶

DAIRY: Owners will consider park

negotiate with the dairy owners for an undisclosed portion of the dairy.

San Marcos City Councilman Mark Loscher, who asked the council to discuss obtaining land at the dairy, said he would like to see a passive park created on top of the knoll. Below the knoll will be ball fields, picnic areas and other activity fields.

According to De Jong, the family has planned to close down the dairy for at least two years as increasing development in San Marcos squeezed out the rural landmark.

The trigger for the move will most likely be the city's planned widening of Mission Road to six lanes in front of the dairy, he said. The road widening is expected to take up some of the dairy land.

"Cows don't do too well on concrete, so that will trigger our movement. I guess that's progress but that's the way it is."

The dairy will be moved to land owned by the De Jongs in the San Joaquin Valley, he said. In its place, the family planned to build a 288-house, 419-apartment neighborhood complete with a shopping center and a 7.5-acre park.

But if negotiations with the city reach fruition, and the large park is created, De Jong said the development will have to be redesigned.

"That's fine. It's not a problem. That will still leave us about 83

> "Cows don't do too well on concrete, so that will trigger our movement."
>
> **ARIE DE JONG, dairy owner**

arces instead," he said.

There are also plans for a school site in the development that would be next to the proposed park, he said.

If the deal with the city works out, De Jong says the family hopes to have its redesigned plans approved before selling the project to a builder.

"We aren't developers," he said. "We'd like to get it all approved and then sell it."

City may purchase Hollandia property

By ROBYN WALTERS
San Marcos Courier staff

The cows won't be coming home for Christmas, or anytime after, for that matter.

For more than 40 years, dairy cows have grazed on the hillside north of Mission Road. Through the years, they have watched the Richland countryside change and grow.

Apartments have sprouted up and traffic has increased immensely in the area, pushing the cows out of town.

It's been nearly a year since residents of San Marcos learned Hollandia Dairy would be relocating and that development may overtake the 130 acres of countryside.

Lately though, plans have changed.

According to City Manager Rick Gittings, the city may become the new owners of a part or all of the dairy land.

The owners of Hollandia Dairy, the DeJong family, have been negotiating with several developers as well as the city for the past year to develop the grazing land.

However, a meeting last week between the DeJong's and city officials may help materialize future plans.

"We have indicated to the family (DeJong) that the city is interested in purchasing either a part or all of the land so we are currently putting together a proposal to buy it," Gittings said.

The city would be purchasing the land for a city park.

"We feel most folks would be pleased about putting in a park," Gittings said, although none of the residents have come forward with comment.

City Councilman F.H. "Corky" Smith is pleased with the city's decision.

"I think making the land into a park is a great idea," Smith said. "Wherever and whenever we can get land for parks we should grab it."

According to Smith, the council began toying with the purchase last year when dairy neighbors discovered Hollandia wanted to sell their land.

"This land has a lot of value for the community because we can combine park space with a

Staff photo by RUSSEL LE

Hollandia Dairy property in San Marcos may become city-owned property.

commercial portion running up alongside of Mission Avenue," Smith said. "This plan would create revenue for us later when our redevelopment money will be done with in 20 years."

The city has not yet made an offer on the 130 acres. According to Gittings, the market value of it varies.

"We could be looking at spending between $25,000 to $50,000 per acre lot," Gittings said.

Although the plan to turn the dairy land into a park may sound good, the DeJong's aren't really pleased about leaving San Marcos, despite the financial gains they expect to receive.

"I'll miss it here, we have all raised our families here," Arie DeJong said, one of the four brothers who own and operate the dairy. "For us, the dairy has been a real good thing."

DeJong's father brought his family to the United States from Holland in 1949 and founded the dairy in 1950.

"I started working here in '52 when I was little kid. I was only about 13 years old," DeJong said. "We have been here a long

time and this property is right in the hub of downtown San Marcos. I have mixed emotions about leaving."

However, the option to buy the land and convert it into a city park is a chance of a lifetime for the city, DeJong believes.

"Once this land is gone there won't be any more like it," DeJong said. "All of our land has the potential of being developed, but I think it would be nice for the city to take this opportunity. It will only come once and it wouldn't be to our detriment."

No matter who buys the land, DeJong said what is most important for their family is to be paid enough money for the land to relocate all four families elsewhere.

"We are losing out here. It's a matter of economics," DeJong said. "But, we are giving the city the first right of refusal or right to buy it."

The plan to move will be completed in three stages. The first will be the actual moving of livestock to family land in the San Joaquin Valley. The second phase will involve the moving of the DeJong family.

Arie DeJong and his brothers

maintain homes on the the hill where the cows From DeJong's house, th a clear view of the pool side and the cows on the ot

"Basically the encroac of growth is pushing us DeJong said. "Cows do too good on blacktop."

Despite his misgiving Jong does not regret the ly's decision to sell the la development.

"We knew it would someday," DeJong said.

Although 1,000 cows s main on the hillside, the has had to bear some burdens imposed by the improvements to street roads. In 1989, the dairy's of improvements to th Marcos Creek was $600,00

When the family move cows to the San Joaquin DeJong says life will res before with the cows and grazing over 800 acres.

DeJong also added "chances are good" th milk plant will simply across the road and operating.

The city will be moving with their plans to buy th within 90 days, Gittings sai

228

The End of an Era
Hollandia Dairy Makes Way for Mission Hills High School,
San Marcos City Park and Mission Hills Church

In 1999, the family was approached by the San Marcos Unified School District, the City of San Marcos and Emmanuel Faith Church, all of whom wanted to purchase acreage parcels from the dairy. In February the following year, after long negotiations and terms agreeable to the family, ninety-seven acres of the dairy holdings were sold and divided into three separate parcels. The largest portion was sold to the San Marcos Unified School District, who built the Mission Hills High School on the property. The City of San Marcos obtained the second largest parcel and built Hollandia Park. The smallest parcel was sold to the Emmanuel Faith Church, in Escondido, who built the Mission Hills Church, on the property in San Marcos.

Pictured left to right: Mary, Jet, Arie, Ellie, Karel, Elso, Kees, Pete, and Tom

All parties involved agreed the sale would be done through imminent domain, which allowed the de Jongs three years to re-invest the monies and would prevent a hefty capital gains tax. Although the land was sold through imminent domain, it was not done in a forceful manner. After living on the dairy for so many long and wonderful years, it was a very sad and difficult time for the family members who relocated.

The dairy had been a source of unity and strength for the family unit. After sailing off to try new business ventures, it was a safe harbor, they could return to. Always knowing they could return home to the open and welcoming arms of family and friends. Hollandia Dairy was a place rich with family memories of love, friendship and of children and grandchildren growing and prospering.

Years earlier, Arie sold a great portion of his acreage back to the family. However, he retained six acres which included the original family home on top of the hill. Approximately a year after he sold the Coast Waste Management trash company, Arie and his wife Anneke went

Karel de Jong (left) as the cows were being loaded at the San Marcos dairy for relocation to Hanford, California

to an estate sale and bought the Melrose Ranch in the hills near Lake Wohlford, just outside of Escondido, California. All of the buildings on the ranch including the main house were in a great state of disrepair, due to neglect and squatters. It was two years before he and Anneke were able to move from the house on the hill in San Marcos to Melrose Ranch. Arie then transferred ownership of the house in San Marcos to his son Eric, who still resides there with his family.

Sadly and reluctantly, Tom and Hinke moved to a condo in Escondido, walking distance from his sister Jet's home. Tom wanted to stay on the dairy and felt truly lost and depressed at having to leave his longtime home. He does admit however, with his love of sunbathing, the lack of flies has made it a much more enjoyable experience and there's no yard maintenance to worry about.

They leased the first unit they moved into and the owner didn't want to sell. The condo next to them came up for sale and his sister, Jet bought it. The owner of Tom's condo got married and decided to sell after all. He purchased and remodeled the condo, and lived next door in Jet's condo during the renovation. They have been happily living there since the spring of 2000.

The original owners of the Hollandia Dairy, Karel, Piet and cousin Rudy de Jong were all getting older. None of their children seemed interested or capable of taking on the huge responsibility of running the family business. In 2005, they put the word out within the industry that the family was looking to sell. There was a vague offer of thirty-seven million. Ten million for seventeen acres of the land and twenty-seven million for all the buildings, equipment, trucks, routes, accounts receivable, etc.

In 2006, Arie Helmut stated he wanted to purchase the dairy with three of his cousins. They felt the dairy had been in the family a long time and wanted to keep it that way. The dairy was purchased by Tom's son Arie Helmut, Pete's sons, Peter and Gerrit, and Karel's son EJ, (Eric

John), insuring the dairy stayed in the family. They retained Henk van Nieuwenhuizen as plant manager. Henk was offered the opportunity to purchase 10% of the shares.

Once the land title changed hands in January of 2011, the expansion and remodeling began. When the sale was complete and bank loans were approved, Henk van Niewenhuizen was placed in charge of the project, to build the new processing plant.

The 50th and 60th Immigration Reunions

After we immigrated, we realized these people here in America were no different than us; they're just looking for a dream. We needed to strive for all we had before us in America and count our blessings. It's one thing to have realized and achieved the dream, but it's another to appreciate it. If you appreciate it, you're never spoiled. True value lies in the little things and they should never be taken for granted. **Teun de Jong**

In 1999, Arie and Anneke organized a family immigration reunion that was held on May 26th and attended by approximately two hundred de Jong family members and close friends, all of whom converged on the Wyoming Picnic Grove in Poway. They arrived in their motor homes

The de Jong family celebrating the 60th re-union at Arie's Melrose Ranch in Escondido, California

and trailers to celebrate the 50th anniversary of the family's immigration to America and set up camp by the creek. This is where the family lived in the three little rock houses after their arrival to Poway.

The four day celebration was kicked off with a barbeque picnic. In order to have authentic Dutch musical accompaniment, Henk van Gaalen, of Winchester, brought his antique Dutch calliope to the picnic grove. The following day, an overnight stay was arranged on Catalina Island, at the Catalina Canyon Resort and Inn. Everyone who wished to participate boarded an Amtrak train at 5:30am the next day that took them to the Union train station in Los Angeles.

From there they were transported by bus to Long Beach Harbor and boarded the boat for Catalina Island.

On the 29th, Arie's daughter, Dorinda and her husband, Ned Van der Pol, arranged a mystery bus trip to Balboa Park for anyone willing to participate, which was followed with another barbeque and party, complete with a live band at the Big Stone Lodge, in Poway. A time capsule was supposed to be buried in the park that day, however, for safety, Arie changed his mind. The time capsule which holds various items, including family photos, a calendar of events revolving around the time of their immigration and a movie of the reunion celebration is safely kept at his Melrose Ranch home in Escondido, California. It was decided the capsule would be dug up after the last of the original immigrating brothers or sisters perish, enabling the newest generation to know what the family had valued and felt was important.

Ten years later, on May 5, 2009, Arie and Anneke once again organized a family re-union party, to celebrate the 60th anniversary of the family's immigration to America, and their arrival to California. Although it was not the date their ship docked in New York, or their arrival in Poway, on the 26th of May, it was a true celebration nonetheless, which began on Tuesday, May 5th and lasted for five days.

This time there were over three hundred family members and friends in attendance. The first day of the five day celebration included a barbecue at Arie's, Melrose Ranch home, in Escondido. Arie's daughters, Dorinda and Serena, organized plenty of entertainment for the youngest members of the family, including pony rides, games, a variety of blow-up jumpers and a petting zoo. The next day there was a trip to Bates Nut Farm in Valley Center, to attend the Barnum and Bailey Circus.

 The big event of the re-union was the bus trip to Disneyland. Everyone who boarded the three buses, were given and wore *de Jong family re-union* T-shirts, that Arie Helmut's wife, Nina, designed and had made for the Disneyland trip. The T-shirts read, *'WE ARE FAMILY, The de Jong Family Re-union.'* The T-shirts were a big success and garnered quite a bit of attention from other families visiting Disneyland. Even the Disneyland staff members stated they had never seen such a large family in attendance. After staying overnight at the Disneyland Hotel, the family went back to Melrose Ranch for another barbecue and dance, that included live musical entertainment from the band, "The Texas Toothpicks."

On the last day of celebration all of the family members had breakfast and attended church services at Arie's Green Oak Ranch in Vista, before leaving for home. The 142 acre ranch easily accommodated the de Jong's large family. The five day event was very successful and a good time was had by all.

Arie planned the 60th re-union celebration to coincide with the liberation of Holland from the German occupation, and his father's birthday, which were both on May 5th.

Hopefully the 60th won't be the last of the re-union celebrations, but it may very well be, since the time of the re-unions several of the immigrating de Jongs have perished, including Arie Sr., Maartje, Kees, Karel and Elso.

Hopefully the younger generations of the de Jong family will continue this tradition of celebrating the family legacy long after the original immigrating family members are gone.

GOD BLESS THE DE JONG FAMILY AND GOD BLESS AMERICA.

Made in the USA
San Bernardino, CA
20 January 2016